Other titles in the Marques of America series
published by Motorbooks International:

Buick: The Postwar Years
Hudson: The Postwar Years

Marques of America

Chrysler and Imperial:
The Postwar Years

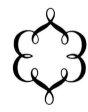

Osceola, Wisconsin 54020, USA

Richard M. Langworth

To Mom and Dad
who always trusted Chrysler

Credits

All photographs credited to the Chrysler Historical Collection except the following:
Briggs Cunningham Automotive Museum, Costa Mesa, California: p.91 (lower left).
G. A. Cunningham: p.111 (upper row and lower right), p.123 (lower left and right).
George Domer: p.91 (upper and lower right).
Paul Hafer: p.30.
Richard Langworth: p.32.

Rick Lenz: p.86 (lower row).
M. W. Martin, Martin's International Newsreel, courtesy *Special Interest Autos:* p.85 (upper left).
Roger Mease: p.19 (center left).
Motor Trend: p.74, p.110, p.121 (upper right).
National Automotive History Collection, Detroit Public Library: p.34 (lower left).
Road & Track: p.66.
The Spectator: p.190.

© 1976 by Richard M. Langworth
ISBN: 0-87938-034-9
Library of Congress Number: 76-19089

All rights reserved. With the exception of quoting brief passages for the purposes of reviews no part of this publication may be reproduced without prior written permission from the publisher: Motorbooks International Publishers & Wholesalers, Inc., 3501 Hennepin Avenue South, Minneapolis, Minnesota 55408, U.S.A.

Printed and bound in the United States of America

Book and jacket design by William F. Kosfeld

Library of Congress Cataloging in Publication Data

Langworth, Richard M
  Chrysler and Imperial.

  Includes index.
  1. Chrysler automobile. 2. Imperial automobile.
I. Title.
TL215.C55L36   629.22'22   76-19089
ISBN 0-87938-034-9

2 3 4 5 6 7 8 9 10

Foreword

This book is a product history. Specifically, it is about the Chrysler and Imperial automobile from the end of World War II to the present, but mainly that fascinating period between 1945 and 1964. It is not a history of the Chrysler Corporation, so it does not deal with corporate decisions and politics, except as they effect the Chrysler and Imperial automobiles.

Writing about Chrysler is at once exciting and sad: exciting because Chrysler built some great automobiles after the war, as well as before it; sad because it's not building great cars today. There are signs — the Cordoba is one — that some interesting new Chryslers will be seen again, now that the worst excesses caused by the ecologists and government-by-hysteria people have rationalized into more honest quests for sensible conservation and automotive safety. Another hopeful sign is the arrival at the helm of Mr. Eugene Cafiero, a product man instead of an accountant. Chrysler may yet rise again. One hopes so. There's a lot of good history behind that name.

I do have a bias in writing about cars. I don't feel any obligation to recount at length their virtues without being cognizant of their faults — given the thesis that to write about a marque at all, it must be relatively virtuous. As my friend Wilson McComb puts it, "we have to be especially careful not to get too misty-eyed and sentimental about the girls *or* the motorcars; we must ask ourselves if they were really that good. Hindsight helps us a little in forming an assessment, but each model should be judged against the background of its own time, recalling the state of the market in those days, what other car makers offered at a similar price, what buyers expected for their money."

Probably, everything good about the postwar Chrysler has already been said by the ad flacks a long time ago. There is, however, no precedent for a work which attempts to put it all together in what I hope is a readable and entertaining form. Possibly this book will point out some of the lesser-known details, and some of the options-never-taken that may have escaped the eye of the enthusiast. If it does that, it will be successful.

I am grateful to those who talked with me, particularly those who were candid, even though many of their names do not appear in the book at their request. Those that do appear are too numerous to mention here, but I would be remiss to omit the names of Virgil Exner, Jr., who talked to me at length about his father and the company; and Raymond H. Dietrich, who told me about an earlier Chrysler and its founder — Walter P. Many others are mentioned and quoted in the following pages. My thanks in advance to them all. I'm appreciative too of Jeffrey I. Godshall for his encouragement, and indeed his ample contributions to these pages; to Jeff, Don Butler and Bill Tilden for helping comb out the nits from the advance draft; to Don and Jeff again for hunting up the many photographs published herein, many of them for the first time. The help of the Chrysler Historical Collection under Messrs. Bunnell and Cheney was priceless, as was that of Jim Bradley of the Detroit Public Library and Mary Cattie of the Free Library of Philadelphia, heads of their respective automotive history departments. Thanks also to George Taylor for help in correcting the second edition.

I also have a list of people who, for better or worse, made me what I am today, beginning with my parents, Harriet and Michael Langworth, who thought it was alright to have a son who liked cars instead of medicine or the law or the florist business; and my wife Barbara, who thinks it's still alright. There are also the people, editors all, merciless and good: Beverly Kimes and Don Vorderman, editor and former editor, respectively, of *Automobile Quarterly*, where I began to learn there were cars other than Kaisers and a period other than the postwar; Motorbooks International editor William Kosfeld and copy editors Amy Parker, Sharin Henricks and Mary Calby, all of whom spent countless hours protecting me from my own failings. Finally there is Tom Warth, president of Motorbooks International, a great Englishman, who presented the opportunity to write the book. He also lent his moral support when I told him I was thinking about freelancing full time.

The opinions and mistakes, as they say, are mine, all mine.

Richard M. Langworth
'Dragonwyck'
Hopewell, New Jersey
April, 1976

Table of Contents

CHAPTER 1
Suggestion of Swagger
page 6

CHAPTER 2
Fabulous Woody
page 28

CHAPTER 3
Silver Anniversary Chrysler
page 40

CHAPTER 4
The Coming of Ex and Tex
page 62

CHAPTER 5
K310 and the Italian Connection
page 80

CHAPTER 6
100 Million Dollar Look
page 100

CHAPTER 7
Looking Forward
page 118

CHAPTER 8
Tailfins to Turbines
page 142

CHAPTER 9
Into the Seventies, Gingerly
page 172

CHAPTER 10
The Present, The Future
page 192

APPENDIX I
The Ghia Crown Imperials
page 198

APPENDIX II
Production Figures, 1946-1975
page 207

APPENDIX III
Literature, 1946-1975
page 211

INDEX
page 214

Suggestion of Swagger

A STORY MAKING the rounds in Detroit during the car-building resurgence in 1948 involved the quality of vehicles then being turned out by the Motor City. A visiting Englishman supposedly remarked, "So this is Detroit, where all the automobiles are made!" A proud native replied, "But we make a lot of things here besides automobiles." "Ah yes, I know," said the Englishman; "I've ridden in some of them." According to *Fortune,* the story especially amused Chrysler Corporation's president K. T. Keller, "because he is so completely confident that the joke couldn't possibly be on *him*. This is in keeping with the suggestion of swagger that has marked the gait of the Chrysler Corporation through its remarkably successful twenty-four year history."

Chrysler, as America's second-largest passenger car producer, faced the booming postwar seller's market with pride, purpose and not a little satisfaction. With minor exceptions — the Airflow being the only one of substance — every move Chrysler made since its origins in 1924 had been the right one.

Beverly Kimes, in *Automobile Quarterly,* described Walter Percy Chrysler as "a glittering personality with a rich, railroadman's vocabulary, short temper and a showman's pride," he had progressed from farm hand to salesman to plant director of American Locomotive; thence to the presidency of Buick. From there Chrysler left to reorganize faltering Willys-Overland, taking a ninety percent cut in salary himself and performing similar salary slashes on company founder John North Willys and making Willys profitable again. From Willys-Overland, Chrysler switched to Maxwell-Chalmers, which became in due course the basis for the Chrysler Corporation.

At the newly reorganized firm appeared the engineering triumvirate of Carl Breer, Owen Skelton and Fred Zeder, that designed the revolutionary new Chrysler of 1924. This brilliant automobile offered something very salesworthy: performance at relatively low cost; with a 201-cubic-inch, L-head six of sixty-eight brake horsepower, and a base price, in the beginning, of only $1,335 for the touring car. For the first time a person could out-drag a Packard, Peerless or Pierce-Arrow for half or a third the price, and Chrysler's future was assured. Chrysler Six production was 32,000 in 1924; it rose to nearly 170,392 for all Chrysler models in 1926. By 1928 three new cars — DeSoto, Dodge and Plymouth — were added to the line and the Corporation had moved up to third place in the sales charts with more than 360,000 cars and trucks produced by all Divisions.

Walter Chrysler's personality pervaded the atmosphere of his company and his cars throughout his tenure as president and beyond his death in 1940. "I first met Mr. Chrysler at the New York Automobile Salon," recalls coachbuilder Raymond H. Dietrich, Chrysler Styling head from 1932-38. "To my way of thinking he was a gentleman all the way through, though a hard master. He was a man who knew what he was doing and how he was

Chrysler's administrative offices and Fluid Drive works were located in Highland Park, north of Detroit.

Chrysler cars were assembled at Detroit's Jefferson Avenue plant.

going to do it, but he had to fight with his engineers, as well as the public at times, to get his points across. There was dynamite in his step, his walk, his smile, and his piercing blue eyes, never doubting what you were saying to him, but always trying to get more out of you. He was a great man."

The prosperity of the Chrysler car through the twenties, and its resurgence after the Depression, was partly based on sister makes cannily added to the line by Walter Chrysler. Before the market crashed he took over Dodge, perennial purveyor of hundreds of thousands of cars a year in the low to medium price bracket, and in 1928 he challenged Ford and Chevrolet with the four-cylinder Plymouth. (In 1932, at the depth of the Depression, he astounded them again with a Plymouth six.) In 1928, too, he launched the DeSoto, plugging the gap between Dodge and Chrysler, and thus his Corporation progressed through the thirties and into the forties, each Division responsible for a definite niche in the automotive marketplace.

The Chrysler car was always at the topmost rung of the price ladder. The company had officially become Chrysler Corporation in June, 1925, and in 1926 produced a Model 70, the numerals standing for its top speed. A smaller Model 58 replaced the Maxwell, while at the other end of the lineup appeared the new $3,100 Imperial E80. But the Chrysler name stood for competitive prowess as well as top-line luxury: In 1928 the potent Chrysler six powered the third- and fourth-place cars at Le Mans, behind a Bentley and a Stutz. With the Depression, Chrysler sales naturally sank, dropping to a low of about 25,000 in 1932. But the economic doldrums did not prevent Chrysler from producing some of its most exciting automobiles ever. Chief among these were the sleek, Cord-inspired open cars that began in 1931, including mighty L-head, eight-cylinder engines and optional four-speed gearboxes.

In 1934 Chrysler Division seemed well along the road to recovery, and accordingly introduced the new, streamlined Airflow, which led the sales campaign at a low $1,245. But its looks never sold well with the public, and it was dropped after 1937, when Chrysler swung all its production to more conventional designs, thus culminating in 1940 with what would be its postwar image.

Engineering always remained (as they've said only recently in advertising) the thing people associated with Chrysler. The marque introduced Fluid Drive in 1938, the first American version of the hydraulic clutch — although GM was bringing out Hydra-Matic at the same time. It was a totally clutchless drive that would ultimately dominate American transmission devlopment. But Chryslers or Chrysler products also introduced fully flexible rubber engine mounts, overdrive as an option in 1934 (standard in 1936), hydraulic brakes, the all-steel body and a new low-friction machining process called Superfinish. Said *Fortune* in 1948, "... these are the things that made the Chrysler Corporation famous. And it is generally accepted that these are the things that made it successful and rich. That the roll call of Chrysler Corporation's more romantic achievements ceases when the active life of Walter P. Chrysler ceases is scarcely a fact to be set with as pure coincidence. It is equally true, however, that Chrysler Corporation hasn't ceased to be successful and it never was so rich, of course, as it is today."

This business magazine was then summing up the postwar Chrysler Corporation as embodied in the presidency of Kaufman Thuma Keller, invariably called 'K.T.' who relieved Walter Chrysler as chief executive in 1935 and became totally dominant when W.P. became ill in 1938. Like his mentor, Keller was a tough, two-fisted ex-railroad man, described as "short, bull-shouldered, profane, his approach as direct and decisive as Dempsey's right to the ribs. He appears to run Chrysler precisely as he pleases, with results that generally please the stockholders." Keller had graduated upward from the railroads to handle the Buick shop foremanship when Walter Chrysler was Buick's president. Later, Keller became president of GM of Canada, and for awhile served as a vice president of Chevrolet. "He runs the job not from any cloistered quarters in downtown Detroit," one reporter wrote, "but from an office building that is placed plunk inside the Highland Park Plant gates. Chrysler has had no Board Chairman since its founder died." Today at Highland Park, the K.T. Keller Building stands in mute testimony to the feats of its namesake.

Says Ray Dietrich of Keller, "K.T. was the same kind of man exactly as Walter Chrysler. He understood. You couldn't pull the wool over his eyes. He was tough, but had a sense of humor too. He would come over to Dietrich, Inc. when I was doing designs for Chryslers and would bring out a little pencil and act like he was going to write something on my drawings. I told him to put it away, they were *my* drawings! When I became associated with Chrysler and K.T. was president, he'd get the pencil out but he wouldn't touch anything, and I'd just keep still. Finally he'd say, 'What the hell is the matter with you? A couple years ago you'd have tore my head off if I tried to touch those drawings.' I said, 'K.T., these are your drawings now, you paid for 'em, you can do anything you want with 'em.' And he laughed like the devil."

Under Keller was B.E. Hutchinson, Chrysler's sixty-year-old vice president and finance committee chairman. Hutch firmly underlined the Chrysler policy of the day: "It is to engineer good products, provide good facilities with which to make them, pay off your debts, and divide what is

Corporate movers in 1933 were finance chairman B.E. Hutchinson, vice president K.T. Keller, Engineering vp F.M. Zeder and president Walter P. Chrysler. The first three were in charge as Chrysler entered the postwar years.

Chrysler Division's Dave Wallace.

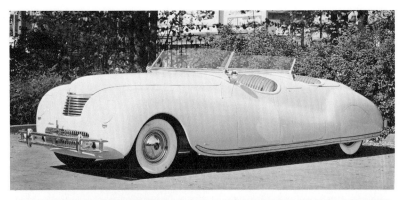

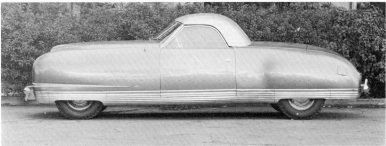

Postwar production styling was greatly influenced by these prewar design exercises: the Newport (upper) and the Thunderbolt (lower).

left with your stockholders, giving them as much of it as you can." William B. Harris noted that this statement said nothing about "leadership" or "contribution," nor contained "any pious reference to the heritage Chrysler has received or the legacy it might leave. It has the cold, clear ring of the countinghouse."

Engineer Fred Zeder was vice chairman of the Corporation, a singularly high honor for a car company to award one of his profession. But those were the kinds of engineers Chrysler had. Zeder dominated what styling or design there was, including the aforementioned Dietrich. Another engineer headed the Chrysler Division, vice president David A. Wallace, an inventor with nearly seventy-five patents for automotive processes and inventions including Chrysler's Superfinish of 1938. Wallace rose to head Chrysler Division in 1937, and remained there for a lengthy twenty-seven years. He was largely responsible for the fabulous Town and Country — of which more anon — and can be considered a critical influence in the postwar Chrysler story.

The engineer's approach was evident in Chrysler's method of plant management and modernization compared with that of its major rivals. K.T. Keller's theory was that auto companies went out of business primarily because they never plowed enough earnings back into plant modernization and new product development. Keller did just the opposite: Chrysler's balance sheet always held plant and equipment at low values, giving the Corporation the lowest ratio of fixed assets to sales of any firm in the industry. In 1941, with Chrysler running at capacity, the ratio was twelve cents to the dollar against about thirty-six cents for General Motors. At the same time, though, enormous funds were poured into plant and equipment, to keep the facilities efficient and the new developments coming.

Depreciation on Chrysler facilities was huge, despite their low rating in the company's books. "Just what the eventual cost of replacing facilities now in use may be is obscure," Keller said after the war, "government indices show that industrial building construction costs have risen eighty-three percent since 1939. There have also been substantial increases in the prices of machinery and equipment. The level at which prices may stabilize is, to say the least, uncertain."

Of all Chrysler's operations, those in or near Detroit comprised seventy percent of the total facilities and employed close to eighty percent of the work force. All major Division assembly plants were in the area: 1950 employment, for example, was 12,000 for Plymouth, 4,000 for DeSoto and 34,000 for Dodge — whose Hamtramck plant built castings, stampings, motors and bodies as well as assembling Dodge cars. Dodge Truck accounted for another 5,000 workers. Chryslers were assembled at a factory on Jefferson Avenue in Detroit, which also produced motors and employed close to 10,000 people. Additional Detroit area plants included Lynch Road (axle and housings), Dodge Forge (forgings), Nine Mile Press (stampings), Winfield (foundry) and Warren Avenue in Dearborn (bodies and motors). At Highland Park on the north side were the executive offices, Styling and Engineering departments; Highland Park also produced Fluid Drive transmissions and miscellaneous minor parts.

New assembly plants were under construction by 1949 in Newark, Delaware (at the old tank plant); Trenton, Michigan; Indianapolis and New Orleans. But Chrysler's operating assembly plants outside Detroit were, for the time being, confined to Dodge and Plymouth facilities in California and a factory in Evansville, Indiana. Transmissions and front-end parts were built in Kokomo and New Castle, Indiana, and minor bits at Marysville, Michigan.

Centralization did create a problem, in that Chrysler lacked the cheaper distribution advantages enjoyed by GM and Ford, whose many

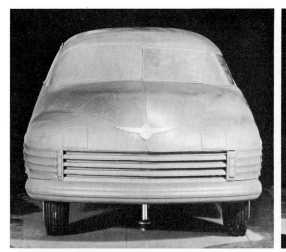

assembly and component plants constructed cars from knocked-down parts in all areas of the country. But Chrysler made more of a profit per car than either of its two major rivals, and this made management less concerned about Plymouth catching Ford or Chevrolet than it was with that ring of the countinghouse. Said K.T. Keller, "How flattering to be considered one of the Big Three."

An early future-Chrysler design was completed in small scale, January 1940: Streamlined with integrated fenders, it emphasized forward motion with extended rear bumpers and sculptured sides announced by a clean, horizontal grille.

Windsor proposal dated May 1941. Again the wraparound molding was featured, along with covered headlights. The 1942 DeSoto actually appeared in production with hidden lights, though the 1942 Chryslers were conventional.

The Chrysler that emerged in the years before World War II was, with the Airflow lesson learned, not at all revolutionary. But it was sound, and extremely well-engineered. As a result, the Division made steady gains in its output from the turning point of 1932:

Year	Calendar Year Production	Industry Standing
1932	25,291	11
1933	30,220	10
1934	36,929	10
1935	50,010	10
1936	71,295	11
1937	107,872	10

The recession of 1937-38 set business back temporarily, but Chrysler again recovered and in 1940 and 1941 posted successive record years:

Year	Calendar Year Production	Industry Standing
1938	41,496	11
1939	67,479	12
1940	115,824	9
1941	141,522	8

Then came December 7, 1941, and the bombs falling on Pearl Harbor. It was quickly realized that civilian automobile production would be halted for the duration of the war, and Chrysler was able to produce only 5,292 units in calendar year 1942 before shutting down the assembly lines in late February.

During the war, Chrysler built a wide variety of defense equipment, and its output (considering DeSoto, Dodge and Plymouth as well as Chrysler Division) was astronomical. There were 120,000 anti-aircraft guns built, half of the Bofors-type and half 40mm 'pom pom' naval weapons; over 18,000 nine-cylinder Wright Cyclone airplane engines; 20,000 land-mine detectors; 2,000 radar units and 1,500 searchlight reflectors; 5,500 Sperry Gyrocompasses, built under license; 7,800 'Sea Mules,' or utility harbor tugs; 29,000 marine engines. But tanks — particularly the Sherman

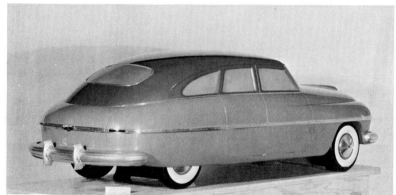

New Yorker proposals from early 1942 bore a family resemblance to the Windsors but with more ornate grilles (one considered skirted front wheels). By this time it was known that car production would have to wait until after the war.

Thunderbolt influence is evident in this full-size 1941 clay model of a proposed coupe.

Wartime evidence of the talents of Chrysler Styling. The armored car (left) is signed by Robert Cadwallader and Buzz Grisinger, the scout car (right) by John Chika. All of these men were hired away from Chrysler by Joe Frazer (Kaiser-Frazer), who had known them from his own days at Highland Park.

variety — were the products for which Chrysler won most fame. More than 18,000 Shermans, out of over 25,000 tanks produced by Chrysler, were built at the Detroit Tank Arsenal, which Keller had constructed for the purpose with government approval. No one can question Chrysler's dedication to the war effort: Not only were its products durable, but its profits as a percent of sales were below average for the wartime motor industry.

The ban on auto production was lifted fairly late in 1945, and Chrysler Division built only 322 cars that year. But it began returning to a semblance of normal production in early 1946. No one was in the least surprised that, like the rest of the prewar auto producers, Chrysler's 1946 cars were only mildly face-lifted from the 1942 predecessors. This has been attributed in Chrysler's case to the postwar material shortages and government controls. But Kaiser-Frazer, which had no prewar models to offer, managed to produce more than 300,000 cars in 1946-48 despite the shortages. It should be understood that no major change of model was deemed necessary out of economic considerations as well as outside factors. Each company knew that for three, four or possibly even five years after the war, it would be unnecessary to rely on anything new or different. It would be foolhardy to let the unamortized dies be scrapped for the sake of brand-new products in 1947 or 1948, unless you were Studebaker, which elected to take a chance and introduce a drastically redesigned 1947 car in the middle of 1946. Chrysler, like the majority, stood pat.

"The plan was for each company to wring the profits out of its old models," one industry executive commented, "and stave off the rapidly rising cost of retooling, right up to the point where the law of diminishing returns began to operate, i.e. the psychological point at which the buyer was beginning to make up his mind about the car he would purchase when he had a free choice. Before that point was reached something new had to be added. But when? For each company the problem was slightly different."

This doesn't mean that no model revisions were considered. Many quarter- and eighth-scale clay models and hundreds of renderings depicting the probable shape of the 1943, 1944 and 1945 Chryslers were well underway before the Japanese unexpectedly ended speculation on their eventual introduction. Most of these designs evolved from lines set down by two significant prewar Chrysler showcars, the LeBaron Thunderbolt and Newport, largely designed by Alex S. Tremulis of Briggs, and Ralph Roberts of LeBaron, which by the late thirties was a Briggs subsidiary.

"Styling at Briggs was almost a 'good will' department," says Tremulis, where Briggs "could offer our clients a fresh viewpoint, free from engineering restrictions and dedicated solely to the task of inspiring top management for future models." The Thunderbolt was a long, low, retractable convertible, a two-or three-seater on a 127½-inch Chrysler chassis featuring wraparound bright molding that formed a full-perimeter bumper. The Newport, a dual-cowl phaeton on a 145½-inch wheelbase, used a rakish envelope body with smoothly flowing fenders and soft lines. Ralph Roberts recalls that the two show cars were originally conceived "more or less for our own amusement, but K.T. Keller was very friendly to us. Like Edsel Ford, K.T. liked to have outside talent around to encourage Chrysler's own designers, though he actually used very little of what we designed in toto. We eventually built six of each car."

Both the Newport and the Thunderbolt eventually made the rounds of the car shows, exhibited under Tremulis' clever title, "The Measured Mile Creates a New Motor Car" — referring to George Eyston's land speed record cars, one of which had been named Thunderbolt. According to Tremulis, this 'hook' — reviving streamlining despite the failure of the Airflow — sold Keller and Chrysler on the notion of producing six each of the cars for publicity purposes.

The Thunderbolt and the Newport strongly influenced Chrysler design during the final prewar months, largely because they greatly appealed to K.T. Keller — especially the former. Many clays were built featuring the Thunderbolt's extruded rub rails, wrapping entirely around some cars to form the grille at the front. On the Thunderbolt, Tremulis had built the curved bumper sections at the corners out of brass, and then had them chrome-plated. This would have proved infeasible (cost-wise) in production, but the idea apparently received more than a little attention, at least for potential DeSoto and Chrysler models. Prototypes also bore hidden headlights, a feature of both the Thunderbolt and the Newport that did see some production in the 1942 DeSoto; but the idea was not revived after the war.

Despite their progenitors, the 1943-45 prototypes were designed entirely by Chrysler, not Briggs. By the early forties, an embryonic Styling department had taken shape. Of course it was directed by an engineer — Oliver H. Clark, chief body engineer, who reported directly to Fred M. Zeder. Ray Dietrich's star at Chrysler, as Styling chief in the difficult post-Airflow period, waned rapidly with the decline in health of his old friend Walter Chrysler. And in 1938, when Chrysler became ill, Dietrich departed. He was replaced by Robert Cadwallader, who was largely responsible for directing the exterior styling studio during 1943-45 model planning.

The small Styling unit eventually came to be known, as at GM, as the Art & Colour Section. Despite its subservience to Engineering, Chrysler Art & Colour possessed ample talent. Two of its best men were Arnott B. 'Buzz' Grisinger and Herb Weissinger, who with Cadwallader would leave for Kaiser-Frazer after the war; there they would respectively head the advanced Frazer and Kaiser studios at Willow Run.

Herb Weissinger was a skilled artist and a clay model perfectionist. Tremulis, who worked with him later at Kaiser-Frazer, says he "was a maestro in the execution of a line on a surface. He regarded a sixty-fourth-inch deviation in a roof line as unthinkable, and would work hours on end seeking its correction. His chrome appliqués were done with the perfection of a Cellini; he was easily the best of us in this area alone. He had the qualifications of a brilliant body engineer, and could cross swords with the best of them in defense of Styling. After forty years in the business I feel qualified to judge those whom I consider best. Herb Weissinger was truly one of the greatest."

Grisinger, Tremulis says, was "the greatest sculptural design modeler of all time. Buzz preferred to work alone. Tremendously talented, he did very little on paper — usually a quick sketch — that was all he needed to attack a full-size clay model single-handedly. In his field he was in a class by himself. The body engineering draftsmen told me that they never had to surface-develop any irregularities in his models; they merely took templates off the clay and used his lines verbatim. . . . Had I the power of decision, I would have locked Buzz up in a small modeling room for twelve hours a day with two assistants to keep piling up clay, and let him work to his heart's content. For lunch I would have shoved a sandwich and a cup of coffee through a trap door. I would have doubled his executive's salary and then gone out and bought more stock."

The staff of Art & Colour never exceeded several dozen, including clay modelers; during the war it lost the services of many young men, including Grisinger, who had been assigned to the Manhattan Project (which produced the atomic bomb). Cadwallader and Weissinger remained, though, and can be credited with much of the stillborn 1943-45 cars, as well as the mildly face-lifted 1946-48 Chryslers.

The production 1946-48's evolved from a design developed by Dietrich and partly by Cadwallader, which was introduced in late 1939 on the 1940 Chryslers: a sort of fat bathtub shape, with separate fenders at each corner and a massive, horizontally-barred, pointed grille. The latter sat between the headlights in 1940, but edged outward in 1941 and finally wrapped itself right around the forward part of the front fenders in 1942, emulating the clay models then being designed in the image of the Thunderbolt. Models like the 1942 New Yorker were fitted with fender skirts, bearing a shiny bauble where the hub cap would be if the wheel were visible, a remnant of the LeBaron days which had filtered down to Chrysler via Briggs. The Dietrich-Cadwallader design emphasized separate, not integral fenders, though the 1943-45 clays all featured completely integral fender lines.

With Chrysler hauling out barely-used prewar dies, the 1946 models were basically 1942's with a new face — but it was an effective one. The multi-bar embellishment of the front and rear fenders was eliminated, save for two strips on the front and one on the back; the grille itself was given vertical bars to create an egg crate effect, which became quite famous as it remained current for three straight years. Some British writers have de-

1946-48 Royal four-door sedan.   1946-48 Royal brougham, or two-door sedan.

1946-48 Royal three-passenger coupe.   Strong ladder-type C38 Windsor/Royal chassis.

plored "the broad, chromium smile" of the postwar Chrysler, while commenting not at all on the comparable plated area of their own Rolls-Royce! In fact, for 1946, the Chrysler looked entirely correct and very current, its smooth fenders washing out at the front doors, its proportions on the longer Chrysler wheelbase far better than the concurrent models of DeSoto, Dodge and Plymouth. Of course its fit and finish were better too, in accord with its price category. The 1946 lineup of models, with original NADA f.o.b. list prices, was as follows:

Model Body Style (passengers)	Price	W.B. (in)	Weight (lb)
Series C38 Royal			
sedan, 4 dr. (6)	$1,561	121½	3,523
brougham, 2 dr. (6)	1,526	121½	3,458
club coupe (6)	1,551	121½	3,443
business coupe (3)	1,431	121½	3,373
sedan, l.w.b. 4 dr. (8)	1,943	139½	3,977
limousine (8)	2,063	139½	4,022
Series C38 Windsor			
sedan, 4 dr. (6)	$1,611	121½	3,528
brougham, 2 dr. (6)	1,591	121½	3,468
club coupe (6)	1,601	121½	3,448
business coupe (3)	1,481	121½	3,383
convertible (6)	1,861	121½	3,693
sedan, l.w.b. 4 dr. (8)	1,993	139½	3,977
limousine (8)	2,113	139½	4,052
Series C38 Town and Country			
sedan, 4 dr. (6)	$2,366	121½	3,917
Series C39 Saratoga			
sedan, 4 dr. (6)	$1,863	127½	3,972
brougham, 2 dr. (6)	1,838	127½	3,932
club coupe (6)	1,848	127½	3,892
business coupe (3)	1,753	127½	3,817
Series C39 New Yorker			
sedan, 4 dr. (6)	$1,963	127½	3,987
brougham, 2 dr. (6)	1,938	127½	3,932
club coupe (6)	1,948	127½	3,897
business coupe (3)	1,853	127½	3,837
convertible (6)	2,193	127½	4,132
Series C39 Town and Country			
sedan, 4 dr. (6)	$2,718	127½	4,300
convertible (6)	2,743	127½	4,332
Series C40 Crown Imperial			
limousine (8)	$3,875	145½	4,814

As can be seen from the above, the four wheelbases were directly related to their work assignments and followed a logical progression. The standard, beetle-shaped four-door and two-door, the latter known as the Brougham in some promotion, gave way to a longer-decked club coupe with a smaller greenhouse and roughly triangular side windows; and finally to the turret-top business coupe with its huge deck and single bench-seat placed ahead of a cargo platform inside the 'turret.' Long-wheelbase models were simply stretched versions of the sedans, the chauffeur's compartment leather-upholstered and the rear sections fitted with quality Bedford cord upholstery. The convertible body relied on a heavier frame for rigidity, hence its greater weight; convertibles were not available in the Saratoga or long-wheelbase models.

The Windsor Six four-door sedan was the most popular postwar Chrysler, and at a starting price of $1,611 it was quite a bargain. It undercut in price, the eight-cylinder Oldsmobiles, all Buicks except the Special, the 1947 Studebaker Land Cruiser, the Kaiser and the Frazer— the last three "all-new postwar cars" it handily undersold despite a substantially pricier 'image.' The New Yorker was the rich man's Chrysler, and the Crown Imperial the pride of dignitaries and politicians, embassies and Mafia chieftains, at the top of the line.

Postwar shortages made whitewall tires unavailable for some time after peace was declared, and Chrysler dealers substituted painted steel or white plastic 'do-nuts' that were hung around the hub caps to separate the plain black tire from the hubs by a modest span of white. Sometimes the do-nuts were offered as standard, but as options they rarely sold for more than fifteen dollars a set, and were quite popular. Chrysler interiors were not known for breathtaking color, but the very luxurious convertibles were well-fitted with two-tone Bedford cord and leather, steering wheels and interior garnish moldings color-keyed to match. Revived from prewar offerings was the brilliant 'Highlander plaid' upholstery, using a tartan design cloth in combination with red leather bolsters. Always unique too was the upholstery of the Town and Country — more of which in the following chapter.

The Chrysler dashboard was, however, one of the most ornate and opulent in the industry, heavily embellished with mottled or solid color plastics, which were then considered rare luxury items. It imparted all vital information in a straightforward way. Behind a massive eighteen-inch-diameter steering wheel was a rectangular panel bearing speedometer, odometer and trip odometer, and the four small minor gauges. A central plastic grid held the radio speaker, and a tall clock was mounted to its right with a row of control buttons below for the usual functions. Chrysler's umbrella-type parking brake locked the driveshaft, rather than the brakes.

The Windsor and New Yorker both offered Chrysler's unique and luxurious Highlander plaid as an optional interior.

The Royal had Chrysler's plainest interior.

1946-48 Windsor eight-passenger sedan used long wheelbase.

1946-48 Windsor convertible.

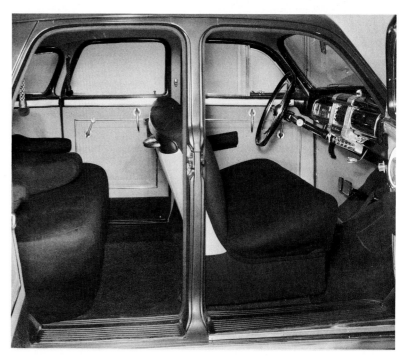

1947 New Yorker four-door sedan of Roger Mease.

1946-48 New Yorker convertible.

1946-48 Saratoga four-door sedan, brougham and three-passenger coupe.

The very plush interior of the New Yorker sedan.

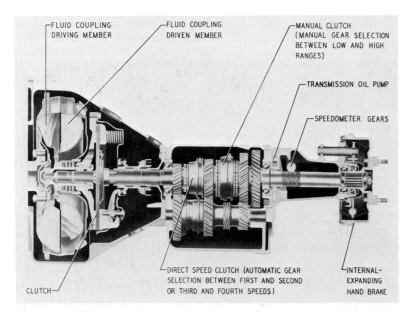

Main components of the M-6 hydraulic Fluid Drive transmission.

A C-29 in production at Jefferson Avenue. Jefferson accounted for all Chryslers and Imperials (except for a two-year period starting in 1959, when Imperial assembly moved to Dearborn), and it still does today.

The main options were the eight-tube radio and dual-output heater. One more important seventy-five dollar option with which most Chryslers were fitted was the inevitable and incredible Fluid Drive, usually coupled with Chrysler's M5 hydraulic transmission — though the two items were listed separately on option lists.

Fluid Drive was one of those intriguing Chrysler engineering feats for which the company earned fame throughout its history. Though generally associated with the postwar days, it had first appeared in 1938 and was standard equipment on the 1939 Custom Imperial. In retrospect, it was probably over-complicated: combining a conventional clutch, a torque converter and electrical shifting circuits which, as one writer said, "afforded the full range of potential transmission trouble."

The system eliminated the conventional flywheel by replacing it with a fluid coupling-type of torque converter. This performed all the flywheel's normal functions — storing energy, smoothing power impulses, carrying the ring gear that meshed with the starter pinion — except providing a contact surface for the clutch plate; so a clutch was mounted behind it. The fluid coupling was a cylindrical drum, eighty percent filled with low-viscosity mineral oil. It contained a casing, or 'driver,' with radial vanes on its inner surface facing a driven 'runner' with another set of vanes running freely inside a cover which in assembly was welded to the opposing drum, making a solid unit. The oil, incidentally, allowed the casing to be sealed by providing permanent lubrication. The fluid coupling was bolted to the crankshaft as a flywheel would be, and the fluid was retained by a leak-proof seal around the rotating central shaft. The filler hole was designed to prevent overfilling.

When the engine was started, the coupling revolved as a flywheel would; but inside, the vanes attached to the casing rotated, throwing the oil outward in a whirlpool fashion. The oil circulated across a quarter-inch gap between the driver and runner and onto the vanes of the latter. The runner then turned through the action of the moving oil, though always a bit slower than the driver. This provided a 'cushioning' effect that accounted for the smooth flow of power for which Fluid Drive was known, with no metal-to-metal contact.

The cushioning effect prevented the engine from stalling when the car was stopped with a gear engaged, allowing the gear lever to remain in position without depressing the clutch pedal. There were two Fluid Drive gear lever positions: *Low* controlled first and second gear of the

1946-48 Crown Imperial eight-passenger limousine. Crown Imperial interior.

transmission, and was used only for extra pulling power; *high* connected to third and fourth gear, and was used for all normal motoring. *Low* was located where second would be on a conventional column shift, and *high* was in its usual place.

To start off, the driver normally shifted into high and stepped on the accelerator. At about 14 mph, he released the pedal slightly, waited for a very audible *clunk,* and cruised on in what was fourth, or high gear. To stop, he braked as he would in an automatic transmission car, and to start again he just stepped on the accelerator. The system eliminated about ninety-five percent of all gear shifting.

Ted West, writing of the Windsor in a 1968 issue of *Road & Track,* noted that the Fluid Drive could actually be used as a conventional four speed. "To shift from high range of low gear to low range of high gear (better re-read that) it is necessary to de-clutch, change the shift lever position to high, re-engage the clutch, press the accelerator to the floor to activate the electrical kick-down switch, and with luck you will continue forward. See how simple and relaxing? To reach high-range high, just let off the gas again . . . you can run through the gears or simply leave it in high, à la Dynaflow (another legend of the Old West), let the torque converter do its stuff. This latter method results in very 'dignified' acceleration and is recommended only for people with several gasoline credit cards."

A conventional friction clutch was mounted between the fluid coupling and the transmission. This allowed Ted West's hot starts, and was used to back up, of course — reverse did not benefit from the fluid coupling. Many drivers were known to ignore this handy set-up and drive as conventionally as possible — the reasons have been, I hope, clearly explained — but Fluid Drive must have been a boon to many neophyte drivers of the day. There was only one strong warning about it from Chrysler: "The fluid used in the coupling must be of the correct chemical analysis and viscosity. This fluid is obtainable ONLY through the Chrysler Parts Corporation, and no other should be used under any circumstances." A small price to pay for all these virtues!

West, who like this writer was weaned on sports cars and to whom the Chrysler Windsor was obviously something else entirely, nevertheless had some favorable things to say about the car, which are worth quoting. "Mechanically, then, the Chrysler Windsor is *not* any great charmer, but 'special interest' cars usually aren't. Mass-produced, reflecting the general tastes of an era rather than the individual mannerisms of a genius, as cautiously inventive as possible, as utilitarian as the price class will allow, such cars are interesting not because they have unique solutions to the automotive problem, but simply because they are in some way 'foreign' to more modern automobiles. The craftsmanship and general feeling of opulence of this car, for instance, clearly distinguishes it from American

The Chrysler production dashboard was less symmetrical than some prototypes predicted. This clay mock-up features rotating controls, centrally mounted radio and clock; note also the side grid, apparently intended as a heater outlet (left). Ornate and amply endowed with lucite plastic knobs, this Saratoga dashboard was typical of the period. Chrysler dashes featured full instrumentation and all controls within easy reach of the driver (right).

cars of the last ten years. It's a luxury car in a way that makes newer cars seem just flashy. If sometimes clumsily conceived, the execution of the car is remarkable and its durability simply outrageous. I grant that this particular example had the benefit of scrupulous care by its original owner, but after 20 years every single foot light, reading light, brake warning flasher, and so on, works perfectly. The clock runs a little slow, but how many auto clocks ever move at all? The radio, of course, is fantastic and, though this may seem unforgivably camp, has lights that shade from cool blue to hot red (phew!) as the tone selector is turned from 'Mello' to 'Speech.' The back seat is fathomless and has folddown armrests and a reading light over the back window! Real late 40's Sidney Greenstreet stuff — perhaps the last example of that particular kind of luxury.

"Except for an elongated cowl (the last gasp of the long, high classic hood line), the body molds are basically unchanged from pre-war Chrys Corp. sedans. Heavy gauge panels are beautifully fitted to each other and the finish is truly amazing. After 20 years the original blue paint is still brilliant, deep and handsome. The car's chrome is also excellent, and, if used so lavishly that it makes the car look nose-heavy, at least the plating is first quality. Finally, the elegant use of high quality plastic (remember when real plastic was a luxury?) here and there puts more modern applications of the material in a very bad light. Handsomely designed and coordinated by the simple crown which symbolized Chrysler in those years, one wonders what could possibly be advantageous about the cheap junk infesting the interiors of even the most expensive later American autos."

I have searched for some years for a statement embodying the feeling one gets from one of these outwardly clumsy, but so very beautifully constructed cars of the late forties. I have taken the liberty of quoting Mr. West at length — his comments are the best summation I have yet encountered of that feeling.

In 1946 the mechanical design of Chryslers was even less altered from prewar concepts than their looks, and the brake horsepower was in fact rated lower. The Spitfire Six powering the C38 series was a 250.6-cubic-inch cast-iron L-head, bore and stroke 3 7/16 by 4 1/2 inches, with four main bearings and 114 bhp at 3600 rpm, carburetor by Carter and 'solar spark' six-volt ignition. The Spitfire Eight used a 3 1/4 by 4 7/8, 323 1/2-cubic-inch L-head of 135 bhp at 3400 rpm. Driving impressions of either of these engines hardly differ, and it takes one highly familiar with Chryslers to tell what's under the hood without looking. The engines provide ample torque, but with leisurely, low-revving horsepower, they are thus quiet runners that take a long time to work up to cruising velocity.

All Chrysler engines boasted Dave Wallace's Superfinish. Said the company, "Superfinish parts are mirror-bright and smooth. They reduce break-in . . . reduce wear . . . preserve compression . . . hold gasoline and oil consumption to an efficient minimum . . . keep Chrysler engines young." The engines rode on sturdy ladder chassis of box-section steel. One customer, watching his car being assembled at the Jefferson Avenue Plant in Detroit, asked if they were sure the frame a crew had just picked off a pile was a good one. "Mister," came the reply, "if we got a bad frame, we wouldn't waste it on a guy like you. We'd send it to the Smithsonian Institution in Washington as a curiosity."

Enthusiasm at the plant was apparently shared by a large number of customers, for Chrysler Division was able to build 76,753 cars in calendar 1946 despite shortages and delays, and finish in eleventh place, just behind Studebaker and ahead of Mercury and DeSoto. One customer bubbled, "Chrysler is the finest car made. Had six since 1929. Hope to have many more." He was echoed by another in home town Detroit: "I drive anywhere from 60,000 to 75,000 miles a year in the territory of Ohio, Michigan and Indiana. In my opinion there is no other car that could stand up the way my Chrysler has. I have driven over 16,000 miles in the last 3½ months — over good and bad roads— not one bit of trouble. Motor purrs like a cat. I also get exceptionally good gas mileage."

On that evidence, there wasn't much need to change. The 1947 Chryslers were introduced in January of that year and aside from serial numbers, were altered only in detail: fender trim, hubcaps, color combinations, carburetors, wheels and instruments in particular. They also began using Goodyear low-pressure Super Cushion tires between August and November 1947. The model lineup was somewhat restructured and the prices were about one hundred dollars higher:

Model Body Style (passengers)	Price	W.B.(in)	Weight (lb)
Series C38 Royal			
sedan, 4dr (6)	$1,661	121½	3,523
brougham, 2dr (6)	1,626	121½	3,458
club coupe (6)	1,651	121½	3,443
business coupe (3)	1,561	121½	3,373
sedan, l.w.b. 4 dr (8)	2,043	139½	3,977
limousine (8)	2,163	139½	4,022
Series C38 Windsor			
sedan, 4dr (6)	$1,711	121½	3,528
Traveler (6)	1,846	121½	3,610
brougham, 2dr (6)	1,691	121½	3,468
club coupe (6)	1,701	121½	3,448
business coupe (3)	1,611	121½	3,383
convertible (6)	2,075	121½	3,693
sedan, l.w.b. 4dr (8)	2,093	139½	3,977
limousine (8)	2,213	139½	4,052
Series C38 Town and Country			
sedan, 4dr (6)	$2,713	121½	3,955
Series C39 Saratoga			
sedan, 4dr (6)	$1,973	127½	3,972
brougham, 2dr (6)	1,948	127½	3,900
club coupe (6)	1,958	127½	3,930
business coupe (3)	1,873	127½	3,817
Series C39 New Yorker			
sedan, 4dr (6)	$2,073	127½	3,987
brougham, 2dr (6)	2,048	127½	3,932
club coupe (6)	2,058	127½	3,940
business coupe (3)	1,973	127½	3,837
convertible (6)	2,447	127½	4,132
Series C39 Town and Country			
convertible (6)	$2,998	127½	4,332
Series C40 Crown Imperial			
sedan, l.w.b. 4dr (8)	$4,205	145½	4,865
limousine (8)	4,305	145½	4,875

Fluid Drive was listed as standard in the Crown Imperial but still optional in other Chryslers. The eight-cylinder Town and Country sedan was dropped after a run of one hundred cars, and a sedan (non-partition) version of the 145½-inch-wheelbase Crown Imperial was added on July 2, 1947. But the main attraction of the new 1947's was the unique Traveler in the Windsor line.

The Traveler was perhaps inspired by DeSoto's more ambitious carry-all project, the Suburban, but the two cars were not simply versions of each other. The C-38 Traveler was mounted on a standard 121-inch wheelbase, had a folding rear seat and a wooden roof rack. The DeSoto Suburban had a long (139½-inch) wheelbase with triple seats that could be folded or interchanged, and wooden planking in the trunk area with no division between trunk and seats.

The DeSoto was probably so much more 'complete' a package than the Traveler because the Briggs Body Company had taken special interest in the project. According to James W. Shank, a DeSoto body engineer interviewed by *Special-Interest Autos,* "Briggs did the trim work [and] interior styling was done by Briggs' styling department in conjunction with the Chrysler people." According to Mr. Shank, "the Suburban came

The 1947-48 Chrysler Traveler was uniquely equipped to handle huge payloads. In addition to the large trunk and more than ample interior, the wood and metal roof rack was capable of holding considerable luggage. The Traveler's durable interior made ample use of vinyl upholstery.

to us as a painted and trimmed body. DeSoto mounted it on the frame and completed it—put on the front end, sheetmetal, etc."

The wood-trimmed Suburban was a true payload hauler, while the Chrysler Traveler mainly shared its wooden luggage roof idea and nothing more. Nevertheless, here were lessons in space utilization from an industry some people say never learned the art—they offer dramatic proof to the contrary. Because the middle seat of the car could be shifted far forward, and its backrests folded flat as well as those of the third seat, a mammoth cargo space could be created behind the driver. The middle seat was happily interchangeable with the front seat, so if you wore one out you still had another, and even with all three seats in use (nine passengers could be accommodated), there was still room for seven or eight large suitcases and a golf bag in the ample trunk.

Originally listing at less than $2,000, the Traveler was surely a bargain in terms of people and luggage-moving; but if its cavernous interior was *still* not enough, it also featured a white ash roof rack. A Traveler option, at $47.00, was a canvas cover for any luggage carried thereon. Typical of the thought that went into Chryslers, the Traveler came with a little step plate that hooked into the rear of the running boards on either side, to make it easier to reach the roof. Only 4,182 Travelers were built for the 1947 and 1948 model years, less than half the number of DeSoto Suburbans, making them among the rarer postwar Chryslers.

Traveler interiors were also carefully designed for practicality in the work for which they would largely be used. They featured Delon and Tolex plastic upholstery in bright shades — cream, red, brown and green. The door panels, inside trunk paneling and forward kick panels were made by Bakelite, Inc., which reproduced photographs of actual wood grain and etched them onto cylinders that printed the photos on sheets of paper. The paper was bonded to a cellulose base. Mike Lamm relates that this core "formed the basis of a 'sandwich' of layers of phenolic resin laminates. The entire sandwich was cured at 350°F before die-cutting and trimming to the final shape. Curved panels, as inside the trunk, came by heat-pressing the laminate in wooden dies. These wooden dies cost about one-eightieth as much as similar steel dies. The final product, even today, looks and feels much like Formica. It resists scratching, scuffing, and the panels inside the Suburban we photographed look as good now as when they left the Briggs plant."

The Chrysler Traveler was not, obviously, a major factor in Chrysler's increasing production for calendar 1947, which totalled 109,195 units. The Division was now beginning to solve its shortage problems and return to a semblance of the volume it enjoyed in 1940 and 1941. The upstarts at Kaiser-Frazer and the Mercury Division of Ford passed Chrysler in this year, but Chrysler surpassed Hudson, which put the Division in the number twelve position. Though the all-new 1949 models were by now close to production, Chrysler again introduced an unchanged line on January 2, 1948:

Model Body Style (passengers)	Price	W.B.(in)	Weight (lb)
Series C38 Royal			
sedan, 4dr (6)	$1,955	121½	3,523
brougham, 2dr (6)	1,908	121½	3,485
club coupe (6)	1,934	121½	3,475
business coupe (3)	1,819	121½	3,395
sedan, l.w.b. 4dr (8)	2,380	139½	3,977
limousine (8)	2,506	139½	4,022
Series C38 Windsor			
sedan, 4dr (6)	$2,021	121½	3,528
Traveler (6)	2,163	121½	3,610
brougham, 2dr (6)	1,989	121½	3,510
club coupe (6)	2,000	121½	3,475
business coupe (3)	1,884	121½	3,395
convertible (6)	2,414	121½	3,693
sedan, l.w.b. 4dr (8)	2,434	139½	3,935
limousine (8)	2,561	139½	4,035
Series C38 Town and Country			
sedan, 4dr (6)	$2,860	121½	3,955
Series C39 Saratoga			
sedan, 4dr (6)	$2,291	127½	3,972
brougham, 2dr (6)	2,254	127½	3,900
club coupe (6)	2,265	127½	3,930
business coupe (3)	2,165	127½	3,817
Series C39 New Yorker			
sedan, 4dr (6)	$2,411	127½	3,987
brougham, 2dr (6)	2,374	127½	3,932
club coupe (6)	2,385	127½	3,940
business coupe (3)	2,285	127½	3,837
convertible (6)	2,815	127½	4,132
Series C39 Town and Country			
convertible (6)	$3,395	127½	4,332
Series C40 Crown Imperial			
sedan, l.w.b. 4dr (8)	$4,662	145½	4,865
limousine (8)	4,767	145½	4,875

As in 1947, hydraulic transmission and Fluid Drive were combined as one option, though its price was up from seventy-five to ninety-five dollars, reflecting substantial inflation in the base price of the cars themselves. On March 31, 1948, whitewall tires and stainless steel wheel-trim rings became available. No changes whatsoever were made in the line. And there was still no automatic transmission.

Chrysler gave *Fortune*, "the impression that it will string along with the Fluid Drive. . . . Perhaps Chrysler is a dissembler on this point — everybody else in the business is scrambling to build something as good as Buick's Dynaflow — but its engineers claim to know of no fully automatic transmission that won't eat more gas than Fluid Drive. Reasonable fuel consumption, plus good acceleration, is a Chrysler talking point; accommodation of interior design to the facts of human anatomy is another; mechanical integrity is still another. In short, Chrysler is selling transportation. K.T. Keller has said, 'Wide as our research interests range, you may be sure that more time and attention, and more money, is spent year in and year out, on these quiet means of individual satisfaction than upon creating revolutionary vehicles and power plants.'"

But if Chrysler didn't find it attractive to do anything very unorthodox in those days, others did, and chief among these was the Derham Custom Bodyworks of Rosemont, Pennsylvania. One of the few coachbuilders still cooking by the end of World War II, Derham developed a number of interesting conversions, mainly to Chrysler New Yorkers and Crown Imperials: a tandem windshield phaeton for the King of Saudi Arabia, equipped with running boards for the game (or peasant) beaters; two Continental-like two-door coupes on stretched wheelbases with greenhouse and deck directly cribbing from Lincoln's classic; a boxy seven-passenger Pullman limousine for cereal fortune heiress Marjorie Merriweather Post; and a number of formal sedans and limousines featuring blind quarter panels and leather or canvas-covered padded tops. A few Crown Imperial chassis were used for funeral vehicles, particularly by Superior of Lima, Ohio, and one Imperial front end was fitted to a Dodge truck chassis and made into a camera crew car for Paramount studios. There were no Chrysler taxis — DeSoto handled that market — but a number of other bizarre one-offs were produced for various commercial purposes.

K.T. Keller's conservatism struck some as strange when cast against Chrysler's long history of engineering breakthroughs. Though admitting that

Derham special bodies on the long-wheelbase Chrysler chassis included (top to bottom) the five-passenger town limousine with padded canvas top; an austere Pullman limousine for Post Foods' heiress Marjorie Merriweather Post; a dual-cowl phaeton for Arabia's King Saud; and the six-passenger Crown Imperial limousine with an automatic raising roof section allowed passengers to enter without stooping.

any auto manufacturer preaching "the homely virtues of sound transportation" is worthy of praise — and how shockingly familiar that comment seems today — *Fortune* found it something of a surprise "to hear the President of Chrysler speaking somewhat sarcastically of 'revolutionary vehicles.' Wasn't the first Chrysler Six a revolutionary vehicle with a revolutionary power plant?" It was, but on the other hand Old K.T. might have told them that once having set the pace, Chrysler's strength was in maintaining the breed. That required an evolutionary approach.

For better or worse, though, nothing very earth-shattering was in the immediate works at Chrysler, and the 1949 models nearing completion in

Windproof and roadworthy. Zippo's unique rolling advertisement on a New Yorker coupe.

late 1948 would not be considered quite as 'new' as those being simultaneously prepared by Ford or General Motors. Nor, in fact, would Chrysler yet go to the fenderless concept, established as early as 1946 by Studebaker and Kaiser-Frazer, and temporarily considered just before the war for the 1943-45 Chrysler.

On the other hand, Chrysler *was* selling cars — 119,137 of them for twelfth place again in calendar year 1948 — and there was no lack of Chrysler glamour wagons. In fact, one series of 1946-48 Chryslers was everything, in its recall of the classic days, that the 'all-postwar' cars were not. It featured considerable leather and woodwork, massive plated embellishments, rode on a long wheelbase and was announced by a long, important hood. It was a Chrysler for which everyone yearned, though as is often the case with such vehicles it was low in quantity and high in price. That aside, it was a truly incredible automobile, and has remained so in collector circles right on through to the present.

We refer, of course, to the Chrysler Town and Country.

CHAPTER 2

Fabulous Woody

IN A SEA of 1942 look alikes built by Detroit after the war, the Chrysler Town and Country was a stunning exception. Of the Big Three manufacturers, it was the only significantly 'new' model, and though new models weren't really needed at the time, it added dash and spirit to Chrysler-Plymouth showrooms. While it was not produced in very large quantities, it proved a valuable sales tool by lending its image to the more mundane models. It was the darling of Chrysler, and of America.

A lot has been written about the appeal of the Town and Country to the moneyed set, and that is so: The list of prominent owners included Cornell Wilde, Bob Hope, Joan Leslie, Clark Gable, Barbara Stanwyck, Ray Milland and Lizabeth Scott. And from that has grown the implication that the Town and Country was a sort of Duesenberg of the forties, which of course it never was. The Duesenberg was mechanically impeccable and generally accepted as an aesthetic triumph, while the Town and Country was mechanically no different from the standard Chrysler and its styling was deplored as often as praised. What sold it to people was its uniqueness at the time, its ability to stand out from the warmed-over prewar cars the industry was peddling during 1946, 1947 and 1948.

Chrysler was not the only company to offer a wood-embellished passenger car. Ford and Mercury built Sportsman convertibles of the same general stripe in 1946, and from 1946-48 Nash built its Suburban sedan, which paralleled the Town and Country sedans. Packard, from 1948 to 1950, offered the distinctive wood-trimmed Station Sedan, though the wood was only structural around the tailgate; on the Town and Country almost all that showed was structural. None of these rivals reached the production peak of the Town and Country, however, so Chrysler is rightfully famous for being the most successful in this limited but interesting field.

The earliest known reference to the Town and Country name by Chrysler is a 1934 Airflow pamphlet, but in its forties application it seems to have been readopted by Paul Hafer, of the Boyertown, Pennsylvania, Body Works. Hafer doodled some Dodge woodies around 1939-1940, on the Dodge Luxury Liner chassis, as proposals for vehicles that Boyertown might build over Dodge engines and chassis. "Whether mine was the first coinage of the name 'Town and Country' I can't say," Hafer told me in an interview for a story in *Automobile Quarterly* in 1973. "The steel front end looked 'town' and the wood portion looked 'country,' so I thought it natural to use that title on my sketches." And in 1941, a Town and Country wagon appeared, bearing some resemblance to Hafer's ideas.

Actually Hafer had proposed three different names, though only one stuck. The other two were Country Club Sport for a kind of landau wagon with a folding rear roof quarter, and Country Gentleman, for a more conventional wagon. But Town and Country was the name that made the biggest impression in the mind of Chrysler Division president David A. Wallace. According to historian Don Narus, Wallace conceived of building

Oh, Cisco! Television's Pancho (Leo Carrillo) was the toast of the town with his longhorn-decorated Town & Country convertible back in 1948. Cowhide upholstery, not visible in the photo, was featured and the cow's eyes lit up, of course. Carrillo also had a conventional hood, for times when he preferred not to be noticed. The car is now in Harrah's Automobile Collection, Reno, Nevada.

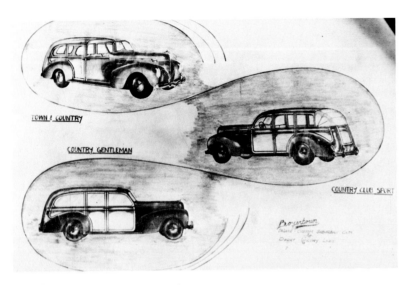

Paul Hafer of the Boyertown Body Works first coined the name 'Town & Country' in sketches for Dodge during 1939. These are his unretouched original drawings.

a Chrysler Town and Country wagon entirely independent of higher management.

The first production Town and Countrys, for model years 1941 and 1942, were station wagons — but with a difference. Rather than follow the upright, boxy designs then typical of estate cars the world over, Wallace and his engineers designed the Town and Country to encompass the basic Dietrich or Cadwallader lines from front to rear, and even used a conventional roof panel from the seven-passenger Chrysler limousine. Draftsmen and carpenters, working only in their spare time on weekends, took two months to create what Wallace was after: a wood-trimmed wagon with the lines of a passenger car, embellished with white ash framing and Honduran mahogany insert panels. Both woods were left in their natural colors, but were varnished to a high luster.

The long wheelbase and roofline made the Town and Country appear very sleek in comparison with any contemporary wagon. At the back, Wallace's designers created a smooth, faired-in wooden deck with a pair of convex doors that swung wide-open like saloon doors. The rear bumper was a standard Chrysler front-end unit and thus one of the first applications of interchangeable features. The all-steel top eliminated the need for an old-fashioned 'trap door' or canvas roof, and the car was entirely stock from the cowl forward. Seven weekends of labor were involved in the prototype's creation. It was presented to K.T. Keller, who thought it was the cat's whiskers, and a few weeks later efforts began to put the car into volume production.

The first Town and Country wagons went unidentified as such (like the postwar Triumph of the same model name), though a script nameplate was adopted on later 1941 models. Chrysler made it more visible with a vigorous advertising campaign: "The *safety* of an all-steel top . . . the *performance* virtues of Fluid Drive and Vacamatic Transmission . . . the swank *appearance* of a specially designed streamlined body . . . the *flexibility* of a seating arrangement carrying up to nine passengers" were the main talking points. And the car was described as a "sturdy, dependable station-goer . . . a car for informal occasions or field expeditions . . . roomy . . . comfortable . . . swift . . . designed for the discriminating owner who wishes exclusive, distinctive transportation."

For 1941 the Town and Country came as a six- or nine-passenger model, the latter effected by an extra seat in the rear. Power came from the Spitfire Six, and the cars were mounted on the C38, 121½-inch wheelbase. Exactly 1,000 Town and Countrys were built for the 1941 model year: 799 (including three for export) nine-passenger, 200 six-passenger, and one experimental nine-passenger on the C39, 127½-inch wheelbase with the eight-cylinder New Yorker engine. The car sparked "spontaneous enthusiasm," according to its maker. "Not only have orders been received from suburbanites and commuters, from owners of country estates and town houses, but also this outstanding car is finding a rapidly growing commercial use — for florists, exclusive dress shops, dry cleaners, interior decorators, photographers, wherever passenger-car comfort, safety and design is desired." Considering the production, there might have been a different occupation for each Town and Country owner!

Nineteen forty-two saw modest changes — sheet metal received the normal face-lift: The door panels were beefed up at the bottom and extended to hide the running board, and there were minor changes in interior details, including a rearranged rear seat on the nine-passenger model. The latter was increased to 849 units, against 150 six-passenger cars, and again an eight-cylinder wagon appeared on the 127½-inch wheelbase. Neither the 1941 nor the 1942 eight has surfaced, though it is believed that the cars did pass to private hands from Chrysler.

Town and Country models sold for between $1,395 and $1,492 during their two prewar years, and even in terms of the 1941 dollar they were bargains. As much like their rival Suburbans as the hare to the tortoise, they were beautifully fitted inside with polished wood and quality upholstery,

sparkling additions to the Chrysler line before the war interrupted all civilian production in 1942. The prewar Town and Country, Chrysler said later, was "utterly different, so much more beautiful and stylish — and so obviously smarter than its predecessors." On this now-famous model, Chrysler engineers and designers were credited with another Chrysler 'first' by that select group of persons throughout the country who know and appreciate fine possessions that look the part.

Prewar Town & Country wagons used a unique door arrangement.

The first production Town & Country was this 1941 wagon. The 1941 Town & Country interior made extensive use of wood.

The successor Town & Country for 1942's short-lived model year.

Custom-designed for a 1942 Ray Milland movie, this cut-down station wagon is credited by some with inspiring the idea of a Town & Country convertible.

A 1946 brochure announced a whole line of Town & Countrys: brougham, roadster, hardtop, four-door sedan and convertible. The first three were never released for production.

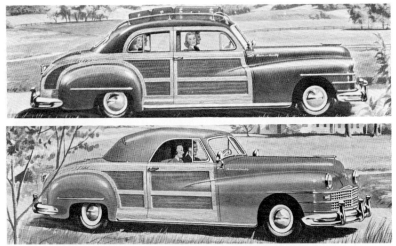

"With the success of the first Town and Country," the company continued, "Chrysler planned a complete line of these smart, utilitarian cars. But they were put aside to make implements of war and it was not until late 1944, when the government permitted development work on new designs, that the [postwar] pilot models were started. Work was again held up, but with V-J day the Chrysler Town and Country *Line* became a reality — another Chrysler Triumph in Smart Motor Cars." (Actually the *line* did not begin until nearly one year after V-J day, though its production was of course assured on that memorable date.)

It is interesting to speculate on whether the Town and Country had begun evolving to its postwar form earlier than 1944. Several sources have indicated to the author that there is evidence for this. They point to a special four-door convertible that was built from a 1942 Town and Country wagon. One former executive says that this car "can be held the genesis of the postwar Town and Country. The basic idea of the wood appliqué and structure, with a conventional type of body such as a convertible or sedan, rather than a wagon. . . ." This individual also explained why the Town and Country wagon models were not revived after the war: "It was decided

early that we would shortly go to an all-steel station wagon [Plymouth's, in 1949], and a continuation of the snazzy Town and Country wagons would have belied progress. It seemed logical, therefore, to shift the Town and Country emphasis to convertibles and regular sedans." Buzz Grisinger, who returned to Chrysler Styling after the Manhattan Project, said the postwar development "was really pretty much of a hurry-up thing. There weren't any clay models or production prototypes as I remember: We just designed up a series of different styles and brushed on wood trim where we thought it looked aesthetically best. Sales took it from there."

Evidently Sales was more enthusiastic than the production planners; for of the five Town and Country body styles announced in a colorful 1946 brochure, only two — the six-cylinder sedan and eight-cylinder convertible — were built in any quantity. The convertible was announced first, on July 17, 1946, using the C39 New Yorker chassis with a 127½-inch wheelbase and the 135 hp Spitfire Eight. It was priced at $2,743 f.o.b., and grew to become the most famous and most favored of all Town and Countrys. The wood trim added much grace and beauty to the by-now familiar lines of the basic Chrysler, and the convertible was the most luxuriously trimmed model in the line.

On the outside, the convertible's white ash framing was basic to the structural rigidity of the doors and deck lid. The wood was beautifully fitted together with interlocking miters, and varnished to perfection. Fine mahogany-veneered plywood decorated the spaces formed by the ash framing, as in prewar models, covering all surfaces from the cowl back, except the rear fenders.

Interior trim matched the convertible's exterior elegance. Standard equipment included two-speed electric wipers, cut-pile carpeting and a

Also stillborn was this Town & Country convertible on the six-cylinder 121½-inch wheelbase.

Definitely not production! This is the interior of the six-cylinder convertible, only one of which was built.

Seven Town & Country hardtops were built, one was used by David Wallace. Originally painted Newport-blue, it was altered to Navajo-brown and given a padded Tolex top with larger rear light. It has survived (lower photo), and is owned today by Allen Bridle of Hinckley, Ohio.

cigarette lighter; options included spotlights for one or both sides, radio, clock and Chrysler's twin-duct heating system. Spotlights are still found on most Town and Countrys, and were standard originally; but some states prohibited them, so they were later relisted as options.

The mahogany veneer finally bowed to inflation and supply problems in late 1947, when Chrysler changed to Di-Noc decals of a somewhat darker shade. "It was essential at that point to cut costs," Buzz Grisinger told me, "and no one could really tell the Di-Noc from the real thing. We were very impressed with it and its adhesion characteristics, and it seemed to hold up well. I believe it was one of the first instances of its use in this particular application, on the outside of a car. Of course it and derivations of it later became very popular, and are still in use today."

Durability was clearly a Town and Country problem. Chrysler shop manuals were at pains to advise owners of the necessarily detailed methods of upkeep of these beautiful bodies, and tried to justify them with the argument that so aristocratic a car required special care: "It has the grace and elegance of a yacht. In fact, the wood paneling is quite similar to the planking of a ship both in construction and treatment. . . . Just as any yacht is refinished every season, so should the beauty and luster of the wood body be maintained by periodic varnishing. [Maintenance] should be thought of in terms of boating rather than motoring. Of the two, the requirements imposed on the protective finish of the Town and Country car are the more severe considering weather extremes, flying gravel, mud splashing, dust and grit, road salt, tar and the many other conditions of ordinary driving . . . special attention [needs to be] paid to all joints, which at all times must be kept thoroughly sealed against moisture."

Not only was maintenance high, but the cost of replacing those beautiful wood-embellished body pieces was formidable. A front door for the concurrent Royal or Windsor, for example, cost $58.17 — compared to $304.78 for a Town and Country sedan. If you dinged your Town and Country trunk lid, a new one would cost you $273.21, instead of only $34.80 for the Royal or Windsor. And a quarter panel for the standard convertible was a paltry $65.71, compared to a whopping $298.02 for the comparable Town and Country convertible panel. "Town and Countrys," comments enthusiast Jeff Godshall, "must have been the Corvettes of their day as far as repair costs go. Can you imagine the cost of hitting one of those babies in the right rear quarter?" Presumably, those who could afford Town and Country in the first place could handle such trifles. . . .

Between 1946 and 1948, the Town and Country convertible changed hardly at all, except in price. It rose from the original $2,743 to $2,998 in 1947, and $3,395 in 1948. The whitewall 'spats' were dropped when whitewalls became available in 1948, and a few details changed; e.g., the

position of the starter button. The car was available with leather or Bedford cord upholstery, in red, maroon, dark green, blue and tan, but could be individualized, due to its hand-built construction. "Chrysler's work or play convertible," said the ads, was "magnificent in its utterly new styling, in the smooth, responsive power of Chrysler gyro Fluid Drive and improved hydraulically operated transmission . . . another triumph of Chrysler's imaginative engineering — first in the field with the developments that really matter!" One can't say Chrysler didn't get as much PR as possible out of the Town and Country: If one totals up all the 'triumphs,' there are enough to make Caesar envious.

With all the commotion the convertible caused, and the impression it made on Hollywood, Newport, Southampton and Palm Beach, the fact that a Town and Country sedan was available went more or less unnoticed in several quarters. The prewar wagons were actually replaced by the sedans, which were announced on January 7, 1947.

Here we arrive at a contretemps, for the N.A.D.A. and *Red Book* used-car value guides both list 1946 Town and Country sedans. Yet Chrysler records indicate that the model was not available until January 7 — which would normally be construed as part of the 1947 model year. Since no firm date is given for the '47 introduction (only the month of January) one can

Considerable handwork was required to fashion the partly wooden body of each Town & Country.

Only in 1946 was an eight-cylinder, 127½-inch wheelbase Town & Country sedan offered; one hundred were built.

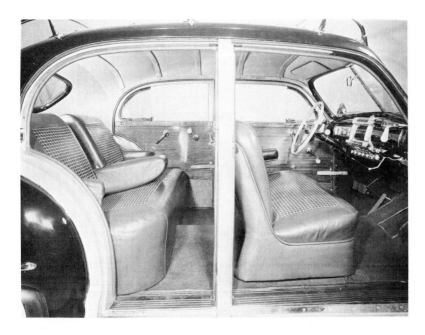

1946 sedan's saran plastic and leather interior.

conclude that the 124 six-cylinder sedans listed by Chrysler as 1946 models appeared prior to the official 1947 changeover date. During 1947, a total of 2,651 sedans appeared; and another 1,175 are recorded for model year 1948.

The longer wheelbase eight-cylinder Town and Country sedan, also announced on January 7, persisted only through one hundred units to the following April 18, 1947, when it was phased out, apparently in deference to the smaller model. In Chapter 1 and the Appendix, the figures are as recorded by Chrysler Corporation, rather than by the used-car value guides.

Town and Country sedan interiors were beautifully finished, as Chrysler put it, "with rich-grained wood paneling and harmonizing cloth headlining and carpets. The seats are spacious, designed for comfort. A choice of fine Bedford cord and rich leather, or Saran (a smart new woven plastic) and leather is available." Don Narus, in his illuminating book, *Chrysler's Wonderful Woodie*, notes that the sedan's Saran upholstery was in combination with leather, but "had a tendency to separate at the seams from the leather and had shown poor wearability. [It was] replaced with a vented vinyl material . . . with tiny pinhole punctures." The same colors as on the convertible were available for the sedan's interiors, and other shades could be ordered for only thirty-six dollars extra.

Sedan interiors were appointed with wood embellishments on the headliners and door panels, all of it superbly fitted and varnished to a mirror finish. Some sedans used a wooden luggage rack and roof runners, which were changed to chromium in June of 1947. This device also became optional on Royal and Windsor limousines at $115 extra. The factory luggage rack became standard equipment on all Town and Country sedans on July 16, 1947, but the chromium model never had the beauty of the wood type, which blended perfectly with the heavily varnished woodwork of the rest of the car.

Particularly intriguing are the three other phantom Town and Countrys announced in the 1946 catalogue but never built — or at least not built in quantity: the six-cylinder brougham and roadster, and the eight-cylinder hardtop, the latter being the first of this body style on the American market. (There was also an experimental six-cylinder convertible which apparently served as the prototypal forerunner of the eight-cylinder production soft top, but this model was not listed in the 1946 brochure.)

The roadster was the first sign of a Chrysler idea that took production form in the 1949 Dodge Wayfarer — a three-passenger coupe body with a longish deck, a large canvas roof and blind quarters. This made for a very streamlined appearance and, had it been produced, it probably would have been the most graceful of the Town and Country models. Unfortunately not even a prototype was built, and its only representation is a drawing from an over-optimistic 1946 brochure. Despite obvious exaggeration of length and minimization of height, it clearly illustrates that the Town and Country roadster would have been a beautiful car. The long deck always gave Chrysler coupes better proportions than the chunkier sedans and broughams, and with Town and Country trim its appearance would have only been enhanced.

Another stillborn Town and Country was the brougham, or two-door version, of which one prototype was built in 1946 and sold to a private owner. This car has not been heard of since, unfortunately. The brougham had better proportions than the sedan, but not quite the lines of the roadster, and would have been available with the usual Town and Country exterior and interior finish.

Most fascinating of the also-rans was the Town and Country Custom Club Coupe, the world's first hardtop. It would have been the only Town and Country sharing the 127½-inch New Yorker wheelbase and eight-cylinder engine with the convertible, aside from the one hundred 1947 eight-cylinder sedans, and it would have been another 'triumph' for Chyrsler to crow about. But only seven were built, and it is not known

exactly why the company stopped there. One hardtop was done for Chrysler's Wallace, and this has survived, currently owned by Allen Bridle of Ohio. Rumors exist of two other hardtops still extant.

The hardtop concept came after the C39 convertible had been worked out, the latter being a Town and Country version of the New Yorker soft top. Someone — and none of those asked are sure who — hit upon the idea of placing a solid steel top on the car to create a pillarless coupe. A Chrysler coupe roof was accordingly sectioned, lengthened and bolted onto a convertible body in late 1946. Although it was not meant to be removed, the roof did predict the later emergence of the bolt-on hardtop, albeit on much lighter machinery: Triumph was the first to offer one as an option, in 1954.

In creating the hardtop, the 'convertible' top and erecting-mechanism framework were lost, but it was not seriously altered otherwise. The roof panel was upholstered in a moleskin-like material with narrow wood framing, and the back seat was slightly redesigned. Armrests were juggled, the hardtop using a set from the DeSoto Town Sedan. The car's courtesy lights were C-40 Imperial under-dash units, set into the blind corners of the inner roof.

The Wallace car, now owned by Bridle, was originally painted in Newport-blue, but later was changed to palace-brick-brown and given a padded vinyl roof of the same color. The padding material was Tolex, an

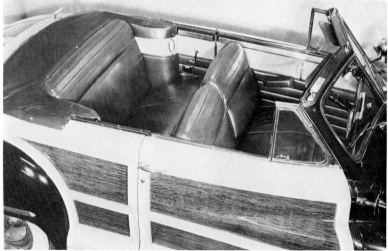

Three types of specially-ordered convertible interiors (top to bottom): all white, with piped carpets, 1946; leather/cloth seats with woven plastic trim and chrome garnish moldings on door panels, 1947; 1949-style seats and plain leather/vinyl door panels, 1948.

In production for all three model years through 1948, 3,950 examples of the six-cylinder Town & Country sedan were made.

alligator-type pattern later used to upholster the 1949-50 Royal wagons. The Tolex was applied to the door panels and seats of the Wallace car, as well as the roof. At the same time, the rear window was enlarged, with plastic instead of glass to keep costs down, and the inner painted surfaces were redone in palace-brick to match the rest of the car. A key starter and power brakes were also fitted at this time.

When Allen Bridle acquired the car it was in excellent original condition, and being Wallace's own, it was easily the most historic Town and Country find on record.

It is rather unfortunate that Wallace and Chrysler did not, or perhaps were not able to, pursue their hardtop idea beyond the seven models built, for the concept certainly was to prove revolutionary. In 1949 Buick's Riviera, Oldsmobile's Holiday, and Cadillac's Coupe de Ville jointly reintroduced the hardtop body style, and it has been around ever since. The decline in favor of the soft top convertible, coinciding with the rising use of air conditioning, made the hardtop a natural choice for those who wanted the sleekness of a convertible with the snugness of a sedan. Only Washington's recent rollover regulations seem to have had any effect on hardtop production since.

Likewise, the Town and Country influenced the creation of the padded top, for in late 1948 Kaiser-Frazer introduced the pillarless Kaiser Virginian, similarly decorated with a swank interior and selling for around the same amount as a Town and Country. Perhaps not coincidentally, the Virginian greenhouse was designed largely by Buzz Grisinger, who had moved to Kaiser-Frazer from Chrysler. The padded top found additional favor in the early fifties on such models as the Lincoln Lido, Ford Crestliner and Kaiser Dragon, and it remains with us today in the popular unpadded vinyl tops offered optionally on nearly everything from Detroit, and on much from Europe as well.

When plans were laid for the 1949 Chrysler line, Styling decided to eliminate the sedan versions of the Town and Country, probably to remove any distractions from the new line of conventional station wagons then being prepared. But they intended to retain the convertibles and re-enter the hardtop field with a production Town and Country pillarless coupe. However, as will be seen, these cars were only shadows of their former selves, and in 1951 the Town and Country line became a conventional

Easily the most famous Town & Country was the 1946-48 convertible on the eight-cylinder New Yorker chassis.

station wagon. The collectability of Town and Countrys is not, however, a direct result of their early discontinuance. Rather it is their unique appearance, luxurious specifications and the old world craftsmanship with which they were built. And of all Town and Countrys, that big, rakishly handsome convertible of 1946-48 is the acknowledged classic.

CHAPTER 3

Silver Anniversary Chrysler

"IT HAS OFTEN *been said, and wisely so, that the supreme distinction of Chrysler cars is the distinction of difference. And this is so true, so evident in the Chrysler Silver Anniversary models. For the new Chryslers are different — and distinctively so. They have a stylish, well-bred look that is unmistakably Chrysler with that rich, conservative charm and good taste so reminiscent of the custom body creations of the famous coach makers of an earlier generation.*

The distinction of difference of the new models is evident also in the comfort, the convenience, and the safety to be found inside the cars. The doors open wide and stay open so you can get in and out with ease and dignity. The deep, soft cushions of Airfoam rubber are chair height so you can sit in a normal, relaxed position. There is 'top hat' headroom, plenty of legroom, and the seats are wide, with shoulder and elbowroom.

There is distinction, too, in the superb performance of these new Chryslers. They are, unmistakably, the greatest performing cars we have ever built. And herein lies the real distinction of difference that makes the Chrysler such a thrilling car to drive, such a completely satisfying car to own."

That was the gospel according to the Sales Department at the executive offices in Highland Park. The actual situation was somewhat different, though the 1949 Chryslers were no less the impeccably-engineered products that Chryslers had always been.

Chrysler Corporation as a whole, and the Chrysler car as part of that whole, had performed in 1949 according to the predictions of the business and automotive press: The cars were fully restyled, entirely different from those that had gone before, but were not bestowed with anywhere near the flair of their rivals at General Motors and Ford. They were boxy, high and ungainly looking, from Plymouth on up, and were totally eclipsed by the sleek General Motors line; they were also surpassed by the new, rounder Fords, Mercurys and Lincolns. As for the independents, Packard's 1948 face-lift of the original Clipper design remained more evolutionary than Chrysler's. And Studebaker, which was a decade ahead in 1947, was *still* a good five years up on anything Chrysler could offer. So were Hudson and Nash; viewed in the context of their time, they were considerably advanced over prewar-styled predecessors. The best one could say of the Silver Anniversary Chrysler was that it was 'practical.' In styling, it was equal to the three-year-old Kaiser-Frazer design; yet Kaiser-Frazer had integral fenders, while Chrysler did not.

Not that streamlining and the demise of the bolt-on fender hadn't been contemplated by Chrysler Styling. Numerous Lincolnesque clays were constructed, and even a few prototypes built, most of them indicating that the 1949 redesign would indeed do away with separate fenders; the majority were considerably smoother-looking than what was actually produced. Even the A109 experimental car, a running model of which was

The Silver Anniversary New Yorker convertible.

Although fastbacks predominated, some hatchback ideas were considered for early postwar Chryslers by prewar stylists.

Nothing too radical or streamlined would be acceptable to the Keller administration, but these ideas were being considered circa 1951-52: The first bears a Chrysler Fluid Drive hood ornament; the second, though much more modern, still shows the prewar prototype's influence.

on hand at least as early as September, 1946, had sweep-through fenders, not quite predicting the eventual production Chrysler Corporation lines. The A109 was a Dodge-DeSoto-sized car that was fully operable. It was tested along with a larger model A116, the Chrysler-Imperial prototype for 1949. But though these two designs were quite close to the final 1949 shape, neither they nor the even more radical alternatives, simultaneously proposed, ever made it into production. Most of those present at the time agree that K.T. Keller was the reason they didn't.

Though the styling activities at Chrysler, as noted in Chapter 1, came under the aegis of chief body engineer Oliver Clark and, in turn, Fred M. Zeder, the final authority over all body proposals remained with Keller. 'Old K.T.' was greatly influenced by the practical, objective, engineer's approach, and while not specifically pointing any fingers at his competition, he was not hesitant about bluntly telling the world that Chrysler would not follow the herd into streamlining at the expense of comfort. Those who attended his address at the Stanford University School of Business in 1948, for example, might have been able to predict the shape of the 1949 Chrysler after Keller remarked: "Automobiles are looked at and admired. The buyer is proud of his car's symphony of line; its coloring and trim express his taste; he welcomes the applause of his friends and his neighbors. But he bought the car to ride in, and for his wife, and children and friends to ride in . . . Though at times one might wonder if even headroom is important. Many of you Californians may have outgrown the habit, but there are parts of the country containing millions of people, where both the men and the ladies are in the habit of getting behind the wheel, or in the back seat, wearing hats."

Reflecting on these remarks, *Fortune* noted that "the '49 Chryslers, Plymouths, DeSotos and Dodges may or may not knock your eye out when you look at them, but they will certainly not knock your hat off. The '49 cars from this manufacturer will be wider, however, a development that Chrysler was planning as far back as 1939. But for practical reasons Chrysler will probably refrain from sucking in the fenders to the point where there are virtually no fenders at all. For one thing, Chrysler has an eye to a wheel design that can accommodate the supersized tires that are now appearing on many new cars. For another, it takes into account the difficulties encountered by repairmen with the oh-so-sleek, self-vanishing fender . . . [the company] appears to be content with a middle-of-the-road approach to the postwar automobile world — 'evolutionary rather than revolutionary,' in the timeless cliché of the industry."

Three-eighth scale clays in Chrysler Styling. The model at left is probably a Plymouth. The club coupe artwork in right background is a DeSoto proposal. Note the raised Imperial(?) taillight in the drawing at left.

Evolutionary would be an optimistic word for it — the Chrysler 1949 design came to be known by some as 'three box styling' — one box, piled on top of two others. But it was approved by K.T. Keller after being proposed by Charles G. Walker of the clay modeling section, and Keller's review was its critical test; Keller in fact liked the boxy shape so much that he envisioned its application to every model throughout the Corporate line, causing a very close family resemblance all the way from Plymouth to Imperial. This would do little to help sales, as time would tell.

Lacking any major distinguishing characteristics vis-à-vis the other company models, the 1949 Chrysler had to rely for its identity on greater length and wheelbase, as well as surface embellishments. It was unfortunate that the latter were necessary, since they created a massive and ornate grille.

The 1949 grille was composed of two heavy tiers of chrome, each bisected by a smaller horizontal bar and five verticals — fewer pieces than in 1946-48, but just as heavy looking. The main members wrapped around the front fenders, and were joined there by large rectangular parking/directional lights. Below was a big, concave bumper with four sturdy guards, the central pair holding the Chrysler logo, which prevented it from being plastered on the hood — until midyear, when just this was done. The hood ornament, as in the past, was a pair of silver wings, and the Chrysler emblem was built into a small strip at the leading edge of the hood.

But the search for uniqueness did produce a clever idea at the other end. In 1949, all Chryslers and the Imperial sedan bore a unique new taillight intended to further separate the Chrysler from its lower-priced brethren: a tall, narrow plastic lens on a chrome base, offering three-way visibility like the Cadillac light introduced the year before. Crown models bore their own special taillights; round units that did not rise above the fender level. A massive deck console carried stop and back-up lights along with an illuminated license plate and a trunk handle. Chrysler's

A 1949 Royal club coupe, somewhat non-stock, bears a non-production rear fender shield and lacks parking lights and taillights (left). The production car at last; stylist's drawing of the 1949 Chrysler (right).

independently housed stop lights were really a good idea; it's too bad they later became unfashionable.

Looking back, it is easy to see an analogy between Chrysler's new design of 1949 and that of Mercedes-Benz throughout its postwar history. If square, unimaginative lines were out of step with the low-slung productions of General Motors and Ford, they were nevertheless entirely sensible in terms of driver and passenger comfort and convenience — Chrysler based its sales campaign largely on this aspect at the time. There was a cavernous trunk, for example, counterbalanced for safety and opened by a straight-forward swivel handle — no buttons, medallions or trick locks — with the spare tire bolt upright, out of the way on the right side. The boxy lines allowed much greater glass area as compared with the '48's, and the windshield was twenty-four percent larger than the year before. The rear window was widened and deepened, "without, sacrificing privacy," of course, and a new dash was designed by Henry King. The latter featured a completely instrumented cluster, including trip odometer, placed smack in front of the driver and hooded to prevent reflection. It was flanked to the right by one of the industry's first padded dashes, a thick, sponge-rubber affair covered with stitched leather. Underneath the pad was a bright metal panel containing the radio and heater controls, a speaker, clock, ashtray and glove box. There were wide, deep window-vents on each door, with knobs that were child-proof — and often adult-proof as well: They were fitted with little knurled buttons that had to be twisted before the knob could be depressed to disengage the latch. Side windows were geared to raise and lower quickly, armrests were big and heavily padded, and window winder knobs were hinged to flop down out of the way when not in use.

One rode high in a Chrysler, with volumes of head, leg and elbow room that might have satisfied Paul Bunyan. In the convertibles, which were almost as large inside as the coupes, smartly tailored interiors were accompanied by a new top with a rear window of huge proportions. Two-tone interiors, introduced by Chrysler some years before, were available in closed as well as open cars and were color-keyed to the exteriors. Altogether there were fifteen basic exterior paint schemes matched with two-tone Bedford cord interiors (maroon/tan, blue/gray, dark/light green), gray or taupe nylon cord, or the now-traditional Highlander plaid and red leather — the latter optional at extra cost. And there was a whole new array of leather and nylon cord combinations for the convertibles.

Mechanically, little had changed from the 1948 models, though both engines featured higher compression — 7:1 for the six and 7.25:1 for the eight, allowing the six to be rated at 116 bhp at 3600 rpm, though the eight remained 135 bhp at 3200 rpm. Fluid Drive now needed no clutch except to downshift or enter reverse; it was renamed Prestomatic, in order to make it more palatable and 'automatic' sounding in the salesrooms, where it was meeting stiff competition from Hydra-Matic and Dynaflow. The ignition was key-start, and waterproofed to insure starting in damp weather and to prevent flooding in wet conditions.

This was an age when a car manufacturer gave trick names to his various mechanical features. For the 1949 Chrysler, one became familiar with Safety-Level Ride, Hydra-Lizer shock absorbers, Safety Rim wheels,

Experimental prototype A109, a Dodge-DeSoto-size sedan, closely approximated the production 1949's when these photos were taken in September 1946. The A109 used production Dodge bumpers and guards and a DeSoto stoplight lamp.

Strongly considered for 1949 was a new Chrysler hardtop, but the project was laid aside until 1950.

The new 1949 six-cylinder chassis with a 125½-inch wheelbase.

Three-quarters front and rear view of Chrysler-Imperial-sized running prototype A116. It strongly influenced 1949 production cars, using the same body as A109 but with a longer hood and front fenders. Fittings were identical to A109 except for a 1946 Chrysler steering wheel. The photos were taken in December 1946.

Full-Flow oil filter and Cyclebonded brake linings. The last three were especially important developments. The Safety Rim was a projecting lip on the edge of the steel wheels, which better gripped the tire casing and held it in place in the event of a blow-out. The oil filter was mounted directly to the engine, without connecting lines, and was standard equipment. And the Cyclebonded brake linings were attached to the shoes without rivets; this, Chrysler claimed, would double the life of the linings.

The 1949 line appeared rather late, owing to retooling delays, and was not ready at the usual new model announcement time, which was then somewhat later than it is now. So on December 1, 1948, Chrysler announced what would later be called the 'first series' for 1949, an unchanged lineup of 1948 models, which was a holding action pending arrival of the true 1949's, or 'second series,' the following March. Since Chrysler would be back on schedule with the 1950 models, the true '49 experienced a relatively short model year, though the reshuffle it ushered in was considerable and would last a few years without many basic changes:

Model

Body Style (passengers)	Price	W.B.(in)	Weight (lb)
Series C45-1 Royal			
sedan, 4dr (6)	$2,134	125½	3,550
club coupe (6)	2,114	125½	3,495
station wagon (9)	3,131	125½	4,060
sedan, l.w.b. 4dr (8)	2,823	139½	4,200
Series C45-2 Windsor			
sedan, 4dr (6)	$2,329	125½	3,681
club coupe (6)	2,308	125½	3,631
convertible (6)	2,741	125½	3,845
sedan, l.w.b. 4dr (8)	3,017	139½	4,290
limousine (8)	3,144	139½	4,430
Series C46-1 Saratoga			
sedan, 4dr (6)	$2,610	131½	4,103
club coupe (6)	2,584	131½	4,037
Series C46-2 New Yorker			
sedan, 4dr (6)	$2,726	131½	4,113
club coupe (6)	2,700	131½	4,048
convertible (6)	3,206	131½	4,277
Series C46-2 Town and Country			
convertible (6)	$3,970	131½	4,630
Series C46-2 Imperial			
sedan, 4dr (6)	$4,665	131½	4,300
Series C47 Crown Imperial			
sedan, l.w.b. 4dr (8)	$5,229	145½	5,250
limousine (8)	5,334	145½	5,295

From these specifications, notable differences can be seen over the previous line of automobiles, underlining new trends in Chrysler marketing strategy aimed at upgrading the image of the marque. The Royal line, for example, was drastically reduced, losing its limousine, two-door brougham and three-passenger coupe; though it later gained a wagon, on June 30. The coupe and brougham, however, were also deleted from the Windsor, Saratoga and New Yorker lines, the theory being that two-door customers were adequately served by the new club coupe. There were no changes in the two-model Crown Imperial series, but a brand-new Imperial sedan appeared on the shorter New Yorker wheelbase, more luxuriously trimmed and priced considerably higher. This was evidence of Chrysler's growing concern with the luxury car owner-driver, for whom a long-wheelbase Crown Imperial was too large to comfortably use for daily transport.

The Town and Country, that entered production on July 8, was bereft of all its former models save the convertible, again with Di-Noc panels on its doors between the white ash planking. A Newport hardtop Town and Country, reviving the 1946 idea, was announced, but only one experimental model was built; by the time the convertible was in production it was late in the model year, and Chrysler elected to offer a Town and Country Newport in 1950 instead, while dropping the convertible.

According to Chrysler, lack of buyer demand had the most to do with the demise of the Town and Country sedans. In their specialty market of luxury/utility vehicles, they were not as practical as wagons. Accordingly "the well known pre-war nine-passenger Chrysler station wagon returns, with new beauty, new style, and many improvements and refinements — and an attractive new price." Interestingly, that price was about $300 more than that of the preceding Town and Country sedan, and it was not even given the snooty Town and Country designation, but was simply called a Chrysler Royal. Unlike the prewar Town and Country wagons, it carried its spare tire on the tailgate, allowing more room inside, but presenting a rather clumsy appearance. Three passengers per seat were easily accommodated; the middle and rear seats were removable to facilitate large payloads.

Shortly after the Town and Country convertibles began being shipped on August 16, dealers were advised that they would no longer come with Di-Noc imitation wood on the doors, which would henceforth be painted the body color. The white ash framing remained, but Di-Noc was now used only on the Royal wagon. This was another step toward the gradual extinction of the Town and Country except as a utility car, which would culminate in the following year. The long-wheelbase Royals and Windsors were also late to arrive, being added on August 17; and only a few more than 600 were built before the 1950 models appeared.

1949 Royal four-door sedan.

1949 Windsor eight-passenger limousine.

1949 Royal station wagon.

1949 Windsor Highlander convertible.

Upper-end models other than the New Yorker were also very late in arriving. The Crown Imperials, featuring new self-energizing disc brakes and distinctive rear-end styling, and a new Imperial four-door on the New Yorker wheelbase were not added until September 23, barely two months before 1950 announcement time. The four-door, with lovely leather and wool broadcloth Imperial interiors, was custom-built by Ray Dietrich, Chrysler's old chief stylist, at a coachbuilding shop he'd set up in Grand Rapids, Michigan. "Ultimately we built fifty of the special Imperials," Ray Dietrich told me, "but it could have been more because demand was high. We spared no expense and insisted on craftsmanship of a quality I knew in the custom body days. The thing I didn't expect was union problems. I wanted to have about six or seven apprentices for each skilled craftsman, but the union wanted six to seven craftsmen for one apprentice. I built a lot of cars, relatively, for the size of the operation, but I wasn't properly financed and the more work I got in, the more money I needed. It was all very frustrating."

The 1950 Crosley Hot Shot is often given credit for the first U.S. production disc brakes, but the Crown Imperial actually had them first, in 1949. The Crosley disc was a Goodyear development — a caliper type with ventilated rotor — originally designed for aircraft applications. Only the Hot Shot featured it. Lack of sufficient research and testing caused reliability problems, such as sticking and corrosion. Drum brake conversion for Hot Shots was quite popular.

1949 Saratoga club coupe.

1949 Crown Imperial limousine.

1949 New Yorker four-door sedan.

The Chrysler disc was more complex and expensive than Crosley's, but far more efficient. It was built by Auto Specialties Manufacturing Company (Ausco) of St. Joseph, Michigan, under patents of inventor H.L. Lambert, and was first tested on a 1939 Plymouth. Unlike the caliper disc, the Ausco-Lambert utilized twin expanding discs that rubbed against the inner surface of a cast iron brake drum, which doubled as the brake housing. The discs spread apart to create friction against the inner drum surface through the action of standard wheel cylinders.

Chrysler discs were 'self-energizing,' in that some of the braking energy itself contributed to braking effort. This was accomplished by small balls set into oval holes leading to the braking surface. When the disc made initial contact with the friction surface, the balls would be forced up the holes, forcing the discs further apart and augmenting the braking energy. This made for lighter pedal pressure than with calipers, avoided brake fade, promoted cooler running and provided one-third more friction surface than standard Chrysler twelve-inch drums. But because of expense, the brakes were standard on Crown Imperials through 1954 and the Town and Country Newport in 1950. They were optional, however, on other Chryslers, priced at around $400. Today's owners consider the Ausco-Lambert reliable and very powerful, but admit to grabbiness and sensitivity.

One of the most astonishing facts about the Silver Anniversary Chrysler was not, however, its mechanical novelty, but the fact that one could be bought for relatively little money. Despite its upgraded image, Chrysler prices remained highly competitive. The Windsor four-door, Chrysler's leading seller, was priced lower than many rivals, yet it offered more interior space than most, and was heavier for its horsepower than nearly everything in its price class — Hudson, Oldsmobile, Frazer, Packard Eight. Still, there was no gainsaying its amazing price of $2,329, and if that was too steep one could settle on a Royal at only $2,134 — well under most of the opposition. This paid enormous dividends, because Chrysler was a better name than most of the marques it competed against, at least in the minds of the public. Herewith, some significant comparisons:

New Yorker upholstery was austere but high quality. The C46 chassis for Saratoga and New Yorker featured a 131½-inch wheelbase.

Model (Red Book Price)	Length (in)	Wheel-base (in)	Weight (lb)	Pounds /hp	Brake hp	Displacement	hp per cid	Compression
Chrysler Windsor ($2,329)	206⅞	125½	3,681	32.3	116	250.6	.462	7.0:1
Hudson Super 6 ($2,207)	207½	124	3,600	28.1	128	254	.503	6.5
Olds 88 ($2,244)	202	119½	3,610	26.7	135	303.7	.444	7.25
Packard Eight ($2,249)	204⅝	120	3,820	29.4	130	288	.451	7.0
Frazer (std.) ($2,595)	207½	123½	3,455	30.5	112	226.2	.495	7.3
Mercury sedan ($2,031)	206¾	118	3,430	31.1	110	255.4	.431	6.8

Chrysler's bargain price (compared with models like the Hudson Commodore, Oldsmobile 98 and Frazer Manhattan), combined with the continuing seller's market in 1949, gave Chrysler Division its best year since 1941, and one of its best in history. There were 141,122 sales in the calendar year, only 400 less than 1941 and about 20,000 more than 1948. But the rest of the industry was also growing and Chrysler's sales position remained static at twelfth place. Though Kaiser-Frazer had slipped drastically for the calendar year, Nash had taken its place, and was about 1,500 units ahead of Chrysler.

It should be noted that Chrysler was inordinately charitable toward its opposition, though perhaps from its then nearly unassailable sales/price position in its class, it could afford to be. "There is little chance of making

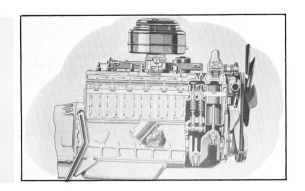

The 1949 Chrysler six now produced 116 horsepower; basically the same as previous sixes, it can be identified by the altered oil and air filters (left). The eight-cylinder engine for Saratoga and New Yorker produced 135 horsepower, still with 323.5 cubic inches of displacement (middle). Cooling system diagram for the eight-cylinder, 323-cid engine (right).

Derham customized this 1949 New Yorker.

a poor investment in an automobile today," read a Saratoga-New Yorker catalogue, "regardless of which make you buy. They are all good. They are all good-looking. And they will all take you where you want to go and bring you back . . . In the fine car field, there are several cars that will meet these requirements. And most assuredly, the Chrysler is one of them." A very mild piece of promotion for a hotly competitive era. If nothing else, it indicated the supreme confidence with which Chrysler faced the future.

And of course 1949 was only the beginning. If Chrysler had only just missed topping 1941 in this year, it couldn't help but beat the record in 1950. This turned out to be a good prediction: 1950 would see more than 167,000 Chryslers produced for the calendar year, a record second only to the monumental 182,000 that Walter Chrysler built in 1928.

You never mess about with a good thing, or at least you didn't in those days when there were five buyers for every two cars. And the 1949 Chrysler was a good thing indeed. Everything was breaking the Division's way; it was in a prime position with an avid following; and the Jefferson Avenue plant — where all Chryslers were built save for a small assembly plant in Los Angeles — was by then at full capacity. With a new design only one

Chrysler stylist Fred Reynolds did these proposals for the 1949 Town & Country; only the convertible was produced.

Town & Country convertible in production . . . and the completed article.

year old, it stood to reason that conservative as that styling was, Chrysler was certainly under no pressure to change it. Thus the 1950 models were not very different in mechanics or design from the 1949's, though certain subtle styling changes were effected that did improve their looks. Generally, the 1950's received a modest cleanup.

Plymouth's trend-setting all-steel station wagon of 1949 (upper) influenced Chrysler's all-steel Town & Country wagon for 1950 (lower).

and 1949's upright taillights were replaced with oblong units faired into the rear fenders. The deck was cleaned up by eliminating the gaudy all-purpose license-plate, stop/back-up light and trunk-handle unit. For 1950, back-up lenses were built into the inner rear fenders and the plate moved down to the center of the bumper. Though the eight-cylinder models used an ornate molding around the leading edges of the front fenders, the total impression was one of grace and refinement that even the offer of six different two-tone combinations did nothing to upset. It was a good job.

Chief identifying factor for 1950 was a three-piece rear window on the closed cars — two vertical bars at each side of the main piece of glass — and an enlargement in glass area of about twenty-seven percent. In the model lineup appeared a new, all-steel station wagon and, for the first time, Chrysler had a spate of mass-production hardtops:

Model Body Style (passengers)	Price	W.B.(in)	Wt. (lb)
Series C48-1 Royal			
sedan, 4dr (6)	$2,134	125½	3,610
club coupe (6)	2,114	125½	3,540
wagon, wood (6)	3,163	125½	4,055
Town & Ctry steel wagon (6)	2,735	125½	3,964
sedan, l.w.b. 4dr (8)	2,855	139½	4,190
Series C48-2 Windsor			
sedan, 4dr (6)	$2,329	125½	3,765
Traveler sedan, 4dr (6)	2,560	125½	3,830
club coupe (6)	2,308	125½	3,670
Newport hardtop (6)	2,637	125½	3,875
convertible (6)	2,741	125½	3,905
sedan, l.w.b. 4dr (8)	3,050	139½	4,295
limousine (8)	3,176	139½	4,400
Series C49-1 Saratoga			
sedan, 4dr (6)	$2,642	131½	4,170
club coupe (6)	2,616	131½	4,110
Series C49-2 New Yorker			
sedan, 4dr (6)	$2,758	131½	4,190
club coupe (6)	2,732	131½	4,110
Newport hardtop (6)	3,133	131½	4,370
covertible (6)	3,238	131½	4,360
Series C49-2 Town and Country			
Newport hardtop (6)	$4,003	131½	4,670
Series C49-2 Imperial			
sedan, 4dr (6)	$3,055	131½	4,245
deluxe sedan, 4dr (6)	3,176	131½	4,250
Series C50 Crown Imperial			
sedan, l.w.b. 4dr (8)	$5,229	145½	5,235
limousine (8)	5,334	145½	5,305

One of the first things people noticed about the 1950 Chrysler was its much neater, cleaner grille, a development most credit to Charles G. Walker. The massive chrome bars were still there, but slimmer in side-section, and the high-tier effect of 1949 was gone, replaced by a full-width horizontal motif and a few more vertical teeth. The bumper was cleaner (and cheaper, without 1949's wraparound feature) and fitted with two streamlined 'buffer guards.' The Chrysler name had shifted to the hood,

The pillarless models, again called Newports, were available in the Windsor, Town and Country, and New Yorker series, and except for wheelbase were of generally similar appearance. The roofline followed the basic idea of the original Newport back in 1946, though it was now an integral part of the body. Chrysler promoted the "low-swept, road-hugging lines of a convertible with a permanent solid steel top that gives the comfort and convenience of a sedan. Its distinctive styling is further enhanced by the graceful three-piece CLEARBAC rear window, with smart chrome division bars, that forms a complete arch around the roof." So much for the air of

1950 Royal four-door sedan.

1950 Royal club coupe.

1950 Royal Town & Country, wood-bodied.

1950 Royal eight-passenger sedan used a 139½-inch wheelbase.

1950 Windsor Newport, with CLEARBAC rear window.

1950 Windsor convertible.

1950 Windsor limousine.

privacy and formality that was touted the year before by virtue of the *absence* of this feature!

Interiors of both the New Yorker and Town and Country Newports were beautifully tailored and designed. Both cars could be fitted with green or tan leather and nylon cord, or black leather with silver-gray nylon cord. The Town and Country, like the Crown Imperial, now featured disc brakes as standard.

Though the Town and Country remained 'un-Di-Nocked' on its door panels, it was still decorated with white ash, which was particularly well-applied in the deck area and still mitered with consummate care. A new Royal station wagon did receive the Di-Noc treatment, doubtless because the look of wood was considered *de rigueur* in a wagon. But Chrysler Corporation was on the way towards changing this: Plymouth's all-steel wagon had appeared in 1949 to break the ice. For 1950, an all-steel Royal wagon was introduced late in September, bearing no trace of white ash or Di-Noc.

In both the wood and steel Royal wagons the spare tire was moved to a subfloor compartment, and third seats were no longer fitted, making them two-seat, six-passenger models. Also unlike the 1949's, the rear seat was not removable, but it did fold flat to create a luggage platform nearly ten feet long, with metal skids provided to allow payloads to be slid easily inside. Finally the tailgate window could be lowered into the tail itself,

eliminating the clumsier two-piece tailgate of 1949. These improvements would gradually spread throughout the industry, but it should be noted that neither Royal wagon was particularly popular in 1950. Only 599 woodies were made, and late introduction of the all-steel model saw only one hundred built for 1950. Nevertheless, the wagon idea caught on, because Chrysler would build more than 3,000 during model year 1951.

The innovative influence of Kaiser-Frazer apparently showed in Chrysler's production of another Traveler in 1950, appearing in the Windsor series and selling 900 copies. Like Kaiser's Traveler and Vagabond, which were introduced in 1949, the rear seat folded like a station wagon's, and there was no partition between it and the trunk. Thus the deck lid could be lifted, and a long or clumsy load inserted without difficulty. The Chrysler Traveler's spare tire appears to have been mounted in various positions: sometimes on the left rear door, sometimes in a well under the floor (like the 1951-53 Kaiser), sometimes even tied or strapped to the floor. One feature of the Kaiser-Frazer model—a second hatch cutting into the roof and encompassing the upper deck and rear window—was not present on the Chrysler Traveler. This didn't allow equal access, but on the other hand it wasn't susceptible to the dust and water leaks that attended the Kaiser models.

The Chrysler Traveler was announced early, on February 20, 1950, and by July the wood-bodied Royal wagon had been dropped, leaving the Traveler as the only utility model in the range. This was rectified on September 26, when an all-steel wagon appeared in the Royal series that finally received the Town and Country designation — for the first time on a wagon since 1942. The name was withheld until then to avoid confusion with the remaining 'real' Town and Country Newports, but by September the latter had disappeared after a run of only 700 units.

Chrysler also offered a specially-built ambulance conversion of the all-steel wagon. This special included a roof-mounted siren and warning light, and a special interior with a split rear seat, allowing a cot to be slid in against the right side of the car and an attendant to sit on the left at the cot's head. Only two or three of these conversions were produced out of the one hundred all-steel 1950 wagons, but they are interesting because they are products of Chrysler rather than of a specialty coachbuilder.

As in 1949, Chrysler grouped the Imperial within the C49-2 New Yorker series, where it was available in a standard and a deluxe trim version (the difference being upholstery), and distinguished by the CLEARBAC rear window otherwise common only to Newports. The cars were never called New Yorker Imperials though, and have been grouped separately in the charts in this chapter. They *were* called Chrysler Imperials, and would be listed as a separate Chrysler model from 1951 through 1954, after which Chrysler took another step by designating Imperial as a make in its own right. The car never lived down the 'Chrysler' prefix, though — of which more anon. The Crown Imperial, lushly upholstered in eight-passenger sedan and limousine form, rode on its own 145½-inch wheel-base as in 1949; and Derham offered the last of its custom-bodied, padded-top, long-wheelbase cars with 'blind' rear roof quarters.

1950 Traveler, in the Windsor series.

Traveler's rear-seat in folded position. The spare tire was either mounted on the door, on the floor or in a sub-floor compartment.

1950 Saratoga club coupe.

Chryslers of 1949-50 featured a new dash with one of the industry's first crash pads.

Aside from visibility, which was improved with the CLEARBAC hardtop and wider sedan rear windows, there were very few mechanical changes in the cars from those of 1949. Even the disc brakes, while important innovations, were confined to the Town and Country and the Crown Imperial. Chrysler took to trumpeting such minutiae as "Bulls-Eye prisms set into [headlight] lenses. This concentrates light rays to give more and better road illumination with less glare for safer night driving." But in sum, the 1950 Chrysler was a beautifully engineered, utterly smooth and silent highway car, and its virtues were solidity, reliability and supreme comfort. These facts were recognized by the newly founded *Motor Trend,* which tested a New Yorker sedan during the summer of 1950, calling it "a car of comfort, a car of class."

Motor Trend's Walt Woron borrowed the car of Lloyd Gregg, who had entered it in the 1950 Mobilgas Economy Run in which he scored 17.11 miles per gallon. "When you slip behind the wheel," Woron noted, "you find that it is easy to reach all of the controls except for the heater, which, after all, is not important to the operation of the automobile. With the seat at the comfortable chair-level height, you are in a position to see the road and around you in all directions. No blind spots are evident. There is plenty of leg room in both the front and rear seats, and there is no problem in removing your foot from the throttle to apply the brakes. Head room is exceptional.

"Steering and cornering characteristics of the New Yorker are very good, considering that the steering ratio is 20.4:1 and that it is such a heavy car. No more mushiness was noticed in this car than is evident in most present-day cars. The amount of sidesway when taking corners at a high rate of speed is not too disconcerting . . . Riding comfort is unexcelled. The car literally floats over bumps and ridges in the road. There is a definite lack of wind noise and tire rumble.

"Acceleration qualities of the Chrysler [Woron recorded 0-60 mph in 19.83 seconds using the Prestomatic low-high shift] are something that even the avid Chrysler owner would not brag about, but it must be remembered that this car is not intended for such use. . . . For normal use, there is sufficient power. For added acceleration, it is possible to use the LOW range and the safety clutch. In this procedure, you shift normally with the clutch, using low gear in the LOW range, shift quickly to the HIGH range (which will put the transmission in third gear), then let up on the throttle

(which causes an automatic shift into fourth gear)." That's how Woron managed to get his 0-60 mph time to less than twenty seconds!

Motor Trend's editor did manage to record a maximum top speed of about 86 mph (it might have been more with a different axle ratio), which was good, but his best fuel consumption was only 17.58 mpg at a steady 30 mph, which meant that the old L-head was no economy unit. He found some brake fade from the twelve-inch shoes, but appreciated the solid design of the car, the practical instrument panel and thick crash pad, and the quality of interior fit and finish.

"For a car of this type," Woron concluded, "it is difficult to suggest improvements, because above all we must consider who and what the car is designed for. . . . Perhaps the biggest improvement will be the addition of the much-talked-about torque converter to be installed on future [it was due the next year] models. As it is, the fluid drive could be improved by having a quicker shifting time from the third to fourth gear (and vice versa). . . . It would be impossible in this article to discuss the many fine

1950 Town & Country Newport.

From a beautifully illustrated 1950 brochure, the New Yorker four-door sedan (upper) and Newport hardtop (lower). Artists stretched the cars and shrank the people to accentuate the feeling of Chrysler style and size.

1950 New Yorker convertible.

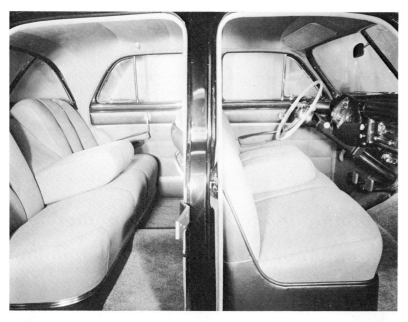

Interior variations on the 1950 Imperial: standard (upper) and deluxe (lower).

1950 Crown Imperial limousine.

features of the Chrysler New Yorker, such as the chemically-treated cylinder walls, the Oilite bearings, the safety-rim wheels, the Amola steel used in the coil springs, etc. If you want a car that you can be proud of, and are looking for a car of the Chrysler-type design and price bracket, then you should consider the New Yorker."

A lot of people did — and they bought other company products, too. In 1950 Chrysler Corporation produced an all-time record 1.2 million cars and 125,000 trucks, about 100,000 units more than in 1949. This was accomplished despite a 104-day strike during the first several months of the year, at the height of the new car selling season, and estimates indicated that another half-million cars and trucks might have been turned out otherwise. Chrysler ended the strike with a new labor contract, and the rest of the year was free of union trouble, though there were still some material shortages.

Meanwhile the Corporation continued to expand plant facilities, particularly at the DeSoto and Chrysler Divisions; both received new body-building shops. At Chrysler, Dave Wallace announced that production, in terms of factory sales, was twenty percent above both 1949 and 1941, the

For the last time in direct coordination with Chrysler, Derham offered a custom town limousine. The roof padding was leather, the rear lights blanked off in the Derham tradition.

two previous high years. With its new body shop in full operation by October, Chrysler built 24,000 cars for a new monthly high. And much of 1950 was spent with the future (and possibly Walt Woron) in mind; installing special-purpose machine tools, automatic conveyors and an assembly line at Jefferson Avenue for a new line of engines destined to solve any performance problems on Chrysler automobiles.

Demand for the 1950's was steady and high. Said sales manager J.A. O'Malley, "The heaviest 1950 volume was in Royal and Windsor lines, the Division's lowest-priced offerings. There was a definite trend, however, to the larger models: New Yorker, Imperial and Crown Imperial; percent of total production in these classes was 24.9. The Imperial, a shorter wheelbase version of the Crown Imperial, showed sales of nearly 11,000 units despite the fact that it was in production for only six months." (Imperial's actual total was 10,650 and it was added to the line on May 1, with the deluxe version appearing on August 14.)

As the new model announcements loomed in the autumn of 1950, some observers indicated that little change was again expected at Chrysler. Most shallow thinkers now thought that the company that had led in innovation during Walter Chrysler's day had settled into harsh conservatism. They couldn't have been more wrong. Though it would take a few years, Chrysler styling was destined to lead the industry. And just around the corner was a stunning new engine development that would send the V-8 pioneers at Oldsmobile and Cadillac back to the drafting boards in search of more horsepower.

A whole new Corporate and Divisional attitude was in the making, and if it was greeted with some reluctance by the more conservative minds at the Highland Park headquarters, they were generally resigned to it. The tingle in the air was transformed into policy change when K.T. Keller forsook the presidency in the fall of 1950 — making way for a new, younger president — and hired an imaginative and brilliant young designer. The new president was L.L. 'Tex' Colbert, the designer Virgil M. Exner. "Stand by," *Motor Trend* reported. "There's going to be some big action and a lot sooner than you think."

CHAPTER 4

The Coming of Ex and Tex

LESTER LUM COLBERT (pronounced "Cull-bert"), who always liked to be called 'Tex,' was a cotton buyer in his youth, but earned enough to go to law school. This provided his entrée into the auto business. After graduation from Harvard in 1929, Colbert joined the New York law firm that was advising Walter Chrysler, and in 1933 he was assigned to Detroit as his firm's resident attorney. Between 1933 and 1935, Colbert attended night school to learn to read blueprints, and he soon became an important administrative aid to K.T. Keller.

In 1942 Colbert was sent to Chicago to build B-29 engines in the huge bomber plant operated by Dodge. The project was so successful that Keller named him president of Dodge Division after the war. Keller admitted that he had 'groomed' Colbert to take on the presidency of Chrysler from that point onward, although the actual event that caused Colbert's succession was Keller's assignment to head the U.S. missile program after the outbreak of the Korean War. Colbert officially relieved Keller, who shifted to the reactivated position of board chairman, on November 3, 1950. "There was no purge in the organization after Colbert took over," the *Detroit News* recorded in 1961. "But as older men retired there was new blood waiting to be used. Colbert used it, on the theory that the organization was getting too big for an old-style centralized operation and that the various divisions deserved more say-so in operations of the company."

Colbert set himself several early goals. He favored a total redesign of all passenger cars as soon as possible, an ambitious program of plant expansion and financing, a hard-hitting sales program reaching from Highland Park to the smallest dealer in the Chrysler family, and the aforementioned 'new blood' transfusion at all levels of Chrysler management. "We all worked as a team," Colbert said in recalling his early presidency. A total redesign would be prevented for three years owing to production lead times, but the man who would produce it was already on hand as part of Colbert's team: Virgil M. Exner.

Exner was one of the earliest members of the styling fraternity generally considered to have been founded by Harley Earl in the late twenties. Exner headed Pontiac styling under Earl from 1934 through 1938, when he switched to the Loewy organization assigned to Studebaker in South Bend, Indiana. He participated in the design of the successful new 1939 Commander, and after the war was mainly responsible for creating the revolutionary 1947 Studebakers, the first entirely new cars produced by a company that had been in existence before the war. Exner had designed the new Studebakers without the knowledge of Loewy, and at the insistence of Studebaker engineer Roy Cole, who was afraid Loewy wouldn't deliver on time. This caused Exner's severance from Loewy after the design was accepted. But he remained a styling/engineering consultant to Studebaker

1951, the revolutionary Chrysler Firepower V-8.

Tex Colbert (left). Virgil Exner (right).

through 1949, competing with the Loewy organization in designing the 1950-52 Studebaker face-lifts.

In 1949, Exner came to Chrysler at the invitation of K.T. Keller. K.T. set him up in an advanced styling studio, relatively independent of Engineering and Henry King, who was responsible for production designs at the time. Here Exner remained until he became director of Chrysler Styling in 1953, and a vice president in 1957. His main interest during his first three years at Highland Park was the remarkable line of Ghia-built Chrysler show cars, which single-handedly held the promise of Chrysler styling during the company's bleakest period of production design from 1949 through 1954. Exner was a thoroughly experienced, imaginative and quite brilliant student of the industrial designs of all countries, a classic car enthusiast, and particularly well-versed in the styling concepts prevalent in Great Britain, France, Germany and Italy. He favored the Italians above all others as creators of the best automotive styling, and the special show cars he built were heavily influenced by Torino. Exner's arrival at Chrysler was one of the more promising signs that the unimaginative boxes of 1949 would inevitably be replaced with something better.

Despite the impending shift in Chrysler management and styling policy implied by the ascendancy of Colbert and Exner, the big public news for 1951 was the introduction of the brilliant new Chrysler FirePower V-8 engine. It had in fact been in the works — long before Colbert, Exner or the '51 models were thought of — as early as 1935. Displacing 331.1 cubic inches (bore and stroke: 3.8125 by 3.625 inches), the FirePower was offered in the 1951 New Yorker, Imperial and Crown Imperial, and in addition to its over-square configuration and 7.5:1 compression ratio, featured the now legendary hemispherical combustion chamber.

In relation to Cadillac's 331.0-cubic-inch V-8, first offered on its 1949 models, the FirePower was identical in displacement but offered twenty more horsepower. It measured slightly less than Lincoln's L-head (336.7 cubic inches) and a bit more than Oldsmobile's ohv Rocket (303.7), but outdistanced all rivals in achieving over one-half horsepower per cubic inch displacement with .544, compared to Cadillac's .484, Lincoln's .457 and Oldsmobile's .455. It used two sets of rocker shafts, arms and pushrods, allowing its valves to be large and inclined. It ran cool with very large, unobstructed, low-turbulence ports for maximum volumetric efficiency. The spark plugs were mounted in the exact center of their combustion chambers, providing complete and even burning of fuel, and the engine was comparatively free from carbon buildup in relation to its rivals, thus providing less chance of pre-ignition or running on. Though the hemi head was developed independent of the basic V-8 engine, their joint adoption was no accident. And the V-8 generally supplied abundant proof that the Chrysler engineering prowess of former days was still in evidence.

James C. Zeder, (brother of the late Fred M.) who was vice president and director of Chrysler Engineering and Research, lucidly described the background of the FirePower in a Society of Automotive Engineers paper in 1951, taking pains to point out that neither its ultra-high compression nor its hemi head was exactly new: "All Chrysler Corporation cars have had high-compression engines since the first 1924 Chrysler, and most people will recall the famous 1928 Chrysler Red Head engine with its then unheard-of compression ratio of 6.2:1. The rest of the industry followed this lead, and compression ratios have steadily increased since that time until reaching their present maximums of about 7.5:1.

"Compression ratio is a measure of how much the fuel-air mixture in the cylinder is compressed before it is ignited by the spark plug. A compression ratio of 7.0:1, for example, means that the mixture is compressed to one-seventh of its original volume before being ignited.

"Engine designers are constantly trying to increase compression ratios because this is one of the most direct ways of increasing the efficiency and power of an engine. Unfortunately, the compression ratio can be raised only so far before a point is reached at which, with available gasolines, the fuel mixture in the cylinder head begins to explode wastefully instead of

Exterior views of the hemi.

burning smoothly. This is the phenomenon — familiar to every motorist — known as detonation, or knock; and it not only reduces efficiency and power but is also very hard on the engine.

"One way of preventing this harmful knock is to raise the octane rating of the fuel. This can be done by changing the chemical structure of the fuel in the refining process or by the use of knock-retarding additives. However, it has become evident in recent years that there is a practical limit to increasing compression ratios merely by increasing the octane value of fuels. Each new increase in octane value requires billions of dollars of new refining equipment and results in a smaller amount of each barrel of crude oil which can be made into automobile gasoline. So in the interest of keeping down costs to the motorist and preserving natural resources, it became necessary to find other methods of improving engine efficiency and power."

The actual development of the V-8 short-stroke engine began during World War II, with the appointment of W.E. Drinkard — more recently executive engineer of Chrysler Vehicle Engineering — in charge of engine development. Drinkard was aided by assistant chief engineer M.L. Carpentier, who had been with Chrysler from the beginning with Zeder, Skelton and Breer. Originally the V-8 was a military project, but its civilian applications were obvious and work continued on it after V-J Day. As at Cadillac and Oldsmobile, where overhead valve V-8's were simultaneously being readied for introduction, it soon became obvious that an oversquare bore and stroke configuration with a well-damped, five-main-bearing crank was the best layout for future engine designs. And like Cadillac's, Chrysler's engineers developed a 'slipper piston,' in which each piston hunkered down between the crankshaft counterweights at the bottom of its stroke, providing smoother running and less friction and wear. The bore, larger than the stroke in Chrysler's design, allowed large valve diameters, while the relatively short stroke paid off in lower piston speed and less cylinder and ring wear. The combination of the two afforded a compact, rigid and relatively light engine block — a major improvement over the blocks then in use.

Before the V-8 project began, in 1937, Chrysler elected to evaluate a variety of valve and head designs then largely on the scrap pile of history, to see if a higher-efficiency design wasn't possible in those areas. Under developmental engineer R.K. Lee, technicians reviewed the two-stroke engine, the Knight sleeve valve and the rotary valve types, but found that none provided a practical improvement on the more conventional poppet

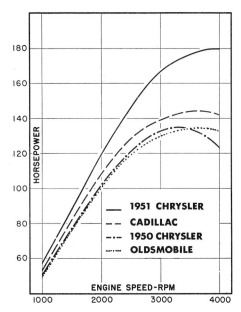

Cutaway side view of the hemi-V-8. Power curve showing the relative power output of the ohv Chrysler V-8 engine versus those of Cadillac, Olds and the Spitfire eight.

valve. The latter then became the basis to work from; methods were explored by which the best sort of poppet valve system could be developed, and these led in due course to the hemispherical combustion chamber.

"Throughout all of this test work," James Zeder continued, "the hemispherical combustion chamber consistently developed the highest efficiency of all the many designs tested. In other words, this chamber was able to put to work more of the heat energy available in the fuel than could any other production passenger car engine in America." In the past, the hemi had been thought to require higher octane fuel, which wasn't widely available, and to idle roughly, which was a consummation devoutly to be avoided on the smooth-running highway cruisers that Detroit then considered essential to the public need. But after building an experimental single-cylinder engine with interchangeable heads in 1946, Drinkard and his staff learned that the feared rough idle simply wasn't there, and that the engine could in fact achieve the same compression ratio as a conventional ohv cylinder head on *lower* octane fuel. To put out the same horsepower, the less efficient engine designs required higher compression ratios ranging up to 10.5:1, and as a result would need much higher octane fuels than the corresponding hemi.

"Equally important to the high performance of the FirePower engine," wrote Zeder, "is the exceptional breathing capacity of this hemispherical chamber design. The cross-section of a FirePower cylinder shows the many features that are conducive to high volumetric efficiency, or breathing. The valves are not crowded together, nor are they surrounded closely by the combustion chamber walls. Both ports are ideally streamlined with a minimum of directional change. The complete separation of the ports, together with the wide space between the valve seats, assures that the incoming charge picks up a minimum of heat from the hot exhaust. In addition, the flow within the cylinder is not restricted by any barriers or tortuous passages.

"The hemispherical chamber has another remarkable characteristic. At 7.5:1 compression ratio, it does not require the high-cost, premium grades of fuel which must be used in other conventional overhead valve V-8 engines (i.e., Cadillac's and Oldsmobile's) at the same compression ratio. In other words, the hemispherical chamber has designed-in octane numbers so that it does not require such a high octane rating of fuel.

"We at Chrysler Corporation are in favor of increasing compression ratios as fast as higher-octane fuels become commercially available. In the interests of economy and savings to the consumer, we intend in the future to use the highest compression which will permit smooth operation with regularly available fuels. But at the same time we intend to pursue all other avenues of increasing engine performance and economy. . . . The hemispherical combustion chamber not only makes [the FirePower] the most efficient engine available today (in terms of pounds of fuel used per brake horsepower hour), but it also makes it better able to take advantage of the better fuels which will be developed in the future."

Like the high compression engine, Zeder remarked, the hemispherical combustion chamber was not a new idea. It was applied to the Welch car and an engine of the Belgian Pipe Company in 1904, to Austro-Daimler in 1910, and to most aircraft engines by the end of World War I. Later it appeared on high-performance sports or racing cars like the Duesenberg, Stutz, Offenhauser and Miller. In *Road & Track,* John Bond noted that the hemi head was also common to the concurrent Jaguar XK-120, where it helped to provide 160 horsepower at 5200 rpm from an engine 120 cubic inches and two cylinders smaller than Chrysler's. "On the same basis," said Bond, "the 331-cubic-inch Chrysler should be capable of 252 bhp — if the tappets would stay on the cam profiles at 5200." Chrysler quickly demonstrated that they would, to the tune of one hundred more horsepower — public demonstrations achieved 352 bhp after a few modifications to the camshaft, carbs and exhaust. And drag racers would later get as much as 1,000 horsepower from the same power plant. So much for any rivalry from Great Britain!

"From a production viewpoint," Bond continued, "it is interesting to note that the cylinder heads are identical and interchangeable, right and left, thus requiring only one cylinder head line in the factory. The intake manifold is also reversible, and symmetrical. A water-jacketed throttle body on the carburetor assures proper control of mixture temperatures. The camshaft is exceptionally large in diameter and runs in five large bushings lubricated from the main bearings. The ignition system is fully waterproofed, spark plugs being located at the bottom of a long tube through the rocker arm compartment. Three rings are used on the slipper-type pistons." Bond also provided an interesting — and illuminating — comparison of the FirePower with the 1950 L-head Spitfire Eight engine:

	1950 Spitfire	1951 FirePower
Bore	3¾	3 13/16
Stroke	4⅞	3 5/8
Displacement	323.5 ci	331.1 ci
Comp. Ratio	7.25:1	7.5:1
Max. Torque	270 at 1800 rpm	312 at 2000 rpm
Max. bhp	135 at 3200 rpm	180 at 4000 rpm
Bhp/cu. in.	.418	.544
Weight, less flywheel and M6 trans.	722 lb	685 lb
Weight, plus flywheel and M6 trans.	1,002 lb	933 lb
Weight per hp	7.58 lb/hp	5.18 lb/hp

The hemi was not without certain disadvantages, however. In comparison with more conventional overhead valve V-8's, it was enormously complex, requiring double the number of rocker shafts (four instead of two). Also required were a set of eight intake and exhaust pushrods, and a set of eight intake and exhaust rockers; each set different. Though considerably lighter than the L-head, it was also somewhat heavier than comparable overhead valve engines: two hemi heads weighed 120 pounds compared to only ninety-four pounds for those of the 1949 Cadillac V-8. The hemi would, as a result, become very expensive to manufacture, but during the next several years it became world-famous.

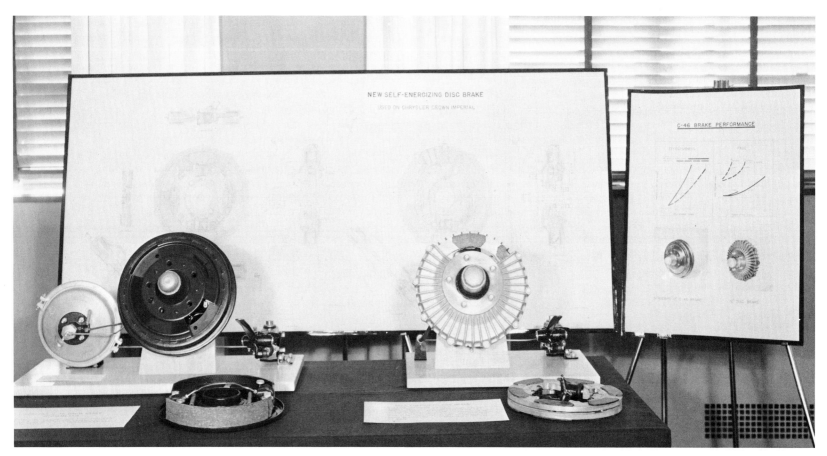

Chrysler's self-energizing disc brakes.

The presence of the hemi engine largely eclipsed three lesser, but still important, developments: ventilated brake drums, Chrysler's first power steering assist and electric window lifts. (The 1950 Imperial was first with electric lifts and the 1950 Crown Imperial had hydraulics.) Brake ventilation was accomplished by spacing the wheel covers one-half inch outward from the rims. Effective fan blades, placed on wheel covers caught the air and drew it in around the brakes, while the raised wheel cover provided an exhaust opening. Power steering, which in true fifties fashion was given a trick name (Hydraguide), was standard on Imperials and New Yorkers and optional on the Saratoga. Fully hydraulic, Hydraguide eliminated four-fifths of the steering effort, making parking and driving the big senior models relatively easy. The hydraulic system was operated by an oil pump driven off the generator. The window lifts were standard on all Imperials, save the Newport, on convertible rear quarter windows, and optional on other models.

Also new in 1951 were two further permutations of the old Fluid Drive: Fluid-Matic ($135 option on Windsors, standard on long-wheelbase Windsors, all Saratogas, Imperials and New Yorkers) and Fluid-Torque ($167 option on Saratoga, New Yorker and Imperial, standard on Crown Imperial). Fluid-Matic was simply the same old fluid coupling-cum-four speed, while Fluid-Torque adopted a torque converter mounted ahead of the clutch. The clutch pedal was used to select the shift ranges, and one shifted by lifting the left foot.

The 1951 line, including the later-announced Saratoga, consisted of the following:

Model

Body Style (passengers)	Price	W.B.(in)	Weight (lb)
Series C51-1 Windsor			
sedan, 4dr (6)	$2,410	125½	3,627
club coupe (6)	2,388	125½	3,570
Town and Country wagon (6)	3,083	125½	3,965
sedan, l.w.b. 4dr (8)	3,217	139½	4,145
Series C51-2 Windsor Deluxe			
sedan, 4dr (6)	$2,628	125½	3,775
Traveler, 4dr (6)	2,887	125½	3,890
club coupe (6)	2,605	125½	3,700
Newport hardtop (6)	2,973	125½	3,855
convertible (6)	3,091	125½	3,945
sedan, l.w.b. 4dr (8)	3,436	139½	4,295
limousine (8)	3,577	139½	4,415
Series C55 Saratoga			
sedan, 4dr (6)	$3,041	125½	4,018
club coupe (6)	3,014	125½	3,948
Town and Country wagon (6)	3,706	125½	4,310
sedan, l.w.b. 4dr (8)	3,937	139½	4,465
Series C52 New Yorker			
sedan, 4dr (6)	$3,403	131½	4,260
club coupe (6)	3,373	131½	4,145
Newport hardtop (6)	3,823	131½	4,330
convertible (6)	3,941	131½	4,460
Town and Country wagon (6)	4,051	131½	4,455
Series C54 Imperial			
sedan, 4dr (6)	$3,699	131½	4,350
club coupe (6)	3,687	131½	4,230
Newport hardtop (6)	4,067	131½	4,380
convertible (6)	4,427	131½	4,570
Series C53 Crown Imperial			
sedan, l.w.b. 4dr (8)	$6,623	145½	5,360
limousine (8)	6,740	145½	5,450

The face-lift this year was confined to the front end, and again the trend favored simplification. Chryslers featured a two-bar grille with the Country Fair badge mounted between the bars. FirePower V-8's were identified by large *V* devices on hoods and decks, while Windsors and the new Windsor Deluxe wore Chrysler script instead. The hood ornament, a curious ring-and-wing affair designed by Ed Sheard of Styling, was common to all models except Imperials, which used a more modest chrome bullet device balanced by a more complicated *V* logo incorporating Chrysler's traditional crown. Imperial was now officially a separate model, although still obviously of Chrysler lineage, wearing Chrysler script on hood and

Full-time power-steering cut steering effort by eighty percent.

deck and an Imperial nameplate on the front quarter panels. The Imperial grille was heavier than Chrysler's, but still much neater than the 1950 design, and Imperial flanks were further streamlined with faired-in rear fender skirts.

Imperials really comprised the only major model change from 1950, for three new body styles were now offered for the first time — a club coupe, convertible and hardtop. The Imperial Deluxe sedan was eliminated, on the logical premise that all Imperials were already deluxe anyway. The Windsor DeLuxe was theoretcially a new model, but in effect it was the old Windsor of 1950 whose name, in turn, was applied to what had been the cheaper Royal. There was a wagon in this cheapest line, as well as an ambulance.

It wasn't until July, however, that Chrysler rocked the industry and the public with the new hemi-powered Saratoga — not the heavy, long-wheelbase Saratoga of 1950 but a lighter version mounted on the Windsor chassis, which had never before been powered by anything but a six. Since the Saratoga was now more maneuverable and lighter than the New Yorker,

1951 New Yorker four-door sedan.

1951 New Yorker Newport.

Styling of the 1951 Imperials was extremely clean. At right is the 1951 Imperial Newport.

it provided marginally better performance; the idea resembled Oldsmobile's placing of its Rocket engine in the light 88 for 1949. Chrysler thus created a stock car champion. The Saratoga immediately became known as Chrysler's hot rod, and it is interesting to compare its performance figures with those of the 1951 New Yorker in contemporary road tests:

	Saratoga Coupe *Road & Track* November, 1951	Saratoga Sedan *Motor Trend* October, 1952	New Yorker Sedan *Motor Trend* May, 1951
Test weight (dry)	3,948 pounds	4,018 pounds	4,260 pounds
0-60 mph	10 seconds	14.8 seconds	14.4 seconds
1/4 mile accel.	18.7 seconds	19.5 seconds	19.32 seconds
Top speed	108.4 mph	107.6 mph	106.01 mph

Road & Track's downright astounding acceleration time was not a typographical error. According to the editors, their Saratoga out-accelerated the Muntz Jet and — up to 60 mph — the vaunted Jaguar XK-120! How so? *Roack & Track* explained: "With selector in low range the clutch was disengaged and the engine revved to about 25% throttle (normal starts do not require use of clutch) . . . depressing the throttle any more than 25% made the Chrysler sit still and peel rubber, losing precious split seconds . . . then with the engine winding to the proper point, the clutch was sharply engaged. At about 35 mph the clutch was again floored, and the throttle was held 'full on.' This put the 3rd gear into play and at around 65 mph the throttle was again backed off to allow the car to drop into 4th. When this is performed in proper sequence a 0-60 time of 10 seconds should result.

"*Road & Track's* test crew seldom, gets excited about American cars, but then *Road & Track's* readers are familiar with this attitude. The Chrysler is an exception. While it has faults, and some of them are serious, we feel that it is outstanding among local efforts." The magazine's lead-footed technique didn't help the gas mileage: The Saratoga returned only 12.5 mpg during the acceleration runs. But a very agreeable 19.4 mpg was obtained at a more normal pace.

Road & Track was also high on Saratoga handling: "Steering is light with, of course, the universal complaint: too high a ratio — 4¾ turns lock to lock. It seems that power steering is the only answer to the nose-heavy

1951 Town & Country, in the Windsor series.

1951 Windsor club coupe.

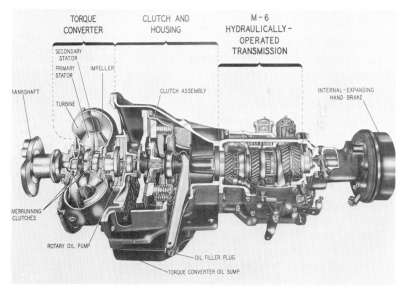

Fluid-Torque remained an option in 1951.

1951 Windsor Deluxe four-door sedan.

The 1951 Traveler in the Windsor Deluxe series continued to look outwardly like a sedan.

Chrysler sold 153 ambulances, built at Jefferson Avenue on Windsor chassis.

American designs. If the steering is 'light' enough for parking and low speed maneuvering, the ratio is too high for safe cornering at speed... Chrysler New Yorker and Imperial are first on the market with hydraulic steering, and this device is optional on the Saratoga. Still, Saratoga's manual steering compares favorably to other American cars of its weight and class.

"The Chrysler has an outstanding quality other than the potent engine... good brakes. Vacuum assisted, they will bring the car to a positive stop from almost any speed without excess pedal pressure. It was found, however, that during the test it was too easy to lock the rear wheels. A slight adjustment should correct this failing. No other car tested by *Road & Track* has approached the Chrysler's braking ability. Brake fade appeared only after repeated severe applications.

"In summation: the tremendous performance of this V-8 is enough in itself to be a strong selling point for the Chrysler. Regardless of the rest of the car's advantages or disadvantages, when you touch that throttle, you know something mighty impressive is happening under the hood."

Motor Trend, which drew similar conclusions about the Saratoga (though a New Yorker tested earlier was faster in acceleration) had already

A proper pace car for the 1951 Indy 500: New Yorker convertible. 1951 Saratoga series Town & Country wagon.

given Chrysler its 1952 Engineering Achievement Award on the basis of extensive and objective comparisons of fifteen representative 1951 automobiles. Of the thirteen criteria, Chrysler led or tied in nine: shortest braking distance, best ton mpg, best acceleration from 0-60 mph and over a measured quarter mile, highest top speed, highest road horsepower, best ratio of pounds per horsepower, highest torque and maximum BMEP (brake mean effective pressure, meaning average 'push' on the head of the piston during its power stroke). Chrysler was bested only in basic mpg fuel consumption (by Studebaker and others), in percent of bhp at the wheels (by Oldsmobile), and in dollars per road horsepower per cubic inch (by Studebaker). Nothing that could not be measured or calculated was included in the tabulation, and in point tally Chrysler scored 176 against 153.5 for Oldsmobile and 145 for Studebaker.

"There are many things the *Motor Trend* Award does not cover," wrote Griff Borgeson: "Safety, suspension, upholstery, appearance, durability, comfort, ease of driving, visibility. Some of these are part of styling, not engineering, and no accurate measurements of such factors have yet been devised. [But] Chrysler had built a car that combines safety, economy and outstanding performance. It is not perfect — yet it is closer to the goal than any other family automobile currently produced in America. It cost the Chrysler Corporation a lot of money to build the new V-8; it took a lot of courage to flout tradition and experiment with design. The Award winner is, in concept, a major step ahead in American automotive history."

The Saratoga was the odds-on favorite to win the 1951 Mexican Road Race, a bruising 2,000-mile cross-country marathon as treacherous as Italy's car-bashing Mille Miglia and Targa Florio. The Mexican run was then becoming highly popular with racing fans the world over, and in 1953 it would be named the fifth and final deciding race for the world's driving championship, following the Mille Miglia, Nurburgring, Le Mans and Tourist Trophy. In contrast to these, however, the Mexicans matched American stock sedans with European sports cars over the same course. No one expected Yank iron to win the event outright, but a splendid battle was always guaranteed for the stock-car class title — and often the stockers came embarassingly close to the likes of Ferrari and Mercedes-Benz.

Two Chrysler Saratogas driven by Tony Bettenhausen and Bill Sterling were the leading contenders; Sterling's car was basically stock but Bettenhausen's was rumored to be putting out almost 300 horsepower. Surprisingly, Sterling drove the better race, finishing first in the stock class and third overall, behind two Ferraris. He crossed the finish line less than eight minutes behind Alberto Ascari and a considerable distance ahead of ninety percent of the European sports cars.

According to Troy Ruttman (in *Motor Trend*), who was fourth in a 1948 modified Mercury, "The greatest single cause for failure on the American cars was brakes. As the years have passed and wheel sizes have diminished, brake sizes have gone down accordingly and the manufacturers have really done little to compensate for this sacrifice. [One wonders what the Saratoga would have done, equipped with a set of Imperial disc brakes.]

"Bill Sterling, the Chrysler third-place winner, was not a race driver in the familiar sense. However, he's an excellent road driver and turned in one of the finest performances of the five-day grind. He used his head every inch of the way, drove fast but kept his machine together and *never* lost a tire on the road. He's a *natural* driver and this, as far as I know, is his

73

AVERAGE BRAKING DISTANCE IN FEET	AVERAGE FUEL CONSUMPTION IN MPG	TON MILES PER GALLON	AVERAGE ACCELERATION IN SECONDS	ACCELERATION OVER STANDING 1/4 MILE IN SECS.	AVERAGE TOP SPEED IN MPH	MAXIMUM ROAD HP	% OF BHP AT WHEELS	DOLLARS PER ROAD HP	LBS. PER ROAD HP	MAX. TORQUE IN LBS.-FT.	ROAD HP PER CU. IN.	MAX. BMEP IN P.S.I.	TOTAL POINTS
Chrysler 90.2	Studebaker 21.41	Chrysler 39.9	Chrysler 10.63	Chrysler 19.32	Chrysler 102.27	Chrysler 104	Oldsmobile 68.1	Studebaker 30.8	Chrysler 42.7	Cadillac Chrysler 312	Studebaker .448	Cadillac Chrysler 142.0	Chrysler 176
Nash Statesman 91.4	Kaiser 19.70	Cadillac 39.1	Hudson 12.52	Hudson 19.41	Hudson 97.09	Lincoln 95	Mercury 67.9	Lincoln 31.3	Hudson 43.1	...	Chrysler .314	...	Oldsmobile 153.5
Hudson 96.3	Nash Statesman 19.07	Lincoln 37.4	Oldsmobile 13.70	Lincoln 19.90	Lincoln 97.08	Cadillac Oldsmobile 92	Studebaker 63.2	Oldsmobile 31.7	Studebaker 43.2	Lincoln 275	Oldsmobile .303	Nash Ambassador 134.8	Studebaker 145
Ford 103.2	Ford 18.28	Oldsmobile 35.2	Cadillac 14.72	Studebaker 20.67	Cadillac 95.44	...	Hudson 62.0	Hudson 32.08	Oldsmobile 43.7	Oldsmobile 263	Mercury .297	Oldsmobile 130.7	Hudson 135
Dodge 104.3	Chrysler 17.98	Studebaker 35.1	Studebaker 15.10	Oldsmobile 20.93	Packard 93.17	Hudson 90	Lincoln 61.6	Chrysler 34.0	Lincoln 46.0	Hudson 257	Hudson .292	Buick 129.0	Lincoln 131.5
Oldsmobile 110.5	Cadillac 17.70	Kaiser 33.3	Packard 15.15	Kaiser 20.99	Studebaker 92.78	Packard 80	Packard 59.1	Ford 34.4	Cadillac 48.0	Packard 230	Lincoln .282	Dodge Studebaker 127.5	Cadillac 130
Kaiser 110.8	Oldsmobile 17.50	Pontiac 33.0	Buick 15.20	Packard 21.04	Oldsmobile 92.54	Mercury Studebaker 76	Ford 59.0	Mercury 34.8	Mercury 49.5	Pontiac 220	Cadillac Packard .277	...	Packard 96.5
Studebaker 111.2	Dodge Pontiac 17.20	Dodge 32.5	Ford 15.31	Ford 21.19	Mercury 91.18	...	Pontiac 58.6	Pontiac 34.9	Packard 51.1	Buick 217	...	Kaiser 126.7	Kaiser 91.5
Pontiac 115.1	...	Buick 32.4	Kaiser 15.40	Cadillac 21.22	Pontiac 87.72	Buick 70	Buick 58.3	Buick 35.5	Kaiser 54.5	Nash Ambassador 210	Kaiser .273	Hudson 125.8	Mercury 90.5
Mercury 116.0	Lincoln 17.07	Nash Statesman 31.2	Lincoln 15.44	Mercury 21.74	Ford 87.25	Pontiac 68	Chrysler 57.9	Cadillac 39.4	Ford 55.9	Mercury 206	Buick .266	Pontiac 123.6	Ford 85
Packard 121.7	Nash Ambassador 16.30	Ford 30.2	Pontiac 16.40	Nash Ambassador 21.75	Nash Ambassador 86.95	Kaiser, Nash Ambassador 62	Cadillac 57.4	Packard 39.8	Pontiac 56.4	Dodge, Studebaker, Kaiser 190	Nash Ambassador .265	Lincoln 123.2	Pontiac 84.5
Cadillac 124.4	Buick 16.20	Packard 30.1	Mercury 16.85	Buick 21.87	Kaiser 83.57	...	Kaiser 54.0	Nash Ambassador 34.9	Buick 57.1	...	Pontiac .254	Mercury 121.6	Buick 78.5
Buick Lincoln 128.1	Packard 14.69	Nash Ambassador 29.8	Nash Ambassador 17.96	Pontiac 22.03	Dodge 83.41	Ford 59	Nash Ambassador 53.9	Kaiser 35.9	Nash Ambassador 58.9	...	Ford .247	Packard 120.4	Nash Ambassador 61.5
...	Mercury 14.62	Mercury 27.5	Dodge 19.03	Dodge 23.68	Buick 82.97	Dodge 50	Dodge 48.5	Dodge 53.4	Dodge 75.6	Ford 181	Dodge .216	Nash Statesman 114.8	Dodge 57
Nash Ambassador 130.9	Hudson 14.07	Hudson 27.4	Nash Statesman 21.98	Nash Statesman 24.47	Nash Statesman 77.19	Nash Statesman 39.5	Nash Statesman 46.5	Nash Statesman 60.7	Nash Statesman 82.3	Nash Statesman 140	Nash Statesman .214	Ford 113.6	Nash Statesman 44

NOTES: All cars tested were four-door sedans. Series and types of transmissions were: Buick Special, Dynaflow; Cadillac 62, Hydra-Matic; Chrysler New Yorker, Prestomatic; Dodge Coronet Diplomat, Gyro-matic; Ford, Fordomatic; Hudson Hornet, Hydra-Matic; Kaiser Deluxe std. with overdrive; Lincoln 74, std. with overdrive; Mercury std. with overdrive; Nash Ambassador, Hydra-Matic; Nash Statesman, Hydra-Matic; Oldsmobile Super 88, Hydra-Matic; Packard 200, Ultramatic; Pontiac Eight, Hydra-Matic; Studebaker Commander, Automatic Drive.

AVERAGE BRAKING DISTANCE IN FT.: Averages of our published braking figures which themselves were averages of many stops from speeds of 30, 45, and 60 mph

AVERAGE FUEL CONSUMPTION IN MPG: An average of scores of readings made with each car under operating conditions ranging from stop and start driving in heavy traffic to a steady 60 mph on the open highway. Mpg with OD not counted.

TON MILES PER GALLON: $\frac{\text{car weight in tons} \times \text{distance travelled in miles}}{\text{fuel consumed in gals.}}$

AVERAGE ACCELERATION: Average of all acceleration figures.

AVERAGE ACCELERATION FOR STANDING 1/4 MILE: Average of two-way runs from standing start over measured 1/4 mile.

AVERAGE TOP SPEED: Average of two-way flying runs over measured 1/4 mile.

MAXIMUM ROAD HP: Engine power output delivered at driving wheels on Clayton chassis dynamometer.

PER CENT OF HP AT DRIVING WHEELS: $\frac{Rhp}{Bhp} \times 100$.

DOLLARS PER RHP: West Coast delivered price

LBS. PER RHP: $\frac{\text{Weight of test car in lbs.}}{rhp}$

MAXIMUM TORQUE IN LBS.-FT.: From Automobile Manufacturers Assn. specifications.

RHP PER CU. IN. OF ENGINE DISPLACEMENT: $\frac{rhp}{\text{cu. ins. displacement}}$

MAXIMUM BMEP: From Ethyl Corp. "Brief Passenger Car Data 1951."

Motor Trend made these comparisons in declaring the 1951 Chrysler, Car of the Year.

1952 Windsor club coupe.   1952 Windsor Deluxe convertible.

background: he's driven a lot of high speed miles over those endless Texas roads; for several months he drove a truck between Mexico City and El Paso, giving him a real knowledge of that part of the road; he drove well in last year's race, was Johnny Mantz's chief contender — or vice versa.

"Sterling's Chrysler can, for practical purposes, be considered a stock machine. Apparently due to the construction of the rear-end gear housing, the lubricant there tended to froth at high speeds, losing its lubricating quality and necessitating replacement of the rear end three different times. This was a problem that plagued only Chryslers and was finally solved when a mixture of white lead and castor oil was used for the rear-end lube.

"Tony Bettenhausen surprised us by making very slow time through the mountains and he told us in Mexico City that that sort of driving was really a novelty for him and that it took him the first two days to get it figured out." Bettenhausen's brakes had been a terrific problem. Apparently he had applied them with abandon coming down the mountains; and as he was rolling into Oaxaca, the first stop on the trek, he kept bumping the curb with his left front wheel to slow the car down. His pit crew finally grabbed hold of the Saratoga and walked it to a stop.

Sterling's Chrysler was the only one in the top ten finishers. To give an idea of the toughness of the race, of fourteen Chryslers that started only six finished.

The excitement of Mexico probably didn't help Chrysler dealers get over the fact that there wouldn't be any new models for 1952 — well, nothing worth talking about, anyway. The 1952 Chryslers were announced in December, 1951; and the only visible change was a redesigned taillight, incorporating the back-up lights with the taillight lenses in heavy chrome bases. The overall lines of the cars were as before. Brochures had to show them with black tires, since whitewalls had been discontinued by government edict owing to defense shortages rising out of the Korean War. There were, nevertheless, certain subtle changes that are often overlooked. The Windsors were stroked slightly (to 4¾ inches from 4½), for a displacement of 264.5 cubic inches and 119 horsepower at 3600 rpm. And a few low-

1952 New Yorker Newport.

Only 251 New Yorker wagons were built for 1952, and the body style was withdrawn from the series the following year.

volume models were missing from the 1952 line up: There was no Windsor club coupe or Traveler, no New Yorker wagon or club coupe, and no Imperial convertible. Also, the Imperial club coupe was phased out in early February, 1952.

Model
Body Style (passengers)	Price	W.B.(in)	Weight (lb)
Series C51-1 Windsor			
sedan, 4dr (6)	$2,518	125½	3,640
club coupe (6)	2,495	125½	3,550
Town and Country wagon (6)	3,220	125½	4,015
sedan, l.w.b. 4dr (8)	3,362	139½	4,145
Series C51-2 Windsor Deluxe			
sedan, 4dr (6)	$2,747	125½	3,775
Newport hardtop (6)	3,107	125½	3,855
convertible (6)	3,230	125½	3,990
Series C55 Saratoga			
sedan, 4dr (6)	$3,240	125½	4,010
club coupe (6)	3,212	125½	3,935
Town and Country wagon (6)	3,950	125½	4,345
sedan, l.w.b. 4dr (8)	4,197	139½	4,510
Series C52 New Yorker			
sedan, 4dr (6)	$3,555	131½	4,205
Newport hardtop (6)	3,994	131½	4,325
convertible (6)	4,118	131½	4,450
Series C54 Imperial			
sedan, 4dr (6)	$3,864	131½	4,315
club coupe (6)	3,851	131½	4,220
Newport hardtop (6)	4,249	131½	4,365
Series C53 Crown Imperial			
sedan, l.w.b. 4dr (8)	$6,922	145½	5,395
limousine (8)	7,044	145½	5,430

Actually the no-change policy and deletion of low sellers were advantages for the Division, because they allowed Chrysler to clean up inventories and place new car introductions on proper schedule. Ever since the war, Chryslers had been announced early in the same year designated, or about three or four months *after* the competition. Kaiser-Frazer, as we have seen, announced its 1951 models only two months after Chrysler announced its 1950's. Korean War shortages prevented any sheet metal changes anyway; and since the 1951 models had only been introduced in February (and the Saratoga not until July), Chrysler was really just having an eighteen month 1951-52 model year. From this point on it would enjoy the normal industry debut dates — the 1953 Chryslers would be announced in October, 1952.

With wartime shortages and defense work again factors, Chrysler would have a hard time matching 1951 sales in 1952. Its production of 167,316 units in 1950 had moved the Division into eleventh place for the first time since 1946; and in 1951 another 162,916 cars were built for a tenth place finish, nosing out Nash by a hair. Nineteen fifty-one also saw large-scale expansion; Chrysler added a new assembly plant at Newark, Delaware, and doubled or tripled its California assembly plant space. Much of the new building was needed for defense work, but the investment would pay off when the war was over. A transmission factory was nearing completion in Indianapolis, and an engine plant of 200,000 square feet was being finished in Detroit. Also in 1951, Chrysler purchased 3,800 acres of land near Ann Arbor in order to construct a proving grounds.

In 1951, Chrysler built 78,000 V-8 powered cars, about one-half of the total production. This was nearly double the past production of the old Spitfire Eight. A ratio of two V-8's to every six was held from July through December, with Saratogas comprising about half of the V-8 total; New Yorkers, thirty-five to forty percent; and Imperials, thirteen to fifteen percent.

But 1952 presented problems other than the defense bind. By the end of the year Ford Motor Company had outproduced Chrysler Corporation

The Saratoga eight-passenger sedan used a Windsor body and 139½-inch wheelbase.

1952 Saratoga four-door sedan.

1952 Saratoga club coupe.

Plush interior of the 1952 Saratoga.   Highlander interior in a 1952 New Yorker.

with a total of 1,004,784 cars against 952,591. Although Chrysler continued to prosper and employ record numbers, Ford's ascendancy was distressing to Chrysler's Sales Department. The Ford threat was less evident at Chrysler Division, however, where the marque moved from third to second place in high-priced car production and scored its usual thirteen percent of total Corporate car output.

Yet only 120,678 Chryslers were built in calendar year 1952. Chrysler blamed the decline from 1951 "almost entirely on government controls, materials shortages and the protracted steel strike," which President Truman had finally ended by temporarily nationalizing the steel industry.

In the first six months of 1952, Chrysler built nearly 40,000 more V-8 engines (due to the six's decline in popularity), over a third more than in the same period in 1951. Chrysler Marine and Industrial Engine Division was moved to the new Trenton, Michigan plant, allowing for still more V-8 production. By the end of 1952 the FirePower was accounting for sixty percent of Chrysler output — the first time it had led the Chrysler six.

The handwriting certainly appeared to be on the wall for six-cylinder Chryslers. While the Windsor and Windsor Deluxe were selling well, they were rather mundane for the new Chrysler performance image. In October, Tex Colbert said the six's time was limited, and that it would soon be common only to low-priced cars. That was good news for those who fancied high-performance Chryslers. Now if only they had styling to match their looks.

They would. Virgil Exner was working on it.

K.T. Keller, with Miss Chrysler Royal at an Automobile Manufacturers' Association function in 1951, had reason to smile, even if there was no longer a Chrysler Royal. The hemi had done well; all the world loves a winner.

CHAPTER 5

K310 and the Italian Connection

IF THE 1952 models exhibited no visible trace of Virgil Exner — indeed no visible trace of anyone's particular style — Chrysler nevertheless displayed plentiful evidence that Virgil was not idle. Exhibit A, forebear of a long line of fascinating Chrysler specials, was Exner's sleek K310 (K for Keller, 310 for its supposed horsepower, though Chrysler archives say it had only the standard 180). It was the first of the spectacular Ghia-built, Detroit-designed Chrysler show cars.

Though many consider Exner to have convinced Chrysler of the merits of Italian carrozzerias, Highland Park had actually dabbled in European designs before he arrived. The first factory-sponsored custom was a neat four-door sedan with striking Cisitalia-like styling by Pinin Farina, on a 131½-inch wheelbase New Yorker chassis. Similar, on a shorter Plymouth wheelbase, was the Ghia-built Plymouth XX500 of 1951, another four-door sedan with a beautiful interior of leather and Bedford cord and clean, chrome-free flanks totally atypical of contemporary Plymouths.

Some time after Exner's death, the writer discussed this era at Chrysler with Virgil, Jr., himself a talented designer now in the employ of Ford. "The XX500 was brought over by Ghia," he said, "to show Chrysler their ability and craftsmanship, and to get Chrysler to give them the business. In retrospect, the XX500 was pretty dumpy, built along the lines of what they were doing in Italy at the time — the Lancia Aurelia for instance. The design didn't scale up too well, but it started the whole idea in Dad's mind that they could do some advanced design and build it as a real car, as opposed to mock-ups as in this country."

Both the Pinin Farina Chrysler and the Ghia Plymouth appealed to Tex Colbert — and certainly to K.T. Keller, who, as the reader will remember, had favored the clean-lined envelope body since the prewar Newport and Thunderbolt. So one of Exner's first roles at Chrysler, long before he became director of Styling, was to work with Ghia toward creating additional design evolutions. Ghia was chosen over Pinin Farina after the XX500 revealed that Ghia could hand-build the cars for a lot less money than Farina. The K310, in fact, cost Chrysler only $10,000, and was crucial in the decision to allow Exner to dabble further in the show car area.

Exner, as his son recalled, "wasn't exactly the most welcome person who ever showed up at that time." Production styling was still under Henry King's men, who viewed Exner as a usurper. "But Dad set up a small studio and began working on his own, without a definite production goal but relatively free to come up with some good workouts. With these he hoped to point Chrysler in what he felt was the right direction," though it bears mentioning that Exner's ideas were often the complete opposites of those visualized by conservative Chrysler managers. "Dad called the Town and Country a 'lumber wagon,'" says Virgil, Jr. "He looked upon it as a car that 'hadn't been uncrated.' He liked the woodie wagons, but was very much a believer in the all-steel station wagon as the practical way to go.

Ghia's first Chrysler special, the Plymouth XX500. Surrounding the car, from left, are styling chief Henry King, Chrysler chief body engineer H.E. Chesebrough, chief engineer Robert Anderson, Plymouth Division president John Mansfield, and Dodge Division vice president R.C. Somerville.

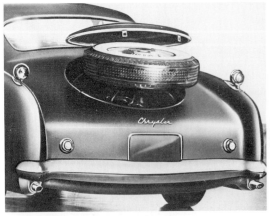  

The K310 takes shape in quarter-scale clay (right). Virgil Exner's first Chrysler show car, the K310, was for its time a marvel of understated elegance. Among K310's advanced features were freestanding taillights (predicting the 1955 Imperial), two-tone blue paint undivided by brightwork and pop-out spare hidden beneath tire outline on deck. The car expressed Exner's concepts of full wheel cut-outs, bold grille and chrome-free body, with sumptuous, all-leather interior.

The wood approach he appreciated but it never really fit into his plans. Of course he thought the 1949 body styles were just awful. Henry King was a pretty good designer, and really his talents were kind of wasted through that era."

Exner's advanced styling group was a three-man show; aside from himself there were Cliff Voss and Maury Baldwin. Voss joined soon after a stint at Kaiser-Frazer and is still with Chrysler today; Maury Baldwin has only recently retired. Says Baldwin, "Virg hired me in 1949, and Ex was hired by Keller, who had really wanted him to come aboard, though there was quite a little opposition from other parties at that time." Virgil, Jr., adds that we should not forget Paul Farrago, "who ran a sports car shop out on Seven Mile Road and was a very good 'seat of the pants' engineer. My dad got to know Paul and he built some racing cars and did some mechanical work for him. Paul became an interpreter for Chyrsler, for people like Luigi Segré, who was then Ghia's chief designer. From then on Paul was pretty well in on every experimental to be built."

According to Baldwin, there was no definite job assignment — Exner, Voss and himself all designed, rendered and made clay models, usually in three-eighths scale. When they were satisfied with a design they had it cast in plaster and sent to Italy. Baldwin recalls that Ghia's method of working with a body was nothing short of amazing: "They worked with practically an eyeball approach, and created it in the sheet metal from the three-eighths scale model. There was no full scale model at all. On the Ghia show cars the front fenders, cowl and body were welded integrally with the frame, and all body joints were filled and smoothed. Their interior work was also fantastic — they were simply beyond criticism, as far as we were concerned."

Exner liked to view the K310 as a successful blend of the best ideas from the British, German, French and Italian schools of design, with other facets that were completely American. The British-traditional school, he told the Society of Automotive Engineers in a 1951 speech, was "characterized by straight, severe lines. Their emphasis has always been on a slim appearance, and on the satisfying effect of sound, detailed craftsmanship." The German-functional school, on the other hand, stressed "classic simplicity — with a strong blend of very functional, mechanical feeling." Strikingly opposite was what Exner called the French-flamboyant school, represented by Figoni et Falaschi, with "heavy, sweeping curves, voluptuous with decoration."

But if the K310 emphasized the ideas of any one European country, that country was Italy. And it was no surprise that what he called the Italian-simplistic school of design was Exner's favorite. The postwar Italian designs, he said, "were thoroughly modern; with subtly rounded shapes and sharp accents indicative of genuine character. One might say that today, the Italian motorcar is a happy blend of early postwar smoothness and the classicism of the early horse drawn carriages. Simplicity has always

on production Chryslers: a one-third, two-third divided front seat; flush door handles; open wheel wells with wire wheels; an egg-crate grille, bomb-site taillights and a spare tire imprint on the deck lid to give the impression, if not the presence, of the 'continental' wheel. It emphasized design unity and a well-integrated upper and lower structure. Though it was a bit slab-sided, Exner applied a 'hitch' to the front fenders, which added character to the design.

Exner used steel for the K310 rather than aluminum, which was used on most experimental cars of that type. "Aluminum was so fragile we didn't think it would hold up," Exner said in an interview with Mike Lamm in 1972. "Now the K310 used a completely production chassis, but everything was completely new on [the body] and there were no production parts used on it whatsoever."

The K310's role was to visit dealerships around the country, attracting the public to the idea that square old Chrysler styling was not going to continue. It was highly successful, and in 1952 Exner had Ghia build a convertible version, the C200, which served the same function. The C200 was mounted on a 125½-inch wheelbase as well, but it was a few inches wider and an inch lower because of its soft top. Painted pale green and black and upholstered in black leather; it too was powered by the FirePower engine.

Next Exner ushered in a new total design of even more elegant proportions, the Chrysler Special, which evolved in due course to a modified, longer-wheelbase Special, the Ghia GS1, and the Chrysler d'Elegance. The Special was first named the SS. It was the first Exner show car to use a modified chassis, a New Yorker unit shortened to a 119-inch wheelbase. The modified Special was built for export vice president C.B. Thomas, who had originally coaxed the XX500 Plymouth out of Ghia. The Specials, and more obviously the d'Elegance, now presented a shape with which everyone is familiar — none other than the Volkswagen Karmann-Ghia!

It has always amused those in Detroit who knew — though they were few — that the Karmann-Ghia's oft-praised styling originated not in some Italian studio but in a back room at Chrysler, where Exner "spent more time in than I probably should have . . . I had this car, the d'Elegance, in the old Ghia shop to be done and, of course, had a very detailed clay model. At that time the shop was operated by Mr. Boano, and at the same time [Ghia was] working on prototypes for the Karmann-Ghia. They had done two or three and Karmann was not satisfied with them. This design of mine came in, and lo and behold when the Karmann-Ghia came out, it was scaled right down to the fraction!"

Though it was not advertised in the United States until 1961, the Karmann-Ghia went on to become a brilliant VW success, selling up to 42,000 a year from 1955 till its recent replacement by the VW Scirocco.

Cast in the image of the K310, the Chrysler C200 arrives at New York's docks, 1952.

been Italy's keynote. It is a theme that can only be expressed by truly fine craftsmanship."

While the K310 was totally unique, it nevertheless reflected Exner's styling considerations. It possessed the simplicity and rounded contours of an Italian design; yet its bold grille was a derivation of British-traditional styling; its rakish two-tone blue exterior harkened back to the French-flamboyant; and its stark side-elevation and greenhouse typified the German-functional. Introduced in 1951, on a 125½-inch Saratoga chassis with a 180-hp V-8 engine, it featured many ideas that would later be seen

Aside from its nose, which was modified owing to the VW rear engine, the Ghia was as close a copy of the d'Elegance as anyone could possibly make. Ghia built only twenty-five of the latter, however, and they had already passed into history when Karmann-Ghia sales began to soar. Exner's memory has often been smudged by those who blame him for the tail-fin craze which developed in the late fifties, the worst excesses of which were partly forced on him. But few realize that he created in the d'Elegance, and indirectly in the Karmann-Ghia, one of the most timeless and longest-lived automotive designs in history, judged by many experts to be one of the finest industrial designs of our time.

The d'Elegance appeared on a very short 115-inch wheelbase in early 1953, simultaneously with Ghia's desire to begin making more than one or two of these good-looking gran turismos. Thus Ghia built 400 copies of the next project machine, the 125½-inch-wheelbase GS1 — a larger-grilled modification of the long-wheelbase Special of 1953 — introduced at the 1954 Paris Automobile Show. The body lines were similar to the Special, except for the new front end and a revision to the side molding. The GS1 was sold in Europe by Society France Motors of Paris, Chrysler's French distributor.

Unfortunately, Exner was even less successful at getting his ideas into production than Ghia was, though he occasionally tried — hard — particularly with the K310 and a lovely DeSoto called the Adventurer I. But, according to Maury Baldwin, "management at that point was still a bit stodgy [despite Tex Colbert]. A lot of people attributed it to the Airflow. They were afraid to make any new inroads."

The C200 duly 'arrived' in 1953 on a commemorative Yugoslav postage stamp (left). C200 dashboard.

Third among Ghia-Chryslers was the 1952 Special sport coupe.

James C. Zeder typified the attitude of which Baldwin speaks. Though Zeder admired Exner's cars, and drove the K310 himself for a few years, he did not take kindly to the idea of a production sports car. In the December 1951 issue of *Motor Trend*, Zeder commented: "We want lighter cars. We want to cut weight as much as we can for better acceleration with greater economy and efficiency. We know that there are diminishing returns in seeking more car performance only through increasing power. . . . Right now Chrysler uses more aluminum and magnesium castings than any other company. But using sheet aluminum in welded body construction is another story, and we haven't licked the cost and fabrication problems."

Thomas Special, a longer wheelbase coupe built for Chrysler Export Division president C.B. Thomas in 1953.

The GS1 saw highest production among Chrysler specials, with 400 sold worldwide.

A 1953 Ghia Special owned by Bob Frumkin of California. Many Chrysler show cars still exist, though the K310 disappeared years ago and has not recently come to light.

Regarding fiberglass, Zeder said it had "basic shortcomings that rule it out of consideration for volume production.... The only plastic materials of which we have knowledge today must be molded and then cured. The curing takes a lot of time. So there would have to be acres of forms to give us enough parts for a day's production."

Zeder assured the public that small, two-seater or economy cars still interested Chrysler, and that the company could build one "in a relatively short time. But to build such a car for sale must mean, first, an assured market of large volume. There is as yet no evidence that such a market exists in this country.... Every sign points to the facts that Americans prefer to buy their cheaper cars in the form of good *used* cars of higher quality, rather than very small *new* cars of reduced comfort, performance, and pride of ownership." That statement would be a joke today, of course, but it was a view largely held by industry planners of the fifties. The failure of the Henry J in 1953, the Hudson Jet in 1954, and the Aero-Willys in 1955 were evidence to managers that the public simply didn't want a small or cheap car. And as Zeder put it, "We can't afford to volume produce cars for hobbyists."

Zeder did point out the advantage of the Chrysler show cars as opposed to the wilder mock-ups of GM and Ford. The Chrysler models *worked.* "We like to see just how these ideas work out in an actual,

operating automobile. Some companies build dream cars which quite obviously couldn't be produced on an assembly line. At Chrysler, our rule is to go all out in building experimental cars, just as long as we don't design a car that we couldn't build in volume." This was the reason Chrysler show cars were less awe-inspiring than those of GM, for example. And the reasoning was valid.

Tracing the early Ghia show cars from 1951 through early 1954, Virgil Exner, Jr., notes that not all should be credited directly to his father. "The ones my father really did personally were the K310, and of course the convertible version C200, the SS or Chrysler Special, and the Adventurer for DeSoto. Ghia was entirely responsible for the GS1, it was strictly their idea and designed to sell as a limited production car, not to be used in shows. Ghia, in the form of Boano, also produced the d'Elegance, though the original clay came from Detroit."

Exner found little he could influence on the 1953 production cars, though they had finally evolved into a more shapely form than that of the 1949-52 cars. But any form was easy on the eye after the upright-oblongs that people had known for the previous several years. There was more glass; windshields were curved, one-piece units; all sense of 'formality' at the rear greenhouse was eliminated by a wrap-around rear window. The hood was drawn further down, and the two-bar grille was spaced closer together. While the Imperial's special grille was a 1951-52 carryover, its near-vertical eagle hood ornament was a unique touch. The dashboard that had first appeared in 1949 was retained, as were the 'chair-high' seats and 'cubic miles' of interior space that were now *de rigueur* at Chrysler.

James Zeder had been quite honest about the desire to reduce bulk: The New Yorker line for 1953 was now reduced to the same 125½-inch wheelbase as the Windsor. The Imperial, renamed the Custom Imperial, grew in wheelbase, however — up to 133½ inches. A new model called

1953 Windsor Deluxe four-door sedan.   Ghia's d'Elegance (upper) directly inspired the VW Karmann Ghia (lower).

the Town limousine, with a division window inside a 133½-inch wheelbase sedan, was added to the line.

The Saratoga name was now eliminated, and that series became the New Yorker, with the former New Yorker series now designated as the New Yorker Deluxe. To the competition-minded this was probably a disappointment, for the Saratoga had made quite a reputation for itself; but the New Yorker name certainly seemed to have more sales appeal, and sales was what Chrysler was in business for. Saratogas had always been low-volume cars; as one dealer said, "neither fish nor fowl, not part of the cheaper Windsor, yet not quite a New Yorker either." The name change helped: five thousand more New Yorkers, née Saratogas, would be sold in 1953 than in 1952.

1953 Crown Imperial and interior detail.   1953 Windsor Town & Country wagon.

In the Windsor Deluxe series, a convertible replaced the club coupe model. The ex-Saratoga New Yorker gained a hardtop, and the New Yorker Deluxe a club coupe.

Model

Body Style (passengers)	Price	W.B.(in)	Weight (lb)
Series C60-1 Windsor			
sedan, 4dr (6)	$2,492	125½	3,660
club coupe (6)	2,472	125½	3,600
Town and Country wagon (6)	3,289	125½	3,960
sedan, l.w.b. 4dr (8)	3,433	125½	4,170
Series C60-2 Windsor Dexlue			
sedan, 4dr (6)	$2,721	125½	3,775
Newport hardtop (6)	3,025	125½	3,775
convertible (6)	3,247	125½	4,005
Series C56-1 New Yorker			
sedan, 4dr (6)	$3,185	125½	4,005
club coupe (6)	3,156	125½	3,925
Newport hardtop (6)	3,522	125½	4,020
Town and Country wagon (6)	3,933	125½	4,265
sedan, l.w.b. 4dr (8)	4,369	139½	4,510
Series C56-2 New Yorker Deluxe			
sedan, 4dr (6)	$3,328	125½	4,025
club coupe (6)	3,299	125½	3,925
Newport hardtop (6)	3,688	125½	4,025
convertible (6)	3,980	125½	4,295
Series C58 Custom Imperial			
sedan, 4dr (8)	$4,260	133½	4,205
limousine (6)	4,797	133½	4,525
Newport hardtop (6)	4,560	131½	4,290
Series C59 Crown Imperial			
sedan, l.w.b. 4dr (8)	$6,922	145½	5,235
limousine (8)	7,044	145½	5,275

Motor Trend tested a New Yorker in late 1953 and found it pleasing. "The luxury car field is as hotly competitve as the lowest priced group. One of the reasons is the Chrysler New Yorker, whose motto might be 'Quality First'." The magazine noted an improvement in riding quality with

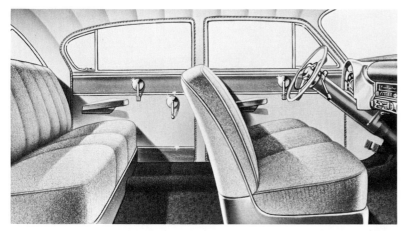

Interiors of the Windsor (upper) and Windsor Deluxe (lower).

1953 Windsor chassis.

no noticeable vibration, road shock or wind noise. As in the past, the New Yorker upholstery was relatively conservative, but of first quality. The car provided up to 105 mph top speed. The 180-horsepower engine had by now been surpassed by Cadillac (210), Lincoln (205) and Buick (188), but the New Yorker remained warmly recommended.

Less pleasing had been Chrysler's 1952 and 1953 performances in the Mexican Road Race. What had started as a promising racing career ended in shambles in 1952, under the onslaught of Clay Smith's Lincolns, with potent new V-8 engines, 'export' suspensions and truckloads of spare tires. Lincoln swept the top four places in the stock-car class ahead of two Chryslers — a 1951 Saratoga driven by Regie McFee and a 1953 New Yorker driven by C.D. Evans. Other '53 models finished ninth and seventeenth. McFee was only thirty minutes behind the winning Lincoln over the 1,934 miles of rugged driving, but nobody remembers also-rans.

Things didn't improve in the 1953 race. The Lincolns again swept the stock class in 1-2-3 order, and Clay Smith became the only co-driver with double victories. The Chryslers flopped. Four cars were entered by E.C. Kiekhaefer, of Mercury marine-engine fame, and were driven by the formidable John Fitch, Regie McFee, Bob Korf and Frank Mundy. But Fitch and McFee were in the sports class, and did not reach the first stop at Oaxaca in the required minimum time, due to transmission trouble, while Korf lasted until Mexico City before the gearbox stopped him. Mundy, who was running fifth at Mexico City, finally was disqualified for exceeding the time limit on a later leg of the race. Chrysler had applied for permission to use its new PowerFlite transmission, which was already being fitted to late-1953 Imperials as standard, but the organizers wouldn't allow it and the drivers had to stick with Fluid-Matic. Other Chryslers did perform reliably, however: Tommy Drisdale was best with his fifth-place finish, though he was forty-eight minutes behind the fourth-place Lincoln — and seven Lincolns finished in the top ten positions against only two Chryslers.

PowerFlite would be common to all V-8 Chryslers by the autumn of 1953. Despite its failure to get into the Mexican race, no one could dispute its technological brilliance. It combined a torque converter with an automatic two-speed planetary gearbox which — unlike Hydra-Matic — did not

1953 New Yorker two-door sedan.

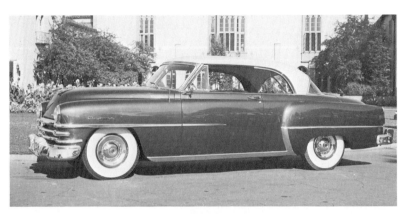

1953 New Yorker Newport.

1953 New Yorker convertible.

have a different gear for nearly every traffic situation and — unlike Ultramatic — offered plenty of get up and go.

As Chrysler put it, PowerFlite "adjusts automatically to any power requirement and to every driving situation. . . . Unlike some other transmissions, PowerFlite gives you, in effect, an infinite number of gear ratios . . . without any mechanical lag or 'jerkiness' in the shifting. Unlike most other automatic transmissions, PowerFlite will not be damaged when the car is started by pushing. And, with as much as 110 fewer parts than the most complicated of competitive transmissions, the Chrysler PowerFlite is built to maintain its superior performance for many, many more thousands of miles."

PowerFlite's planetary gears had a torque ratio of 1.72, while the torque converter ratio was 2.6:1, giving a torque multiplication of 4.47:1 when starting from a complete stop. This provided excellent acceleration, since the drive position started the car in low or first gear, then shifted smoothly to high at about 25 mph under normal conditions. It could be held in low, or kicked down via accelerator, all the way up to 65 mph. In normal use it would automatically downshift to low at 11 mph, or the driver could downshift manually, using the gear lever. But in most situations low was not required.

Aside from its smooth shifting and outstanding acceleration characteristics, PowerFlite evidenced good design in its external controls. The selector lever, for example, was 'gated,' with strong detents to tell the driver what gear he was in, and holding that gear until the lever was firmly pulled up for a shift. The driver didn't have to move through a forward range to get to reverse (as was the case with Hydra-Matic), and the smooth shifting allowed Chrysler to advertise "the right power for any road condition."

Fortunately, Chrysler's 1953 competition hopes didn't ride entirely on the outcome of what Tom McCahill called "that Mexican clambake." In Europe, a Chrysler New Yorker surprised a lot of people (while cheering Highland Park) when it ran off with the American car class at Belgium's Francorchamps race in the capable hands of Paul Frère. Later Frère won the touring car class in the rough-and-tumble Mille Miglia — a tremendous accomplishment for a car of the New Yorker's weight and bulk. This victory alone might have been enough to satisfy Chrysler that year, but it was totally eclipsed by the Le Mans performance of Briggs Swift Cunningham.

Since 1950, this wealthy sportsman and motor enthusiast had taken American racing blue in search of conquest on the road courses of Europe.

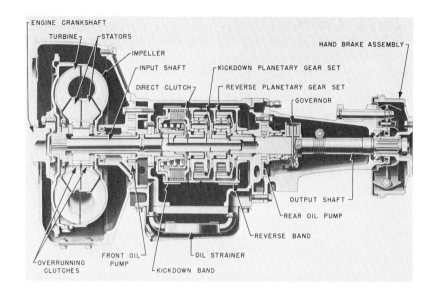

For the Le Mans twenty-four-hour race that year, he had entered two Cadillacs, one a stock Coupe de Ville and another with a special racing body, nicknamed *Le Monstre* by French enthusiasts. The latter finished a respectable tenth, followed closely by the Coupe de Ville, both powered by Cadillac V-8's putting out considerably more than the stock 160 horsepower.

Cunningham waxed ecstatic when he saw the Chrysler hemi, and determined to install it in his new C-2 racing car for the 1951 Le Mans race. The C-2 was mounted on a one hundred-inch wheelbase, with all coil-spring suspension and a de Dion rear axle, and it cost $100,000. But it

Chrysler's PowerFlite automatic transmission.

Chrysler-powered Cunningham C-2 photographed at Watkins Glen, 1951. Briggs Cunningham and the street-version Cunningham C-3.

disappointed Cunningham by finishing no higher than eighteenth, in the opinion of many because of its excessive weight — some 700 pounds more than its nearest competitor.

Cunningham's faith in the FirePower engine was unshaken, however, and for 1952 he built the C-4R racing car — 600 pounds lighter than the

Francorchamps, Belgium, was one bright spot for Chrysler in pre-1955 racing.

C-2, with a 300 horsepower hemi and five-speed gearbox. Seemingly, all the sources of '51 troubles were eliminated, and the C-4R looked formidable indeed. But lubrication troubles with the gearboxes forced a last-minute substitution of Cadillac three-speeds for the endurance race, and these put the C-4R's at a terrific disadvantage when braking for Le Mans' sharp turns at the end of its long straights. Three C-4R's were entered, a coupe and two roadsters. The coupe quit with valve trouble and one roadster dnf'd with similar problems after running solidly fifth overall for four hours. Cunningham himself drove another roadster, and finished fourth overall at an average speed of 87.15 mph.

Le Mans '52 thus provided the prelude for Cunningham's great feat in 1953. His mount this year was the C-5R, considerably modified from 1952 but with standard 7.5:1 compression in order to be happy with French petrol. Cunningham drove the C-5R to third place, averaging 104.14 mph, against 105.85 mph for the winning Jaguar C-type! His back-up car, a C-4R, finished tenth. And the following year two 330-horsepower C-4R's ran again, finishing third and fifth overall.

Nineteen fifty-three might have been even more exciting for Chrysler had not the Indianapolis 500 disallowed displacements of more than 275 cubic inches at the last minute. Chrysler engineers had built four hemis for the Memorial Day race, which developed over 400 brake horsepower with Hillborn fuel injection, from the standard 331-cubic inch displacement. In late 1952, a Kurtis racing car powered by one of these engines averaged over 135 mph in Indianapolis tests, running for 900 miles without even a change in spark plugs. When the Indy organizers suddenly reduced the displacement limit in early 1953, Chrysler cut displacement to 271 cubic inches and registered up to 375 horsepower on methanol fuel. But the small hemis could not match the performance of their predecessors in mid-range speeds. Thus Indy was not the almighty rout it might have been had Chrysler been allowed to compete with the standard 331-cubic inch block. Like the Mexican disappointment, Indy was an unhappy show.

Sales, however, rallied from the wartime depths of 1952 and for 1953 were almost back to '51 levels. A reorganized Sales Division was set up in late 1952, and for the first time Chrysler had its own merchandising, advertising and used-car merchandising managers. A special assembly line of two million square feet was set up for the Imperial at the Jefferson Avenue plant, and three or four Custom Imperials an hour were scheduled for construction.

But again in 1953 Ford out-produced Chrysler, and now seemed to be pulling away: Where Ford had led by only 50,000 cars in 1952, the gap was now 300,000. Chrysler had an answer for this: At the end of the year it announced that the "explosive reassertion of [our] production sales prowess seems imminent." The grounds for its assertion was the purchase of the Briggs Manufacturing Company.

Briggs had been in business since 1909; its main customers included Ford and Packard as well as Chrysler. The Chrysler business developed in 1930, when Briggs began to build Plymouth bodies, and continued to improve through the forties and early fifties. Briggs-built Chrysler Corporation bodies were always well-constructed and extremely durable, though it is interesting that this reputation did not last after Chrysler began building the bodies itself. When company founder Walter O. Briggs died in January 1952, inheritance taxes made it impossible for his family to remain in business, so they sold the company to their biggest customer — Chrysler — on December 29 for $35 million.

Chrysler acquired ten body plants in Detroit, one in Youngstown, Ohio, and another in Evansville, Indiana — a total of 6,544,584 square feet of floor space, and 30,000 new employees. The purchase made Chrysler the largest single employer in the Detroit area, with about 133,000 workers. The Chrysler takeover displaced one other customer— Packard — which had had its bodies built exclusively at Briggs since the advent of the Clipper in 1940. Since Chrysler naturally wanted all of Briggs' output, Packard was

1953 Custom Imperial Newport.   1953 Custom Imperial four-door sedan.

forced to find another body plant. It compounded its problem by buying a small Chrysler factory on Conner Avenue, Detroit, instead of reviving body manufacture at its East Grand Boulevard plant. Conner Avenue was too small, and was plagued by production and quality control problems that helped cause Packard's demise.

Several production changes made in the 1953 Chryslers may explain features on surviving models. These included the removal of the front seat's center armrest on the Windsor Deluxe and the New Yorker, discontinuation of two-tone paints on Windsor coupes and sedans in January, and the option of wire wheels in two sizes on January 23. Two-tone paint was discontinued on the Windsor Deluxe sedan in March, and two outside front bumper guards were made standard on all models in June. PowerFlite appeared on Custom Imperials on June 3. On September 1, special New Yorker club coupes and sedans offered the Bermuda Beauty option. They featured two-tone cream and green paint, or two shades of blue with cream. On March 10, 1953, a Custom Imperial Newport was added on a shorter 131½-inch wheelbase.

Chrysler Division began 1953 in vigorous fashion, with two shift assemblies running between January and June and a daily output of 800 to 900 units. But production slowed in March and April due to strikes in allied industries, and in July was cut back to 650 units "to adjust for market conditions," i.e., low sales. This slowdown was followed by an inventory shutdown in August and the suspension of the second shift. Pump-priming methods were tried, including a March price cut of $115 to $225; but at 1954 model announcement time, prices were up again about $130 on New Yorkers. Late in 1953 Dave Wallace retired as head of Chrysler, his place taken by E.C. Quinn, former vice president and general manager of the Division, who proclaimed higher output and cheerful optimism.

Quinn, as it turned out, couldn't have been more wrong. For 1954 Chrysler introduced a warmed-over line of cars that were not significantly different from what had carried the Division for the last five years. And a disastrous slide was in the making.

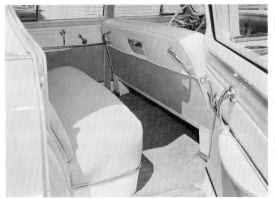

1954 Custom Imperial Newport.

1954 Windsor interior. Windsor Deluxe Newport.

By the end of 1953 the seller's market had abated. Chrysler was about to learn a painful lesson, predictable after K.T. Keller had railed at longer, lower, streamlined cars back in 1949 but now assured following the cutbacks in length and wheelbase in 1953. The public wanted big cars and, by God, Chryslers were supposed to be big. And getting bigger. If they weren't, well, there wasn't much reason for buying Chryslers.

"Sell more in '54" was the Chrysler sales slogan as the new model year opened in October, 1953. And on the surface, it seemed as if the Division couldn't miss. All models, save the Windsor (the Windsor Deluxe had been dropped) were now V-8 powered. There was 195 hp on the New Yorker and 235 on the New Yorker Deluxe and Imperials, putting Chrysler again in the lead in the horsepower race. PowerFlite automatic transmission had spread to all models except the Windsor as standard equipment, and was being fitted to ninety-eight percent of 1954 production by December, 1953. Full-time power steering, standard on the Crown Imperial, was also available for $140 on other Chryslers, and Airtemp air conditioning was more widely ordered than in 1953. The new Chryslers were retrimmed inside, and minor revisions created a sleeker exterior. The dashboard, which had survived intact since 1949, was altered to a more modern motif, but still featured heavily-padded safety cushions and a big console full of large,

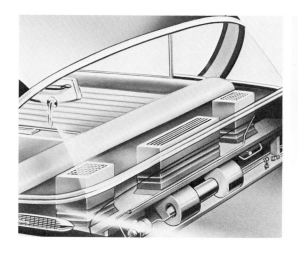
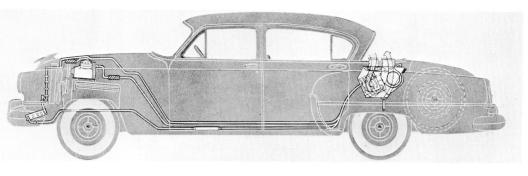

Schematics showing layout and delivery system of Airtemp air conditioning, 1954.

1954 Windsor Deluxe convertible.

1954 Custom Imperial four-door sedan.

legible instruments. Inflation, commonly represented as a two-headed dragon by Dwight Eisenhower's administration, had been appeased by no price increase in the Imperial and a $150 cut in the cost of the Windsor Deluxe.

Nineteen fifty-four marked the re-emergence of automotive air conditioning in the industry after a thirteen-year hiatus, following tentative experiments by Packard in 1940 and Cadillac in 1941. Walter Chrysler had seen to the invention of Airtemp air conditioning back in the thirties for the Chrysler Building, and had ostensibly offered it on cars in 1941-42, but none are known to have been sold in the latter form until 1954. Brilliant in comparison with the complicated, cumbersome rival car air conditioners of 1954, it was easily the most efficient. It recirculated, rather than merely cooled, the air inside the vehicle, and it was also the highest-capacity unit available on any automobile.

Like PowerFlite, Chrysler Airtemp was disarming in its operational simplicity. A single switch was placed on the dashboard, marked with low, medium and high positions, which the driver selected as desired. That was about all he had to do. The system was capable of cooling a Chrysler from 120° to 85°F in about two minutes, and of completely eliminating humidity, dust, pollen and tobacco smoke at the same time. Since it relied on fresh air — and drew in sixty percent more of it than any other system — Airtemp avoided the staleness associated with more primitive rigs. It was silent and unobtrusive. Instead of the gawky plastic tubes mounted on the package shelf, as on GM and other cars, small ducts directed cool air toward the ceiling of the car where it filtered down around the passengers instead of blowing directly at them— this, incidentally, is a feature that cars have since generally lost. Outside, instead of the clumsy pod scoops of the competition, Chrysler designed a modest flush-laid air intake grille. Finally, Airtemp Division made such notable progress in miniaturization that the

1954 New Yorker two-door sedan.

Crown Imperial limousine; note Airtemp scoops at rear quarters.

For 1954, Exner specials bore DeSoto, Dodge and Plymouth heraldry, while reflecting the inspiration of previous Chrysler specials. Here, the Plymouth Explorer, mainly a Ghia exercise.

Golden Falcon was a special New Yorker with custom paint and trim.

Chrysler air conditioner took hardly any trunk space away, and used an underhood compressor measuring only one cubic foot. The condenser panel was mounted diagonally in front of the radiator, where it received adequate fresh air without blocking the cooling system.

The '54 Chrysler line introduced in October, 1953, follows:

Model Body Style (passengers)	Price	W.B.(in)	Weight (lb)
Series C62 Windsor Deluxe			
sedan, 4dr (6)	$2,562	125½	3,655
club coupe (6)	2,541	125½	3,565
Newport hardtop (6)	2,831	125½	3,685
convertible (6)	3,046	125½	3,915
Town and Country wagon (6)	3,321	125½	3,955
sedan, l.w.b. 4dr (8)	3,492	139½	4,185
Series C63-1 New Yorker			
sedan, 4dr (6)	$3,229	125½	3,970
club coupe (6)	3,202	125½	3,910
Newport hardtop (6)	3,503	125½	4,005
Town and Country wagon (6)	4,024	125½	4,245
sedan, l.w.b. 4dr (8)	4,368	139½	4,450
Series C63-2 New Yorker Deluxe			
sedan, 4dr (6)	$3,433	125½	4,065
club coupe (6)	3,406	125½	4,005
Newport hardtop (6)	3,707	125½	4,095
convertible (6)	3,938	125½	4,265
Series C64 Custom Imperial			
sedan, 4dr (6)	$4,260	133½	4,355
Newport hardtop (6)	4,560	131½	4,345
Town limousine (6)	4,797	133½	4,465
Series C66 Crown Imperial			
sedan, l.w.b. 4dr (8)	$6,922	145½	5,220
limousine (8)	7,044	145½	5,295

La Comtesse, in pink and white, was the lady's version of the transparent-top 1954 show car.

Masculine counterpart was Le Comte, in bronze and black.

Top to bottom, the 1954 DeSoto Adventurer II, Dodge Firearrow sports coupe and convertible.

All the former Windsors and Windsor Deluxes had now been compacted into the Windsor Deluxe line — plus a convertible, which had been unavailable the previous year (though only 500 soft tops would be built). The New Yorker, New Yorker Deluxe, Custom and Crown Imperial models were the same types as offered in 1953, though one Custom Imperial convertible and two special Town limousines were built experimentally and for show purposes. Virgil Exner's influence was still not obvious in the new cars — the parking lights had shifted back under the headlamps again and the grille was a bit fussier with a curious artificial air-scoop mounted dead center. As before, the six-cylinder cars bore Chrysler script on the hoods, and a chrome *V* designated hemi-powered machines.

Nineteen fifty-four saw more limited-edition sales campaign cars, following the path of 1953's Bermuda Beauty. On March 17, Chrysler began the spring selling season with two specials named Golden Falcon and Bluebird. They came with custom gold and gray or blue exterior paint, special upholstery, chrome wire wheels and whitewall tires. Power steering and brakes, radio, heater, Solex tinted glass and PowerFlite were standard. Golden Falcon and Bluebird trims were available on the Windsor Deluxe

Old K.T. with Ken Murray and friends at a 1952 A.M.A. party. The women are dressed to represent new models. Left to right: Misses DeSoto Firedome, Aero-Willys, Dodge Ram, Chrysler Highlander, Packard Mayfair, Nash Ambassador Studebaker Commander, Hudson Hornet. Woman seated in the middle of the C200 is Miss Henry J. Vagabond. Ah, Miss Vagabond, wonder where you are today....

A major development in 1954 was construction of the Chelsea, Michigan Proving Grounds. A banked oval allowed sustained speeds of faster than 140 mph... while rough sections were provided for endurance testing.

and New Yorker sedan, club coupe and hardtop, and the New Yorker Deluxe sedan and hardtop. On March 24, some leftover 1953 upholstery from the New Yorker series, including Highlander plaid, was offered on the Windsor Deluxe club coupe and sedan. And on June 24, these same cars appeared with Summer Special trims: two-tone paint; whitewalls; New Yorker Deluxe upper door moldings; rear-seat center armrests on sedans; white plastic steering wheel; color-keyed dash, steering column and interior garnish moldings, painted to match the lighter of the exterior colors.

Virgil Exner's Ghia specials for 1954 were confined to the Plymouth Explorer and four varieties of the Dodge Firearrow; the last spawned the Dodge-based Dual Ghia. Another show Plymouth, the Belmont sports car, was a fiberglass non-Exner design study done by Briggs. No Chrysler-based Ghias were relased that year, and the only Chrysler show cars were La Comtesse and Le Comte — a pair of Imperial Newports with plexiglass roof panels, wire wheels, special interiors and rear-mounted spare tires. The Comtesse/Comte relationship was emphasized by doing the former in pink and white and the latter in black and bronze. These two cars toured the auto shows and major dealerships, much as the K310 and its descendants had in earlier years.

A much-heralded Corporate development for 1954 was the new proving grounds in Chelsea, Michigan — and there in hangs an amusing tale. Chelsea was to be Chrysler's first such facility. Its 4,000-acre site was chosen after an exhaustive aerial survey of the countryside around Detroit, followed by a CIA-type investigation to determine how many separate lots of land would have to be purchased to make it up. The total turned out to be fifty-two. A New York law firm bought up the land piece by piece, through another lawyer in Ann Arbor who did not even know whom the New Yorkers were working for! Purchases began in 1947 and were completed in 1952. The secrecy was not so much directed at competitors as at keeping the prices down until Chrysler had most of the real estate under its belt — but the scheme backfired.

Today the 'consumer advocates' would probably raise a terrific flap about the whole maneuver, forgetting as usual that the people being 'exploited' were pretty shrewd themselves. It didn't take Chelsea's canny locals long to learn that someone very big was after a large chunk of property — so they all began to raise their selling prices! Toward the end, Chelsea real estate had risen to levels comparable to the Chicago Loop. "Most womenfolk feared that the government was setting up an A-bomb factory," wrote Don MacDonald in *Motor Trend*, "but the men wistfully held to the theory that a nudist camp was planned."

Chelsea was dedicated in mid-1954, and the residents were generally happy with it and the several hundred new jobs it created. In early 1954 two million cubic yards of earth were moved and construction began on the 4.71-mile banked oval track. The dedication was attended by a bevy of Indy cars, and Jack McGrath broke the track in with a few laps at close to 180 mph.

The Chelsea proving-ground course was normally adequate for up to 140 mph in stock Chryslers if, as MacDonald quipped, they were capable of such speeds. He didn't know it then, but they soon would be.

CHAPTER 6

100 Million Dollar Look

THOUGH CHRYSLER WAS prepared as never before to sell cars in 1954, it failed miserably, on both the Corporate and Divisional levels. K.T. Keller's strategy of building boxy, practical cars had run up against a public that wanted precisely the opposite. And Chrysler had no effective reply. But Keller's derision of streamlining was not the only reason Chryslers looked the way they did. The shape of the 1949-54 Chrysler was planned long before Keller made public his philosophy of design — it was rooted in Chrysler product planning after the end of World War II.

After the war, *Fortune* relates, Chrysler management had "noted that there were nearly seven million more passenger cars on the road than in 1941, and predicted that congestion inevitably would grow worse before it got better. The public, Chrysler engineers reasoned, would want cars not only comfortable but highly maneuverable. Road visibility was given a high priority. Someone had coined the slogan, 'bigger on the inside, smaller on the outside.' This was what the engineers and designers set out to achieve in Chrysler's 1949 models. Basically this was an engineer's, not a stylist's approach to design. The '53 models were, of course, a great improvement over the '49's, but the Corporation's engineering department designed them with the same basic concept in mind.

"There was only one fallacy in this approach, but it could not be discerned so long as a car-hungry public was buying anything on four wheels. The fallacy lay in the fact that Americans, when they have a choice, like and buy a big package, and adapt as well as they can to what they find inside. In 1953 . . . the public for the first time could choose, and Chrysler soon found out from its dealers that the customers . . . were reluctant even to investigate the inside of cars that didn't look as long as buses".

The psychological stand-off between Chrysler and the public was manifested where it counted most — in the sales charts. Ford, which had traditionally ranked third in total passenger car production, surpassed Chrysler by a hair in 1952; and by 1953, the second-best year in the history of the industry, Ford was well ahead. Of the more than six million cars sold that year, Ford produced over twenty-five percent, against only about twenty percent for Chrysler. And though Chrysler had promised to reverse this trend with the 1954 models, its early sales to dealers in late 1953 were disappointing.

Of course Chrysler had introduced its 1954 models earlier than Ford and GM, so demand naturally slackened sooner. The problem was that it more than slackened — it started to plummet! Chrysler dealers simply weren't buying. They were all well-stocked with new models and refused to go into the hole for more.

The softening of the market for Chrysler Corporation cars was most evident in the Dodge and Plymouth market, but the big Chrysler dealers felt it too. A rumor early in 1953 held that Chrysler dealers were discounting — two months after introduction of the new models. And the rumor persisted

into 1954 because it was true. The situation worsened when Henry Ford II declared that, having caught and passed Chrysler, he was now going after GM, and began shipping huge quantities of cars to his dealers whether they had ordered them or not.

What the industry later called the 'Ford blitz' began in July of 1953. Ford built 679,500 passenger cars from July through December, against half a million in the first half of the year; Mercury increased output from 125,000 to almost 200,000 during the same period. GM naturally reacted with vigor, holding its own production schedules to the first-half pace instead of backing off, as was traditional before the model change. This produced a glut of GM and Ford cars on dealer lots. Since the customer was now in the saddle, price wars ensued, with disastrous effects on the new car market for the independents and Chrysler. Some Chrysler dealers resorted to 'bootlegging' — selling cars to out-of-state used-car lots at well under list prices.

It is interesting to view Chrysler's crisis of the fifties in the light of recent charges by an assortment of demagogues claiming to represent the benighted consumer. Detroit, they say, has always dictated to the public — the public never has a say in what kinds of cars it wants, and thus has to spend more than it wants or needs to for meaningless styling changes, excess bulk and weight. One wonders how the same people would explain Chrysler's problem of 1953-54. In direct opposition to the concepts of GM

Directly inspiring the 1955 Chrysler line were Exner's Parade Phaetons of 1952 (upper) and 1955 (lower).

Design sketches of '55 Imperial details.

1956 Imperial Parade Phaeton.

and Ford, Chrysler shunned the lower-longer-wider approach to build beautifully-engineered, good-handling, relatively compact machines with minimal styling changes — none of any substance between 1951 and 1952. Chrysler had concentrated on building value into the cars. Besides quality interiors, rugged chassis and efficient powerplants, rust on a 1949-52 Chrysler body was almost a physical impossibility. And as soon as the seller's market expired, the public shunned Chrysler products in droves.

K.T. Keller greeted this repudiation of his all-too-prominently-touted philosophy with characteristically blunt honesty. "I have seen," he remarked, "the error of my ways. Christ, we can't afford another mistake." (Detroit Free Press). Tex Colbert agreed — and determined to do something about it, bloody quick.

Colbert recognized early that some decentralization of the Corporation — delegating more responsibility to Division managers — was necessary to spark creativity and sales. But decentralization was anathema at Chrysler, a forbidden word smacking of General Motors. So Colbert called it 'divisionalization,' instead — and won the blessing of the old guard. One of his first steps on assuming the presidency — before the sales problems had even developed — had been to divisionalize. The heads of Plymouth, Dodge, DeSoto and Chrysler were told to take the talent they needed from the central office and tackle their respective problems. They did. Division purchasing agents studied and challenged their budgets; Division engineering staffs studied ways in which they might one-up the opposition and even rival Chrysler Divisions. There was even talk about Divisional, rather than Corporate, production and engineering staff. Each Division's task was clear: Produce not only product but profit.

Colbert had been largely responsible for the acquisition of Briggs, Chrysler's longtime body supplier. While this was seemingly a step back from decentralization, it had the advantage of immediate savings and the integration of much of the company's production processes. For the short term it made sense — the cars were not, after all, totally different from each other. Then in early 1954, Colbert engineered a $250 million, one-hundred-year loan from Prudential Insurance to provide more integration of production processes, and to buy new plants and more automatic machinery. Many people scoffed, saying that Prudential was now Chrysler's de facto owner, that we'd soon see a Rock of Gibraltar model. But Colbert let them laugh, took his 'piece of the Rock' and put it to work.

Finally, Colbert determined that Chrysler would have to shake off its old image as a very conservative company building very conservative cars for very conservative people. On a tour of his dealers in 1953, the most common complaint Colbert heard was that rivals were calling Chryslers "conservatively styled." This, the dealers said, was worse than calling them just plain lousy. Colbert initiated the late-1953 price cuts, held the 1954 models to the same price or less, and together with K.T. Keller called in Virgil Exner for his first full-production assignment. The result appeared in November, 1954. Chrysler called it the "Hundred Million Dollar Look," which was probably a fair approximation of the cost of Colbert's managerial overhaul.

Exner had been named director of Chrysler Styling by Colbert and Keller late in 1952, but his influence on the 1953-54 cars was limited because of corporate lead times. "Dad had gotten involved a little bit in 1954 ornamentation," said Virgil Exner, Jr., "though the basic sheet metal was already set. I can remember him doing some of the details — the 1954 taillight and some of the side ornamentation and a bit of the grille, back in 1952. But the Hundred Million Dollar Look for 1955 was all new, and was inspired by one of Dad's specials — the Imperial Parade Phaeton."

The Parade Phaeton, on a 1952 Crown Imperial chassis stretched slightly to a 147½-inch wheelbase, was another example of unique Exner styling which even Virgil didn't anticipate seeing in production. Three cars were built, by Chrysler rather than Ghia. According to Virgil, Jr., they "came from strictly full-size clay models in Dad's studio, from scratch." The cars were assigned to New York, Detroit and Los Angeles, and were used to carry distinguished guests in parades, hence their name. Bearing 1952 Imperial front ends, they were distinguished by color scheme: The New York car was black with a light-gray interior; the Detroit model was metallic green with natural pigskin upholstery; the Los Angeles Imperial was cream with a rose-red interior. Later the cars were reworked to 1955-56 Imperial configurations, repainted and reupholstered. The New York and Detroit cars became off-white with red leather interiors, while the L.A. car was done in metallic silver-blue with white upholstery. One of the off-white models survives in the collection of Paul Stern of Manheim, Pennsylvania.

Virgil, Jr., continues: "There came the day when K.T. Keller asked Dad's opinion on what the 1955 stuff was going to look like. Dad told him, 'lousy.' K.T. kind of liked that — he was quite a strong character. 'Okay,' he said, 'you put it together and you've got eighteen months.' They quickly swiped ideas off the parade cars and managed to put the 1955 line together in time. [It should be noted that by 'line,' Exner refers mainly to the Imperial, Chrysler and DeSoto. The 1955 Dodge and Plymouth, while also all-new, were not take-offs on the Parade Phaeton. Maury Baldwin designed the Dodge, and the Plymouth was done at a different studio.] The Parade Phaetons can easily be seen to predict the 1955 production cars. They had the same side treatment and the hopped-up rear fender as the 1955 Chrysler and Imperial. They were all identical in design — long, clean-lined and sleek."

The most obvious descendant of the Parade Phaetons was the new 1955 Imperial (one of the classic designs of the fifties) — uncluttered, an understated style if one discounts the gaudy bird ornament on the hood and deck, a throwback to the ornate heraldry of the K310. Like the K310 and C200, Exner's Imperial had a large, divided, egg-crate grille and free-standing 'gunsight' taillights. The 1955 Chrysler offered a smaller egg crate, similarly divided, placed atop massive grille bars — which was not as imposing nor as expensive to manufacture as the heavy Imperial die casting. These 'twin tower' taillights were huge vertical units in heavy chrome frames that were rather un-Exner-like but gave identity to the rear end.

Club coupes and eight-passenger sedan models were absent from the Chrysler line, the latter being wholly the province of Imperial. There was a declining market for long-wheelbase models, and even Imperial failed to sell 200 of them. Both Windsor and New Yorker received the designation 'DeLuxe,' though there were no non-DeLuxe models, and both used a 126-inch-wheelbase chassis. The Imperial was on a 130-inch wheelbase, down 3½ inches from 1954, and again did not offer a convertible model, though one was built for evaluation. The aforementioned long-wheelbase Crown Imperials now adopted a 149½-inch wheelbase — four inches longer than that of 1954.

Colbert's earlier prediction that the Chrysler six was as dead as a dodo was now borne out: the 1955 Windsor DeLuxe used a new, smaller V-8 of 300.5 cubic inches, with an over-square bore and stroke of 3.63 x 3.63 inches; developing 188 horsepower at 4400 rpm and 275 foot-pounds of torque at 2400 rpm. Retaining a link with the past, it was called the Spitfire V-8. It had many of the modern features of the 331.1-cubic-inch FirePower engine, which at 250 hp continued to power New Yorkers and Imperials. The Windsor power plant featured rotor-type oil pump, full-flow oil filter, hydraulic valve lifters, dual-throat carburetor with integral automatic float, and tin-plated aluminum-alloy pistons. But the Spitfire was a poly, rather than a hemi.

Poly refers to what Chrysler called a polyspherical combustion chamber, a feature of the Spitfire V-8 as well as the smaller V-8's for Plymouth (Hy-Fire) and Dodge (Red-Ram). It wasn't a particularly new idea; Sir Harry Ricardo, the pathfinding British engineer, had come up with the idea back in the teens. Unlike the hemi, the poly's intake and exhaust valves were placed diagonally across from each other rather than directly opposite. This allowed it to use a single rocker shaft in each bank of cylinders instead of two, as in the hemi, and made the spark plugs more accessible. The poly's heads weighed less than the hemi's, and with single

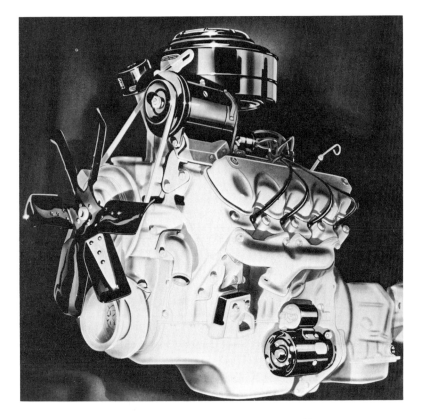

The 'poly head' Spitfire 188-hp V-8 for 1955.

1955 Windsor Deluxe Newport.

1955 Windsor Deluxe Blue Heron.

1955 Windsor Deluxe Green Falcon.

rockers the engine was much less expensive to manufacture. At the same time, much of the desirable breathing qualities of the hemi were retained, as was its ability to run on lower-octane fuels.

A fifteen-horsepower increase — to 250 — in the 1955 New Yorker/Imperial FirePower hemi was obtained through a one-ratio increase in compression and a redesigned four-barrel carburetor with vacuum-controlled secondary throttles. These came into operation when the primaries were more than half open. Dual exhausts were standard equipment, and all other engine measurements remained the same as 1954's.

PowerFlite automatic transmission remained optional on the Windsor DeLuxe, at the price of $189, but was standard on other Chryslers and all Imperials. A miniscule number of Windsor DeLuxes retained the three-speed column shift (a chrome plate covered the dashboard hole on such cars). The PowerFlite control lever's location surprised many. It was moved to a dashboard stalk at the right of the steering wheel, and caused charges

about irreverence to the safety god. Chrysler claimed the stalk was made of special malleable metal which would bend in an accident rather than harpoon an occupant. In any case the feature was short-lived, being replaced by something even more exotic the following year. The 1955 Windsor brochure also implies that a column-mounted PowerFlite control was available, though this is unconfirmed by observations in the field.

Including the 300, of which more shortly, the 1955 line of Chryslers and Imperials looked like this:

Model Body Style (passengers)	Price	W.B.(in)	Weight (lb)
Series C67 Windsor Deluxe			
sedan, 4dr (6)	$2,660	126	3,925
Nassau hardtop (6)	2,703	126	3,930
Newport hardtop (6)	2,818	126	3,925
convertible (6)	3,090	126	4,075
Town and Country Wagon (6)	3,332	126	4,295
Series C68 New Yorker Deluxe			
sedan, 4dr (6)	$3,494	126	4,160
Newport hardtop (6)	3,652	126	4,140
St. Regis hardtop (6)	3,690	126	4,125
convertible (6)	3,924	126	4,285
Town and Country wagon (6)	4,209	126	4,430
300 hardtop (6)	4,110	126	4,005
Series C69 Imperial			
sedan, 4dr (6)	$4,483	130	4,565
Newport hardtop (6)	4,720	130	4,490
Series C70 Crown Imperial			
sedan, l.w.b. 4dr (8)	$7,603	149½	5,145
limousine (8)	7,737	149½	5,205

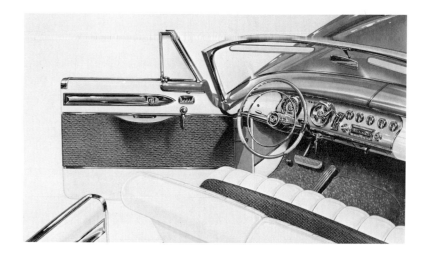

1955 New Yorker convertible.

New Yorker convertible interior.

There is no doubt that the 1955 Chryslers were beautiful cars, not only in the context of their time, but over the years. They still look clean and stately today, well-balanced without too much of the stylistic hokum of the fifties. If one forgives the garish Chrysler taillights and some of the inevitable two-tone color schemes, they were nicely-executed cars, especially in comparison with their peers; e.g., Oldsmobile, Buick and Mercury.

1955 New Yorker four-door sedan.

1955 New Yorker Town & Country.

Trim differences between the 1955 New Yorker Newport (upper) and St. Regis (lower) hardtops.

Dealers were pleased that the Windsor no longer looked like a New Yorker that had started smoking too young. Despite the fact that the two lines had moved from about $500 apart in 1954 to about $800 apart in 1955, the Windsor shared the wheelbase, body and much of the trim with the senior line. It *looked* like a Chrysler, and with its new Spitfire V-8 it performed like one too. The Windsor was now competitive in the sales race. Nearly 100,000 copies would be sold in 1955 — the most since 1950, and better than double the number sold in 1954. (Chrysler would sell about 163,000 of the 1955 models against 105,000 of the '54's; hence the Windsor's improvement was about double that of the other models.)

A number of different trims were applied to the Windsor models: from a very conservative nylon cloth and vinyl upholstery in the sedan and cheaper Nassau hardtop; to nylon and pleated vinyl in the Town and Country wagon; and to colorful V-motif leathercloth and nylon, with full carpeting, in the convertible and Newport hardtop. By offering two hardtops Chrysler acknowledged the growing popularity of that body style. Differing on the outside only by their rear roof quarter nameplates, the Newport's $115 premium was represented mainly by a fancier convertible style interior than was found in the Nassau.

Windsor Deluxe sedans and Nassau hardtops originally appeared with rubber mats in the front compartment, but buyers demanded carpets, and they were offered beginning February 23, 1955. Originally Windsors had only a thin chrome strip on their flanks, with two-toning restricted to different-colored tops. But in April, two special models were announced that featured more exotic decors — the Green Falcon and the Blue Heron.

These two special trim options for the Windsor Deluxe hardtop and sedan came in platinum/blue and platinum/green, with color-keyed upholstery and carpeting. They sold for an extra $65.80. Unfortunately, the non-platinum color was applied over the deck, along a part of the rear fenders, and through to the front fender in a tapering sweep.

Other semi-custom Windsors were built at various times during the model year, which accounts for the occasional strange one discovered by

Imperial Newport interior details.

There was no mistaking the 1955 Imperial, at either end....

From any angle, the Imperial Newport for 1955 was magnificent.

collectors. Many were fitted with fabrics left over from earlier model runs — as were some New Yorkers and Imperials — including the ever-popular Highlander plaid with red leather. On May 23, dealers were advised that specially-modified Windsor Deluxe sedans would be available for conversion to airport limousines, ambulances or funeral cars, though there are no records to indicate how many were built.

For the 1955 New Yorker, Chrysler flacks went all out: "This is not only the most beautiful of all Chryslers, but the first regular production car to achieve all the slimness, tautness, and feeling of motion that should be the natural marks of a fleet, land-borne vehicle." (Whew.) Like the Windsor, the New Yorker was called a Deluxe, though no standard model was offered. The line included a four-door sedan, Town and Country wagon and, like the Windsor, two hardtops — the Newport and the St. Regis. Unlike the Windsor coupes, however, the difference between these two was on the outside — the St. Regis roof, hood and upper third of the body sides were painted in a color that contrasted with the rest of its body; while

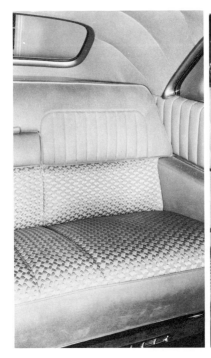
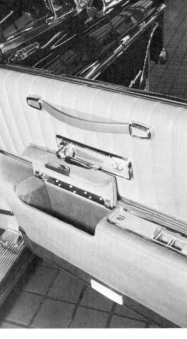

Interior details of the 1955 Crown Imperial.

1955 Crown Imperial.

The Summer Special combined both Newport and St. Regis trims.

the Newport came in one color, or with a contrasting roof and a slim sidesweep. The hardtop was the only New Yorker trimmed in the St. Regis pattern; other models used the Newport style. Few people bothered to specify one-color New Yorkers, though the cars that were painted that way naturally look better today — two decades after the era of Crayola-box paint schemes.

New Yorker interiors were tasteful and lavish, trimmed in leather and nylon on all models except the sedan, which used a less-luxurious cloth; and the Town and Country, which relied on plaid linen-and-vinyl combinations. Both the New Yorker and Windsor wagons offered as an option a completely removable third seat. Other options included air conditioning (except on wagon and soft top), Solex tinted glass, radio with or without signal-seeking ability, rear-seat speaker, two- or four-way electric seats, power steering, tubeless whitewalls, wire wheels (with tube tires), electric window lifts and a 'custom accessory group' including exhaust pipe deflectors, outside rearview mirror, custom steering wheel and windshield washer. Standard on the New Yorker, but optional on the Windsor, were power brakes (standard on Windsor wagons only), electric clock, rear-center folding armrest in sedans and a lighting group including back-up, trunk, glovebox, brake warning and rear-door dome lamps. Initially, wire wheels were optional on all 1955 Chryslers, and they looked especially nice on New Yorkers. But on February 1, dealers were advised that they would no longer be fitted to wagons or Imperials, possibly because of weight considerations.

Like the Windsor, a radically two-toned New Yorker appeared in June of 1955. Called the Summer Special, it featured a combination of Newport and St. Regis two-tone panels and cost $8.60 extra plus the regular two-tone charge. Summer Specials were confined to hardtops, and sedans. Less than 2,000 were sold. Among the four Chrysler hardtops, the plainer Windsor Nassau and the gaudier New Yorker St. Regis were the preferred models. The Nassau outsold the Newport in the Windsor line by eighteen to thir-

teen, while the New Yorker St. Regis topped the New Yorker Newport eleven to six.

All Chrysler cars for 1955 were said to possess "The Forward Look," Chrysler's name for styling which leapfrogged the opposition by being, at least in Chrysler's opinion, two or three years ahead. But the finest expression of The Forward Look was the magnificent 1955 Imperial. Unlike the Chrysler models, it was never dressed up in exotic two-tone paint schemes; the Division even preferred that Imperials be painted solid colors, without so much as a contrasting top. As many of the 1955 customers desired some semblance of 'fashion,' more than one Imperial was two-toned in the dealer's paint shop. The Imperial was swathed in leather and the finest fabrics, replete with deep pile carpets and numerous passenger amenities. Its aforementioned bold grillework was its most dominant feature, making the car easily recognizable. It seemed like the ultimate, but then on February 8, 1955, Chrysler announced a car with an Imperial grille that behaved like no Imperial, past or present — the legendary Chrysler 300.

It must, by now, be understood by nearly everyone that the Chrysler 300 — or C300, officially — was one of the great performance automobiles of all time. Perhaps Tom McCahill of *Mechanix Illustrated,* was best-qualified to sum it up in his own inimitable style. "Here is the most powerful sedan in the world, and the fastest, teamed up with rock-crushing suspension and a competition engine capable of yanking Bob Fulton's steamboat *over* the George Washington Bridge. . . . This is definitely not the car for Henrietta Blushbottom, your maiden schoolmarm aunt, to use for hustling up popsicles. In fact, the 300 is not a car for the typical puddling male to use. This is a hardboiled, magnificent piece of semi-competition transportation, built for the real automotive connoisseur." It was that. And naturally enough, a connoisseur was behind its conception.

A special Derham-modified Crown Imperial limousine, shown with the characteristic Derham blanked-out rear quarters.

Bob Rodger, 'father of the 300,' poses with his 1963 300J ram-tuned V-8.

His name was Robert MacGregor Rodger, chief engineer of the Chrysler Division.

Bob Rodger was born in northern New York in 1917, to dairy farmer parents who helped point him towards a technical career. He graduated from Clarkson with a degree in mechanical engineering in 1939, and

Design sketches of the 300 show Styling's ideas for modest revision to the stock front end. Sketch at left was made close to production, while sketch at right shows 1956-type grille and radically non-stock sculpting at rear quarters.

journeyed to Detroit to enroll in Chrysler's prestigious Institute of Engineering, from which he emerged with a masters degree in automotive engineering in 1941. Rodger had been on the engineering team that developed the hemi, and with Tex Colbert's 'divisionalization' was sent to head Chrysler Division Engineering in 1952. Later Bob would become chief engineer of Product Planning (1960) and special car manager for competition (1964). He died, before his time, in 1971 from leukemia. Says Chrysler 300 historian Ray Doern, "Bob had a host of friends in all walks of life. He was not flamboyant and seemed almost out of place among the racing crowd. His desires in life were rather simple and he never made unreasonable demands of his associates. Nevertheless, he inspired those under him to great accomplishments and had their unquestioned loyalty."

The hemi engine naturally prompted Chrysler to join myriad backyard hot rodders in thinking about the horses that it might produce with a little educated tweaking. As we have seen, more than 300 versions of the engine were built soon after its introduction, including Chrysler's own 310-horsepower unit which was rumored to be — but was not, in fact — under the bonnet of the K310. Following introduction of the hemi, Exner's designs were the second step toward the 300. Their clean, flowing, aggressively handsome lines appealed to the same kind of man who enjoyed the potent hemi engine shielded by its smooth hood. Virgil Exner, a sports car enthusiast himself, often dreamed of a production Chrysler sports car, though James Zeder and others preferred to ignore this low-volume market. But the idea of a flaming-hot hemi installed in a stock Chrysler was not beyond the realm of possibility.

Early competition experience with the hemi heightened the interest of Chrysler men in a spirited stocker, one capable not only of out-dragging Olds 88's at stop lights, but also of destroying them (along with Hudson Hornets) on NASCAR ovals — with attendant publicity for Chrysler. Briggs Cunningham had added proof of the big engine's capabilities with the tuned hemis in his C-2, C-4R and C-5R racing cars for Le Mans, and the FirePower had performed creditably in the Mexican Road Race and at Indianapolis.

Bob Rodger personally attended many of Chrysler's competition efforts, and was encouraged to develop a super-stock model by stylist Exner, who yearned for a hot Chrysler. Early in August of 1954, Rodger finally broached the subject to Division general manager Ed Quinn. Quinn's reaction was favorable, but he and Exner insisted that the car's styling not deviate very much from the 1955 models already in production — for purposes of both identity and economy. Chrysler was in debt to Prudential, whose loan largely went into the 1955 revival program on which many felt the survival of the Corporation depended.

Exner, Cliff Voss and Tom Poirier of Styling went to work on the car, relying on production Chrysler and Imperial components. Any significant die changes had been ruled out. In November, the result of their efforts — a combination of Chrysler and Imperial components — was recommended to Ed Quinn: New Yorker hardtop body; Windsor rear quarter panels; and Imperial grille, parking lights, front bumper and wire wheels. Quinn gave a tentative okay.

Tacking the Imperial grille onto the New Yorker front end was not as easy as it may have looked. But a mock-up of the 300 was run through the Imperial assembly line in October, only ten weeks after Rodger had received Quinn's go-ahead. Voss and Poirier, with Rodger, then tried a number of identifying emblems on the bare body, finally deciding on the one they liked best and the proper place to locate it. Their choice was a checkered flag on an inverted trapezoidal emblem subtly placed on the deck and hood. The car bore no hood mascot, and its flanks were clean except for a Windsor chrome strip and a small '300' near the tail.

Bob Rodger personally supervised construction of the 300's engine. A standard 331 hemi block was used, but the cam grind was reportedly the same as in the 1954 Le Mans Cunninghams; solid valve lifters and a second four-barrel carburetor were fitted. The engine developed exactly 300 horsepower. A tight suspension was created to hold all this brute force down. When McCahill drove the 300, he compared the suspension to "a New Hampshire winter [but] on the beach I made a number of hard cuts and full, fast, 360-degree turns and found that there just wasn't the slightest bit of 'plow' in this rig. It was as solid as Grant's Tomb and 130 times as fast."

The 300's engine provided breathtaking performance. McCahill's times at Daytona, for example, were 0-60 mph in 9.8-10 seconds, 0-90 mph in

16.9 seconds and an honest 130 mph top speed. "I also realize," said the impressed *MI* road-tester, "that the guy who buys this for his one-and-only family hack has rocks in his head. It's too masculine for a pet."

The 300 was listed as part of the New Yorker series in November, and was slated for introduction in February. But before the year was out, Exner had made some revisions, rendering the production car still cleaner than it had started out. Considering the Imperial bumpers too bulky for the lean fire-breather, Exner specified Chrysler bumpers and parking lights, with Imperial-type bumper guards set far apart. The Imperial dashboard, which had no tachometer, was used instead of the Chrysler version. (The absence of a tachometer was not too serious, since the 300 came only with PowerFlite transmission in 1955.)

The guy who did buy one of the 1,692 300's of 1955 (an additional thirty-three, including one bare chassis, were built for export) had relatively

Assembly of the 300. Engine bolted to chassis; body is dropped; and the big hemi fits snugly under the hood.

The production 1955 300 displaying quarter, interior and rear views.

limited options to choose from. McCahill's model listed for $4,055.25 (NADA quoted $4,110 f.o.b. Detroit) and was equipped with a radio, heater and power steering, for a total of $295.50 extra. The steering, Uncle Tom said, was useful, but trying to park a 300 was still "like playing ping-pong with an anvil." According to Chrysler brochures, rear-axle ratios of 3.54, 3.73, 3.91 and 4.10 were available — as were power seats, brakes and windows; clock; Solex tinted glass and wire wheels; in addition to the options noted previously. Chrysler did not even offer air conditioning,

The 300 immediately went to work, running Daytona at faster than 127 mph.

As in 1955, the 1956 New Yorker came with a fancier St. Regis trim option.

The New Yorker four-door hardtop gained Newport script at midyear.

back-up lights or outside rearview mirrors on the 300, though the last two items were probably installed on most of the cars by dealers.

The first 300 off the line was painted platinum-white, followed by ten tango-red cars. All 300's were done in these two colors or black, and all had tan leather upholstery. The 1955 brochure indicates that New Yorker hub caps were fitted, but actual photos reveal Imperial-type wheel covers with special checkered center ornaments. Wire wheels were optional.

McCahill questioned the 300's ability to win events like the Mexican Road Race, despite its power, because of its two-ton curb weight. But Mexico was never run after 1954; the 300's venue was NASCAR tracks and the sands of Daytona, where it was nearly unbeatable. The 1955 Hudson was a face-lifted Nash, so that marque was out of the NASCAR running, but even the Hornet of 1954 was no match for the Chrysler 300. The 300 won the NASCAR Grand National at 92.05 mph, sped through the Daytona flying mile at over 127 mph, took the standing-start mile record for its class at 76.84 mph and won thrity-seven NASCAR and AAA races of more than one hundred miles in 1955. Chrysler's name as a synonym for performance was now established, to the benefit of the overall sales picture. From just over 100,000 units in calendar 1954, the Division romped back with 176,039 for calendar 1955, 15,000 more units than all of American Motors production combined.

In 1955, Chrysler Corporation, as a whole, had the highest dollar volume and unit sales in its entire history. Its cars represented 17.1 percent of American retail sales, compared with only 13.2 percent in 1954, and at Chrysler Division the market percentage was up from 1.8 percent in 1954 to 2.2 percent. New car sales peaked in February with 17,076 units, and again in April, with 16,793. Chrysler introduced the first transistorized car radio in regular production in April, and during the year added a new assembly plant, increasing its production capacity to 1,200 cars per working day. By every measure of success — racing, sales and reputation — 1955 was a vintage year. Dealer doubts were washed away and confidence returned as the '56 models were introduced during a series of twenty-seven dealer meetings beginning on September 16, 1955, built around the theme of 'conquest.'

But 1956 was an anticlimax, for the industry as well as Chrysler. Almost two million fewer cars were sold, and production was down in all Chrysler Divisions — the Corporation as a whole was down .8 percent in market penetration too, to 16.3 percent. With Imperial counted as a separate make, Chrysler production totaled only 95,356, and was surpassed by DeSoto — for the first and last time — which had not suffered as great a cutback. Cadillac and AMC also squeezed past Chrysler Division in the production race, knocking the marque back to twelfth place, where it hadn't been since 1949. It didn't seem quite so bad with the whole industry in decline, but 1956 production was hardly better than 1954.

With the exception of slogans, the 1956 line hadn't changed much. 'The Hundred Million Dollar Look' was now replaced by 'Powerstyle,' and the one new body design was a four-door hardtop:

Model Body Style (passengers)	Price	W.B.(in)	Weight (lb)
Series C71 Windsor			
sedan, 4dr (6)	$2,870	126	3,900
Newport 4dr hardtop (6)	3,128	126	3,990
Nassau 2dr hardtop (6)	3,005	126	3,910
Newport 2dr hardtop (6)	3,041	126	3,920
convertible (6)	3,336	126	4,100
Town and Country wagon (6)	3,598	126	4,290
Series C72 New Yorker			
sedan, 4dr (6)	$3,779	126	4,110
Newport 4dr hardtop (6)	4,102	126	4,220
Newport 2dr hardtop (6)	3,951	126	4,175
St. Regis 2dr hardtop (6)	3,995	126	4,175
convertible (6)	4,243	126	4,360
Town and Country wagon (6)	4,523	126	4,460
300B 2dr hardtop (6)	4,419	126	4,145
Series C73 Imperial			
sedan, 4dr (6)	$4,832	133	4,575
Southampton 4dr hdtp (6)	5,225	133	4,680
Southampton 2dr hdtp (6)	5,094	133	4,555
Series C70 Crown Imperial			
sedan, l.w.b. 4dr (8)	$7,603	149½	5,145
limousine (8)	7,737	149½	5,205

Chrysler wheelbases remained the same in 1956, though the cars grew longer by virtue of stretched quarter panels and larger bumpers with extensions. Restyling was confined to a new, more unified frontal aspect and the first refined Exner tailfins. Coupes and convertibles used quarter panels three inches longer than those on sedans. Imperial wheelbases were increased, however, from 130 to 133 inches.

On the New Yorker and Imperial, the hemi engine was bored out slightly to 3.94 inches; it now displaced 354 cubic inches and developed

1956 Crown Imperial limousine.

280 horsepower at 4600 rpm. The compression ratio accounted for the increase, going from 8.5:1 to 9:1. Also new were a twelve-volt electrical system, redesigned intake manifold that allowed improved combustion, and a higher-winding PowerFlite for better acceleration. The poly-head Windsor was also bored out, to 3.81 inches from 3.63, and now displaced 331 cubic inches, like the 1951-55 FirePower. Brakes were improved: Called Center Plane, they used a molded-lining construction with floating-shoe action for a self-centering effect and uniform shoe-to-drum contact. Following the industry trend, the newest body style was a four-door hardtop offered in the Windsor, New Yorker and Imperial lines. But there were no other model changes, and both Windsor and New Yorker lost the unnecessary 'Deluxe' appellation, being available in only one trim style — except for the Windsor Nassau/Newport and New Yorker Newport/St. Regis two-door hardtops. Chrysler Corporation four-door hardtops for 1956 were a year behind those of GM. Plymouth's and Dodge's, in particular, seemed to reflect hasty preparation. In design they appeared less integrated and somewhat more ungainly than their GM rivals. But the Chrysler and Imperial were so well-designed in the first place that the four-door hardtop looked perfectly correct.

Not widely known is the fact that management had considered dropping the Windsor entirely, leaving room in its field for the lower-priced DeSoto. But Chrysler dealers rebelled, and so did Chrysler Division's newly independent leaders. Divisionalization had bred the competitive urge Colbert had hoped for, though at the dealer level it was probably always there. The Windsor had, after all, accounted for nearly two-thirds of

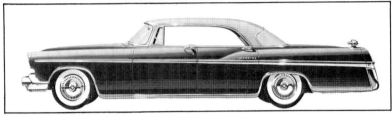

1956 Imperial four-door sedan (upper) and Southampton four-door hardtop (lower).

At the 1956 Mobil Gas Economy Run, Imperial topped its class.

Chrysler sales in recent years; and retailers were naturally reluctant to let it go. So the Windsor was retained. This may have been the decision that spelled death for DeSoto, incidentally, for that make expired in 1961.

The Windsor was a terrific automobile. Uncle Tom McCahill rated it as the best buy in its field for 1956, and if its poly head made any difference in performance compared with the hemi, he wasn't aware of it: "Here is a full bred, full powered, big Chrysler V-8 that'll satisfy a lot more pocketbooks than will the New Yorker. And, with the addition of a power package which costs about the price of a case of scotch, it has a barrel full of moxie." The Windsor engines's 225 horsepower could be increased to 250 hp with 'power-pak,' which meant dual exhausts and different carburetion. The latter setup gave McCahill a 0-60 mph time of 10.5 seconds, barely slower than the 1955 300, and a recorded top speed of 111 mph. Clearly the 1956 Windsor was no slouch.

The Chrysler New Yorker, priced almost $300 above its 1955 counterpart, ushered in (with Dodge) the Corporation's first three-tone paint job, one of the most questionable aspects of fifties quackery. Three-tones were applied to the St. Regis hardtop, the usual subject for such tarting up, commonly with a regimental-red and cloud-white body and raven-black top. It is not known whether this combination was available on other New Yorkers. It was not offered on Windsors, though owners could have had them painted that way by the dealer, and some probably did.

The New Yorker was distinguished from the Windsor by a more ornate, finer-meshed grille, a series of little shark gills along the rear fenders, more lavish interiors and, of course, the hairier hemi engine. To give the car its due, it was impressive for its time, and some of the milder color combinations suited it admirably. The New Yorker was also sumptuously upholstered. There was sculptured brocatelle and satin petit-point in sedans, brocatelle and leather in convertibles and hardtops and plaid cloth and vinyl for the Town and Country station wagons.

Like Chrysler, the '56 Imperial line also had a four-door hardtop, but for the first time it used a different and unique name — Southampton. This name was also applied to the two-door hardtop, a befitting one for a beautiful luxury car. Imperial interiors were spacious and trimmed in fine leather and a special fabric called Imperial Eagle faille. All were color-keyed to match the exterior. Gunsight taillights were retained though the fuel filler was now hidden behind the corner of the right fender instead of under the taillight mount. "Imperial is, by our firm intent, conservative," said its maker, for whom 'conservative' had been a naughty word just two years before. "But in this reserved refinement is a modern new note of

1956 Windsor convertible.

design that gives the Imperial its own unique distinction that immediately identifies it and separates it from other cars, both here and abroad. . . . In the Imperial [we] have striven to create a style, a design that is, first of all, in impeccable taste, a perfect complement to the other fine possessions of those for whom this car was expressly designed and created." In this writer's opinion, that particular bit of ad copy was 'right on' — the 1956 Imperial (with the '55) was the most elegant example of the marque ever produced. It wore its modest fins well; they never intruded on, and actually enhanced, its classic lines. It was a winner, and still is; when The Milestone Car Society added it to their list of outstanding postwar cars, they were only acknowledging its pre-eminence.

At the top of the line, the 1956 Crown Imperial soldiered on for yet another season. This was to be its last year, though Ghia would take up the manufacture of a new Crown in 1957 (for details see the Appendix). Once again, the Crown Imperial was offered as either an eight-passenger sedan or limousine, with air conditioning the only significant option. In a curious move for design-conscious Exner, the Crown retained its 1955 fenders but attempted to present a new look by adding a tacked-on fin. Only fifty-one sedans and 175 limousines were built before the Chrysler-manufactured Crowns were phased out in mid-1956. Management recognized the fact that the 1956 Crown was really no different from the 1955 by retaining its 1955 C70 series designation.

Nineteen fifty-six may be remembered as the year the manufacturers tried to sell safety — and the public responded by buying performance.

Ford made the biggest splash, with its deep-dish steering wheel, safety door locks, padded dash and seat belts, none of which were exactly new ideas by then. But Chrysler pitched hard too. Its list of safety features was massive, and included some items that really had nothing to do with safety — pushbutton gearshifting, for example. Some important items, though, were safety door latches; wider-swept windows, front and back (they still called the rear window CLEARBAC); padded dash; oversized brake pedal; outrigger front bumpers; illuminated trunk compartment and big, three-way visible taillights — still 'twin towers,' but now nicely faired into the fenders. Pushbutton PowerFlite was a refinement of the dash-mounted 'joy stick' of 1955, and theoretically, the Windsor could still be ordered with a three-speed column shift. Chrysler offered Airtemp on all models, and for those who say inflation has destroyed our purchasing power, it is interesting to consider that this option cost $567 in 1956, far more than it would today.

There was no plethora of midyear changes in 1956, though a Windsor Spring Special did appear: special color combinations, body moldings and upholstery on the two- and four-door hardtops and sedans. These were announced early, on March 1, 1956 — sales were slogging, and some stimulus was deemed necessary.

The 1956 Chrysler 300B was a logical refinement of the 1955 model, again using a Chrysler hardtop body with special identification and an Imperial grille. It was introduced at the Chicago Automobile Show in January of 1956 — a bit behind the rest of the line, as usual. With a bored-

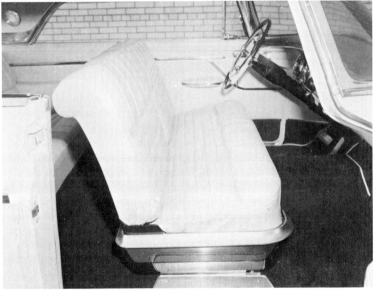

1956 Chrysler 300B, with interior detail.

Back at Daytona, the Kiekhaefer team's 300B ran as far up the scale as 139.7 mph.

out 354-cubic-inch hemi, the 300B pumped out 340 horsepower with 9:1 compression and offered 10:1 as an option with 355 horsepower. This would be the only 300 to ever exceed one horsepower per cubic inch of displacement. Tom McCahill of *Mechanix Illustrated* loved it, and called the B a "mastodon of muscle."

McCahill's test car belonged to Brewster Shaw of the Kiekhafer Mercury Outboard Racing Team, and was equipped with a rare 300 option for 1956 — a three-speed column shift. Since PowerFlite now dominated production, the stick was a $70 optional extra. Shaw's car didn't break 1955's speed record during his Daytona tests — but that of his teammate Tim Flock did — with a 139.373 mph average. McCahill found the stick awkward to use, though the car was a tiger once in gear and went from 0-60 in only 8.4 seconds. Uncle Tom had a suggestion: "I'd buy the New Yorker, which has the same basic 354-cubic-inch engine as the 300B. I'd order it with the solid valve lifters of the 300B, the 300 cam and a *single* four-barrel carburetor. With this combination I could stay with the Chrysler 300B up to well over 100 mph from a standstill, wheel turn for wheel turn, as my torque would be exactly the same. But at slower speeds around town I'd have a car as smooth as a vanilla ice cream soda that has been standing in the sun for ten minutes.

"If I wanted the 300B I would tell them to remove the two four-barrel carburetors and manifold and give me the New Yorker hook-up. This would be a much more satisfactory outfit, in my opinion, for anyone not planning to enter competition. I'd also stick with the pushbutton transmission unless the gearbox has been smoothed out considerably." This was significant: For the first time Unk, the inveterate shifter, had recommended an automatic over a stick! He had realized, he said, that American automatics were no longer the power-robbing slush boxes they had once been, since the advent of four-speed Hydra-Matic, Dynaflow and Ultramatic. It was quite an admission. The following year McCahill and others would view the Chrysler line and make another surprising admission — that American cars now *handled*. But we digress.

The 1956 300B could be tailored by the owner, though whether Chrysler would consent to detune one as McCahill suggested was a moot question. But there were all kinds of 300 rear axles, for example, from 3.08 all the way to 6.17; the car must have done 0-60 mph in four seconds with

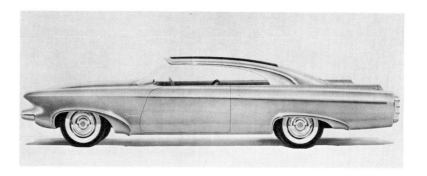

Replacing the previous year's PowerFlite shifting stalk, this 1956 pushbutton adaptation became a Chrysler tradition for many years to come.

One that didn't make it. Virgil Exner's cantilever-roofed Norseman sank with the *Andrea Doria*. Designed only for testing, this car would not have seen an auto show.

the latter. Two engine options were available, as noted, and one could specify three-inch-diameter dual exhaust pipes. These factory goodies allowed the 300B to be 'prodified' to good advantage. Again the car dominated NASCAR, Kiekhafer's Tim Flock winning the Grand National 160-mile race at a 90.836 mph average. Close on Tim's heels at the Daytona speed trials was Vicki Wood, who set a new women's record of 136.081 mph in another 300B.

Chrysler offered other options on the 300B to make it more civilized, if that was desired. Air conditioning was now available, as was Solex glass, power windows-seats-brakes-steering, a self-winding clock mounted in the center of the steering wheel, 'instant heat' heater, radio and Chrysler's latest accessory, Highway Hi-Fi. In the days before tape casettes, Highway Hi-Fi was revolutionary. Built for Chrysler by RCA, it operated from the regular electrical system and played through the radio speaker. The turntable used special 16⅔ records and a needle and arm that stayed grooved. The unit was mounted centrally under the dash, and seemed like quite a comer until the tape decks appeared. Then, of course, it became clumsy and inefficient by comparison.

One Chrysler-based special designed by Exner was to have no influence — because of a shipwreck in the Atlantic Ocean. This was the Norseman, a fastback hardtop with a unique cantilevered roof supported entirely by the rear pillars. There were no windshield or door pillars — the glass just butted together. The Norseman was the only 1956 show car of the period powered by a Chrysler engine, using the 331-cubic-inch poly-head Windsor unit and PowerFlite transmission. Unlike the other Exner specials, it was not designed for the show circuit — its designer said it was being brought over on the S.S. *Andrea Doria* specifically to be wrecked — rolled over at Chelsea to see how well the cantilevered roof design would hold up in a crash. The Italian liner did the job ahead of time. It collided with the *Stockholm* and sank in 300 feet of water.

During 1956, most Exner show cars were other than Chrysler-based, hence not technically part of this story. A look at them is useful, because some of the ideas they expressed did influence Chrysler production cars.

Exner's other show cars included the Plainsman, a Plymouth-based experimental station wagon; the Falcon, a DeSoto-powered sports roadster with lovely lines, which came close to being put into production; and the DeSoto Adventurer II, a sleek, long, Ghia exercise on a stock DeSoto chassis. The Falcon introduced Exner's squared-off, prominent grille, which would influence the styling of the 1957 Chryslers. The Plainsman predicted other coming features with its hardtop-wagon styling and spare-tire compartment in the right rear fender.

In late 1955 two other show cars appeared, called Flight Sweep I and II, a convertible and hardtop respectively. Maury Baldwin had a lot to do with their designs, and they were to be significant. Both 170-hp DeSoto engines and were mounted on stock 120-inch-wheelbase DeSoto chassis. But their importance was in their rakish, dazzling design, which wowed the show audiences in 1955-56 as it would later on the 1957 Chryslers.

The Flight Sweeps featured a bold, squared-off central grille of egg-crate pattern, heavily-lidded headlamps, flowing lines and strongly-upswept rear-fender fins. The K310's spare tire outline had returned to the deck. Chrysler said these features were portents of things to come, and Chrysler was right, of course, since by that time Highland Park knew *exactly* what was to come. It officially arrived in October, 1956. Virgil Exner called it "the new shape of motion."

CHAPTER 7

Looking Forward

FEW WOULD DISPUTE Chrysler's claim that its 1957 model was "the most glamorous car in a generation." Despite good 1955 styling, Virgil Exner had wiped the slate clean again, and 'The New Look of Motion' bore no resemblance whatsoever to any Chrysler of the past. If the cars weren't any longer — the Imperial wheelbase in fact decreased from 133 to 129 inches — they looked it. Long, tapering, graceful fins supplanted the tacked-on affairs of 1956; grilles spread full width, yet were narrower and better-integrated with the bumpers. For the first time, four headlights were available — though they were not standard, since, at announcement time, nine states had yet to approve them. There were new interiors and brighter colors inside and out. Glass area increased, and on Imperials the windshield even wrapped around at the top. Yet all Chrysler products used a more mildly-angled A-pillar to eliminate the sharp corners of the traditional wraparound windshield.

The 1957 models culminated Virgil Exner's long struggle to alter Chrysler's styling image. Though Ex had instituted the wire-wheel option and minor trim changes through 1954, and had created a distinctive-looking line for 1955-56, even the latter were not entirely new, albeit beautifully executed. For the 1957's, he and his team were in total command of styling for the first time, and they created a shape that soon had all of Detroit scrambling to emulate it.

"The '57's were just sensational," says Virgil Exner, Jr., "The most important thing about them was the fact that they were *sculptured*. Now, you look at them today and they don't look nearly as sculptured, and you say, gee, what was I thinking about back then? But if you compare them with the 1957 Ford and Chevrolet, which were fat looking, you realize that the most important aspect of these new designs was their slimness." They were also a lot cleaner, with little of the tinsel of GM and Ford. And of course, their most prominent feature was their huge tailfins.

"My father was a real staunch believer in fins," Exner continues. "Like a lot of designers at that time, he was tremendously influenced by Italian designs — the Alfa BAT and the Cisitalia, for example. The idea of the fin was to get some poise to the rear of the cars, to get them off of the soft, rounded back-end look, to achieve lightness. To my dad, Italian design represented these characteristics, and was good at achieving a sculptured effect, a very contemporary proportion. At the same time, he never forgot the long hood-short deck proportions of the Duesenbergs of his childhood — and these in turn were also characteristics of the 1957 Chrysler line. You can see the classic influence in the radiator shell of the 1957 Chrysler 300, for example, in the spare tire outline on the Imperial deck, and in the full, open wheels, which he very much liked. But it was the tailfin that captured the eye of the beholder."

The Exner fins touched off a debate that has never ceased, and in the superficial analysis common to TV-orchestrated exposes of the sins of Detroit, they are often held up to ridicule as having been a waste of time, talent and resources. The fact is that the fins of the 1957 Chrysler and

Imperial were far more than gimmicks; they were quite practical affairs — regardless of the excesses which resulted from attempts to copy the idea; e.g. the 1959 Chevrolet and Chrysler's own 1960 models. Says Maury Baldwin: "We did quite a bit of aerodynamics work. The fins were fully aerodynamic in the first concept. Wind tunnel tests proved conclusively that they aided stability at speeds over 60-70 mph. Later on, they did become a styling thing, with one company striving to out-fin the other. But they were never *conceived* as a gimmick, as for example those three-tone paint jobs of the period. It's too bad that they got out of hand." It's also too bad that Exner has been saddled with the 'blame' for the tail-fin era all these years. It is obvious, when one talks to those who were there, that his original concepts were grounded in engineering and design practicality.

Experimental Flight Sweep I indicated the look of future Chryslers.

Flight Sweep II was the hardtop version. Both cars were designed mainly by Maury Baldwin.

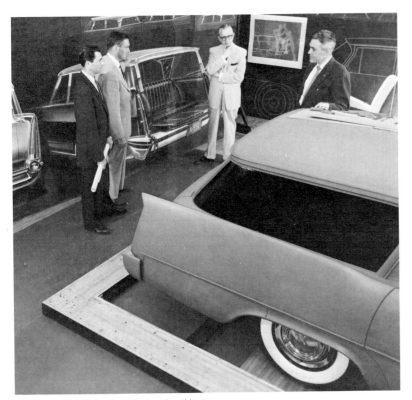

Henry King was still director of Styling when this photo was taken at Suburban studio in early 1956. Left to right: DeSoto chief stylist Richard Baird, ornamentation studio manager Henry Keene, Henry King, Suburban chief stylist James Higgins. Clay model is the 1957 DeSoto.

Neither does this imply that Chrysler Styling was altogether blameless. To illustrate this, one need only point to prototype car number 613, an early possibility for the 1957 Chrysler 300 series, and one that did influence the 300 front end as well as the greenhouse of the 1957 Plymouth. This prototype was pure 1957 Chrysler 300 up front; at the back, it was pure horror.

The frontal aspect of the 613 featured a Ferrari-like oblong grille cavity, narrower at the top than the bottom, and a flared-out bumper. The shape of the entire 1957 line was there. As it turned out, only the 300 used the squared-off 'classic' grille, though derivations of it appeared throughout the line in 1960 and persisted through the 1964 models.

But the 613's stern was something else again. Enormous fins were the dominant feature, and they were not too far from the actual production fins of the 1959 Plymouth. The exterior-mounted spare tire that had so long fascinated Virgil Exner appeared in full outline, but it appeared to be tacked on and did not blend well with the rear deck lines. Inside the car was a center console, first on a Chrysler, and another feature that would appear in production — on the 1960 300F. Overall, car 613 was a clean, forceful design, but the fins and dummy spare detracted from it, and indicated that Exner, too, sometimes got carried away.

One of the many traditional rules that governs the normal activities of the Motor City is the alternation between styling and engineering developments: You don't, they say, introduce anything radical in one department the same year that something revolutionary is being introduced in the other. Yet in this year of major styling change, Chrysler violated that rule — from Plymouth to Imperial, its cars now featured torsion-bar front suspension.

Though torsion bars were not a breakthrough on the scale of Maurice Olley's 'knee action' independent front suspension on 1934 Cadillacs, Buicks and Oldsmobiles, nor as important as the independent rear suspensions then under development on both sides of the Atlantic, they were significant for the auto industry. Like all suspension ideas of the last twenty years, knee action — suspending front wheels to allow for independent vertical travel — had been an attempt to improve ride. Torsion bars were a step in another direction: an attempt to improve handling.

American cars had been criticized for a generation for their sloppy handling, and the torsion bar wasn't the first attempt to deal with this problem. One of the early-fifties suspension improvements had been a wider track — widening the lateral spring base by increasing the front track, and mounting the rear leaf springs outside the frame rails. Increasing the distance between spring lever points improved roll stiffness by a ratio of 1:5 — i.e., a five-inch increase in distance meant a stiffness increase of twenty-five percent. Coupled with the newer, low-center-of-gravity bodies, this made for better handling without compromising ride quality.

As suspension geometry became a popular field of study in Detroit, engineers began to raise the roll centers of some cars by making small setting changes in the A-frames. They created more accurate rear-steering qualities by varying spring lengths and spring shackle angles. Anti-sway bars, uncommon in the past, became widespread; gradually the bars became thicker in diameter. Torsion bars, common to some European cars for years, were tried as early as 1946 (on the stillborn front-drive Kaiser), but it was another ten years before they were seen on an American production car — the 1955 Packard.

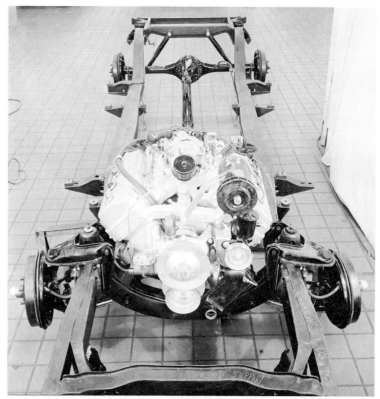

Various approaches to the suspension problem were considered. Above, torsion bar front suspension with live axle and semi-elliptic leaf springs in rear. Below, same arrangement using coil springs at rear. The date is November 1955.

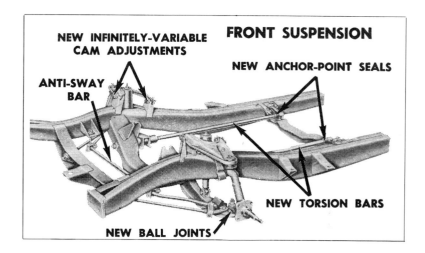

Features of torsion bar front suspension.

    A conventional leaf or coil spring sends the force of road bumps directly up into the car in accordance with the simple laws of physics. But the torsion bar absorbs much of this force, by winding up against its anchor point. This twisting motion eliminates most of the upward force of road irregularities. Packard's system, designed by the brilliant engineer Bill Allison, took this principle and added a new touch — interconnected front- and rear-wheel torsion bars. This system achieved excellent pitch characteristics by linking pairs of wheels at the opposite ends of the car, as reaction points for each other. Allison also included in his system an electronic motor to 'load,' and therefore level, the car — compensating for the weight of passengers or cargo — though this complex feature was susceptible to dampness and corrosion. Including solenoids and control box, the motor required no less than seven electrical switches.

    Those who expressed surprise at Chrysler's simultaneous radical styling and engineering for 1957 would have better understood the situation had they realized that torsion bars were originally planned for the 1955 or 1956 models. Packard's sudden announcement of the torsion bars, in a crash program necessitated by that company's deteriorating health, took the industry by surprise and caused Chrysler to postpone its own introduction. According to one executive, the Sales Department reasoned "that it wouldn't do to come out with torsion bars on the front of our cars while

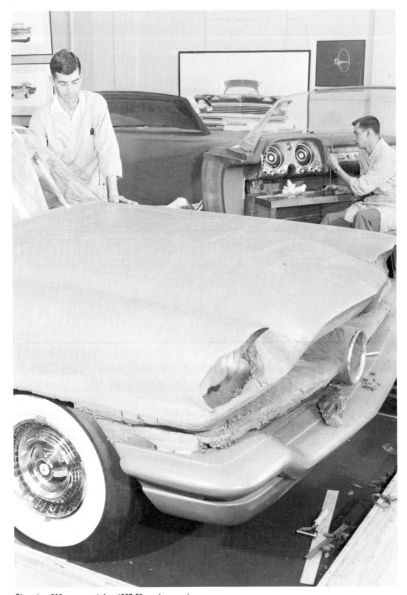

Chrysler 300 proposal for 1957-58 underway in the Imperial studio. In the background is a nearly complete Imperial instrument panel.

Packard had them all around. We could easily anticipate their claiming that their system was twice as good as ours!"

Despite the inherent advantages of torsion bar suspension, most engineers then and now feel that Chrysler's Torsion-Aire Ride was aimed more at gaining engine compartment space and impressing sales prospects than it was at producing a better ride or handling. Nevertheless, Chrysler 'roadability' reigned supreme, and Torsion-Aire was a much simpler explanation than the 1957 models' wide lateral spring base, lower center of gravity, stiffer spring rates, higher front roll center and improved rear steering geometry. The new system also sent GM and Ford scurrying to reply with unique suspension ideas of their own (like the notably unreliable air bags of the late fifties), which would never have been offered on anything but limited-edition cars if it hadn't been for Torsion-Aire. Obviously the bars were no threat in their relatively sophisticated form on low-volume Packards, but on the front ends of Chrysler products they were a serious sales menace to Ford and General Motors.

Chrysler torsion bars were longitudinal, replacing conventional coil-type front springs. They were coupled with strange-looking rear leaf springs that were slim and extended at the rear, to insure a soft ride, but short and thick in front (and seven times more rigid), to cut down on roll and slop. Space saved by deletion of the coils meant a lower hood could be adapted; this allowed Chrysler hoods to drop to fender level for the first time, and let Exner create a radically low beltline with a large glass area, while using less steel in the process.

Added touches of refinement on the new Chrysler suspension included rubber insulation throughout — which was said to eliminate small shocks that caused fatigue on long trips — and a reduction in wheel size to fourteen inches with low pressure (22 psi) tires. These features, Chrysler claimed, "aided steering and provided better ride and longer tire life." The engines were the old blocks, bored out to achieve more horsepower. The poly-head Windsor now measured 3.94 by 3.63 bore and stroke, for 354 cubic inches, and developed 285 horsepower at 4600 rpm, or 295 hp in the Saratoga, which had returned to the lineup. The New Yorker/Imperial hemi was bored and stroked to 4.00 x 3.90, 392 cubic inches, 325 horsepower at 4600 rpm; the 300C produced 375 and 390 horsepower.

A new automatic transmission, introduced the previous spring in the Imperial, was on hand for 1957. Called TorqueFlite, it was a three-speed affair with manual override on first and second gears, and controlled, as in 1956, by a push-button panel. It was standard on all but the Windsor, where it cost $220 extra. Normal starts were made in first gear, with a 2.45:1 ratio, shifted through second (1.45:1) and up to high via a direct torque converter, unassisted by planetary gears. The converter was capable

of a torque increase of up to 2.7 times, providing up to 6.62 multiplication on take-off, for astounding acceleration. But rear axle ratios were at the same time allowed to go higher, improving economy if the car were driven moderately. Both the lower gears had lockouts to prevent them from engaging if their buttons were pressed when the car was traveling faster than 25 mph (first) and 70 mph (second). The transmission also skipped second as the car came to a stop, avoiding any lurch — an overrunning brake prevented transmission torque during the downshift.

Imperial studio, March 1956. Model in foreground uses stillborn front-end proposal, probably considered for 1958-59. Background models are variations of the 1957 theme. At right, the 1957 Imperial fiberglass prototype develops.

Depicted here, clay and finished version of Exner's outlandish no. 613.

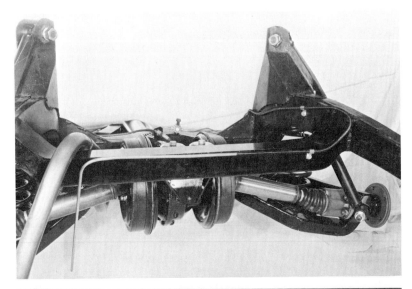

Experimental car no. 618, early 1956, using centrally mounted differential and swing axle with both coil (upper) and leaf springs (lower).

Collectively, the 1957 Chrysler and Imperial lineup was as follows:

Model / Body Style (passengers)	Price	W.B.(in)	Weight (lb)
Series C75-1 Windsor			
sedan, 4dr (6)	$3,088	126	3,995
hardtop, 2dr (6)	3,153	126	3,925
hardtop, 4dr (6)	3,217	126	4,030
Town and Country wagon (6)	3,575	126	4,210
Series C75-2 Saratoga			
sedan, 4dr (6)	$3,718	126	4,165
hardtop, 2dr (6)	3,754	126	4,075
hardtop, 4dr (6)	3,832	126	4,195
Series C76 New Yorker			
sedan, 4dr (6)	$4,173	126	4,315
hardtop, 2dr (6)	4,202	126	4,220
hardtop, 4dr (6)	4,259	126	4,330
convertible (6)	4,638	126	4,365
Town and Country wagon (6)	4,746	126	4,490
300C hardtop (6)	4,929	126	4,235
300C convertible (6)	5,359	126	4,390
Series IM1-1 Imperial			
sedan, 4dr (6)	$4,838	129	4,640
Southampton hardtop, 2dr (6)	4,736	129	4,640
Southampton hardtop, 4dr (6)	4,838	129	4,780
Series IM1-2 Crown Imperial			
sedan, 4dr (6)	$5,406	129	4,740
Southampton hardtop, 2dr (6)	5,269	129	4,755
Southampton hardtop, 4dr (6)	5,406	129	4,920
convertible (6)	5,598	129	4,830
Series IM1-4 LeBaron Imperial			
sedan, 4dr (6)	$5,743	129	4,765
Southampton hardtop, 4dr (6)	5,743	129	4,900
Crown Imperial (Ghia)			
limousine (8)	$15,000	149½	5,960

Model expansion was the rule for 1957: The Saratoga was revived in three versions and there was a new Imperial Crown series along with the first production 300 convertible. This resulted in a large variety of body styles, since the only deletions were the four hardtops in the 1956 Windsor and New Yorker series, and the Windsor convertible. Prices had gone up some $200-300 across the board — and had even doubled in the case of the Crown Imperial limousine, now built by Ghia.

The bottom-line Windsor now cost more than $3,000. Its untrimmed lines looked very clean and sleek, but this wasn't necessarily advantageous in 1957. So Chrysler soon offered a 'Flite-Sweep-insert' color panel — dart-shaped from mid-fuselage to tail — to go with duo-tone roofs. A three-

Production 1957 chassis.

1957 prototype is identical to production Saratoga, though here it bears New Yorker script.

quarter-length body side-molding was made optional later in the year. Together with the New Yorker, the Windsor Town and Country offered an 'observation package' in May, whereby a customer could order a rear-facing third seat, electric tailgate window and four Captive-Air tires — the result of a no-spare tire policy dictated by the addition of the third seat. (Exner was already solving this problem: His experimental 1956 Plainsman station wagon carried a spare in its rear fender well, and the same feature was standard on Plymouth wagons beginning in 1958.) The new Saratoga, neatly slotted between Windsor and New Yorker price brackets, was a shade more luxurious and ten horsepower more powerful than the Windsor. The New Yorker came in at $4,424 and was certainly the handsomest of the line, with a slim two-tone color sweep running from front to rear. Rear-fender fish-gill strips were an identifying holdover from 1956. For 1957, Chrysler revised its door handles: In 1955, they'd been a push-me-pull-you type that was subject to failure; they were replaced by a pull-type in 1956; and a pull-up affair in 1957 — the latter to persist for some time.

Chrysler dashboards were also revised. Full instrumentation was again provided, grouped in two dials in front of the driver and flanking a smaller, centrally-mounted clock. Control buttons were grouped closer to the driver, and extensive padding was used. The aforementioned new windshield, inspired largely by prototype 613, was an impressive improvement, intruding less into the entranceway than the windshields of GM, Ford, AMC and Studebaker. Exner had seen to every detail: Even the license plate housing was streamlined, set in a shadow box on the deck lid. Options included the usual items, plus rear-window defroster, dual rear antennae and a six-way power seat with an eighteen-degree tilting feature.

The 1957 300C, technically part of the New Yorker line, appeared at the New York Automobile Show in December, 1956, two months after its general introduction. Here Exner kept ornamentation to a minimum, adopting a simple chrome strip toward the rear and a new red, white and blue 300C medallion as the only decoration. The device was used, Chrsyler said, "to remind people this is truly an American car. We use the circle because what makes a car different from a boat or plane is the circle or wheel."

True to Exner's classic precepts, the 300C featured a special squared-off grille, slightly trapezoidal to emphasize the wideness of the car and honeycombed with egg-crate bars. It was flanked by small intakes, channeling air directly to the front brake drums, which also benefited from a lining area of 251 square inches. All these were features suggested by the 613.

Mechanical refinements of the 'big C' included SilentFlite fan drive, which automatically cut out fan action at 2500 rpm to boost power, and torsion bars forty percent stiffer than those of the New Yorker. Power steering was a useful option on 300's, as it required only three and one-third turns lock-to-lock. Like the Windsor — but unlike any other Chrysler — the 300 could be ordered with a three-speed stick instead of TorqueFlite; and in addition to its 375-horsepower, 392-cubic-inch engine a high-lift cam could be specified which increased output to a towering 390 horsepower. Most 390's were equipped with stick shifts, which must have made them awesome to behold on dragstrips and less-official race 'tracks.'

1957 New Yorker Town & Country.

Sketch showing extent of cargo space available in 1957 New Yorker Town & Country. On three-seat models, spare tire was eliminated and 'captive air' tires were fitted. However...

... three-seat experimental 1956 Plymouth Plainsman pioneered storage of spare in rear fender.

A convertible, representing twenty percent of 300 production, was now available in the series for the first time; but, as in the past, trim options were limited. Interiors came only in natural tan hide; exteriors in copper-brown, parade-green, cloud-white, Gauguin-red and jet-black. Some model 300 details varied from car to car — they came with two or four headlights, depending on the state in which they were to be sold. An occasional example is found without air intake screens or bumper guards, and the '300' logos vary.

By now Tom McCahill, among others, had become thoroughly enamored of the Chrysler 300. His 1957 test car, Unk said in *Mechanix Illustrated*, was "the most hairy-chested, fire-eating land bomb ever conceived in Detroit." McCahill ran the 0-60 mph sprint in 8.4 seconds with TorqueFlite, indicating greater alacrity in the 'C' — since his 300B stick shift had only matched that figure the year before. He calculated a top end of 150 mph with the right gearing, and maintained that the 300 would be a racing terror in spite of its bulk and weight. Unfortunately, the Auto Manufacturers Association picked 1957 to initiate its infamous ban on motor racing; the 300C was not able to defend its title as stock car champion. But it did take the national standing- and flying-mile championships at the Daytona Beach Speed Weeks early in the year. In the standing mile, Brewster Shaw exceeded 130 mph with the 3.73 rear axle.

The 300C was "motorized dynamite," McCahill warned his followers, "not for the faint of heart." Some road-testers even exceeded Tom's 8.4-second time for the 0-60 mph sprint, one getting a 300C down to 7.7 seconds. It was a fast one, and no mistake.

The newly-independent Imperial, with a greatly expanded model range and full identity as a make stood at the top of the line. There was no interchange of body panels between it and regular Chrysler models. This was to be the banner year for Imperial, its best on record, with close to 38,000 sales for the calendar year — just edging out Lincoln. Never again would Imperial sell anything like this huge number of cars.

Front and rear photos of the 1957 New Yorker convertible.

The sleek 1957 New Yorker hardtop, and interior.

1957 Windsor hardtop with Flite Sweep insert.

Why did it do so well? The car looked right, for one thing. It featured gracefully swept fins; gunsight taillights now integrated into the fenders rather than perched on top; a massive grille and sleek fuselage; much glass, including the first compound curved side windows on a regular production car; and a luxurious interior. The Crown series set the Imperial sales pace and, indicative of a growing preference, was offered in a four-door hardtop guise — 7,843 of these were sold in the model year. Four-door hardtops were approaching sedan sales in the Chrysler lines too, and were in such demand that Imperial offered another version in the LeBaron series beginning in January, 1957. The Crown Imperial limousine was now built by Ghia (see Appendix).

By the end of model year 1957, Lester Lum Colbert could look with pride on the design rebirth he had fathered. Starting with an undistinguished line in 1950 — mundane styling, old-fashioned engines, mush suspension — Chrysler had rallied with vividly styled cars, the hemi- and poly-head V-8's and excellent roadability. Throughout the industry it was generally conceded that 1957 had been Chrysler's year; Chrysler was the car to beat in 1958. Its styles were the most widely imitated; its torsion bar suspension had the competition scrambling to imitate it; its TorqueFlite was perhaps the most perfect automatic transmission yet. Chrysler's 300C was the hottest car around. Its dollar sales were the highest in history — . $3.5 billion, up 34.5 percent over 1956 and 2.9 percent better than the previous record year of 1955. "Chrysler in 1957 aggressively established Imperial as

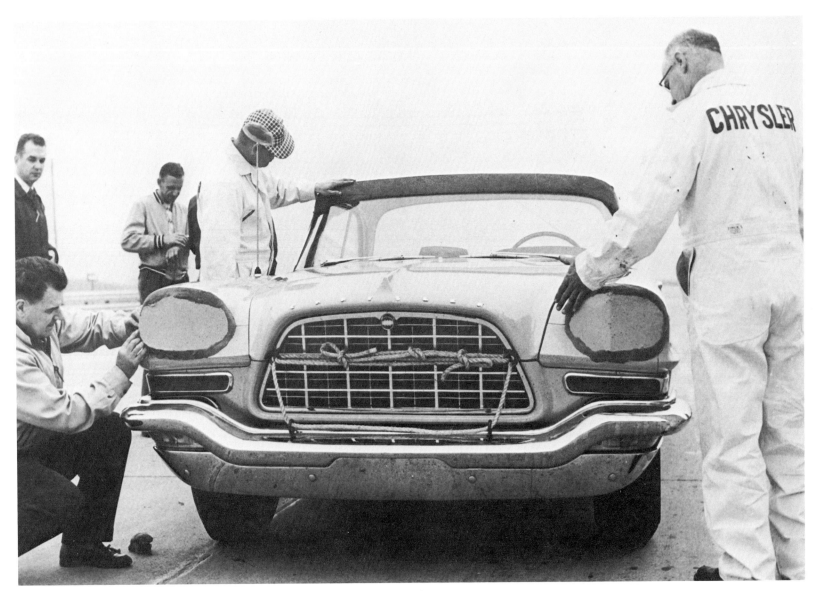

Speed run with the 300C. To aid streamlining, Chrysler mechanics faired in headlamp and windshield header sections; they also encouraged the hood to stay closed.

a volume automobile line," Colbert reported. "The Division's U.S. production in calendar year 1957 jumped 45.8 percent over 1956, but Imperial accounted for more of the increase than did the Chrysler line; this, despite the fact that the '57 models featured the addition of a new series — the Saratoga. . . . Built in the calendar year were 156,679 cars, including 118,733 Chryslers and 37,946 Imperials. . . . Thus the Imperials jumped to 24.2 percent of the Division's annual volume, from 11.3 percent in 1956.

1957 300C hardtop and convertible.

1957 Imperial's 392-cid FirePower engine.

1957 Imperial four-door sedan and Imperial four-door Southampton interior.

1957 Imperial LeBaron and interior.

1957 Imperial Crown convertible.

Office of the 1958 New Yorker convertible.

1958 Windsor Dartline option included new trim with color flash, available as sedan, two- and four-door hardtop and wagon. Special colors included frosty-tan, fireglow and Bimini-blue.

About half the sales of Windsors, Saratogas and New Yorkers were 'conquest' sales to owners of rival makes, and in the fine car market Chrysler and Imperial upped their penetration to 22 percent, against 15 percent in 1956."

Significantly, sales per dealer were up too. In an attempt to weed out some of the weaker links and improve the quality of its dealerships the Division opened 1958 with 2,754 Chrysler dealers against 2,854 a year

before, while those handling the Imperial were cut from 1,834 to 1,580. Fewer outlets and a popular 1957 product made it obvious that little change would occur in 1958. With the exception of a shortened (to 122 inches)

Windsor wheelbase, the lineup was literally identical. The Windsor's only change was the use of front fenders similar to the DeSoto Firesweep; previous Windsors had shared front ends with other Chryslers.

Model
Body Style (passengers)	Price	W.B.(in)	Weight (lb)
Series LC1-L Windsor			
sedan, 4dr (6)	$3,129	122	3,895
hardtop, 2dr (6)	3,214	122	3,860
hardtop, 4dr (6)	3,279	122	3,915
Town and Country wagon (9)	3,803	122	4,245
Town and Country wagon (6)	3,616	122	3,860
Series LC2-M Saratoga			
sedan, 4dr (6)	$3,818	126	4,120
hardtop, 2dr (6)	3,878	126	4,045
hardtop, 4dr (6)	3,955	126	4,145
Series LC3-H New Yorker			
sedan, 4dr (6)	$4,295	126	4,195
hardtop, 2dr (6)	4,347	126	4,100
hardtop, 4dr (6)	4,404	126	4,240
convertible (6)	4,761	126	4,260
Town and Country wagon (9)	5,083	126	4,445
Town and Country wagon (6)	4,868	126	4,435
300D hardtop (6)	5,173	126	4,305
300D convertible (6)	5,603	126	4,475
Series LY1-L Imperial			
sedan, 4dr (6)	$4,945	129	4,950
Southampton hardtop 2dr (6)	4,839	129	4,640
Southampton hardtop 4dr (6)	4,945	129	4,795
Series LY1-M Crown Imperial			
sedan, 4dr (6)	$5,632	129	4,755
Southampton hardtop, 2dr (6)	5,388	129	4,730
Southampton hardtop, 4dr (6)	5,632	129	4,915
convertible (6)	5,759	129	4,820
Series LY1-H LeBaron Imperial			
sedan, 4dr (6)	$5,969	129	4,780
Southampton hardtop 4dr (6)	5,969	129	4,780
Crown Imperial			
limousine (8)	$15,075	149½	5,960

Styling changes were minimal, yet not all of them were successful. There was a busier grille, and heavier chrome lids covered the Windsor's now-standard four headlights. At the rear it was change for the sake of change, with 1957's beautiful taillights shrinking to about half their former size. Since the taillight cavity remained the same, the taillights looked as if they'd shrunk in a hot oven. Side trim was also slightly revised. The New Yorker lost its contrasting color sweep in favor of a more restrained silver anodized aluminum insert, while on Saratogas the color sweep was

1958 Saratoga two- and four-door hardtops.

abbreviated, starting on the front doors instead of front fenders. Windsors wore a single side strip or their optional Flite-Sweep panels, and in the spring were offered in a Dartline variation. This consisted of special side molding incorporating a contrasting anodized aluminum panel, altered roof and sill moldings and three horizontal chrome strips on either side of the license plate box. The sill, roof and deck trims were also available on senior models." Here was a good example of fine styling being altered just to look changed," says Virgil Exner, Jr. "The public was attuned to the annual change, and in those days to not come out with it was anathema. So you had compromises, infringing on the purity of the original design, just for the sake of a different look."

Model trims were also shuffled in 1958. Metallic vinyl made its entry into the Chrysler world, combined with jacquards of various patterns — Fontainebleu, chainmail and Bahama, respectively — on New Yorker,

1958 New Yorker four-door sedan.

Saratoga and Windsor. The Bahama jacquard was not durable. "We had a helluva time with it," says one member of the Chrysler trim department. "Many, many replacements were fitted under warranty, and God only knows how many people suffered with the stuff whom we never heard from. Considerable research went into finding replacements for the jacquard, but we eventually went to nylon based fabrics like the rest of the industry."

Those who urge Detroit to stick with good styling once it is achieved would probably have been unhappy with the 1958 Chrysler. But they would have loved the Imperial. Except for a mild shuffle of regalia, a change in grille meshwork and the replacement of square parking lights by round ones, the "Triumphant 1958 Imperial" was unchanged from '57. But it did feature two Chrysler firsts — the first automatic driver speed control and the first integrated electro-mechanical door locking system on American cars. On the inside, Imperials showed some very lovely new fabrics: diamond-glow jacquard and vinyl on the LY1-L (which, like the 1957, bore no model name), crown pattern jacquard and vinyl on Crowns, and wool broadcloth on LeBarons.

Mechanical changes were also slight on the 1958 models. Compression increases pushed Windsors and Saratogas to 290 and 310 hp respectively, while the New Yorker now produced 345 hp and the basic 300D, 380 hp. All Chryslers now featured 10:1 compression ratios, sad reminders of a vanished age of high octane. Three-seat station wagons were listed as separate models in the Windsor and New Yorker series, the price premium over two-seat wagons being $187 and $115 respectively. Captive-Air tires were again *de rigueur* on the Town and Country. Imperials ran 9.50 x 14 tires, but offered 11.00 x 14 optionally, the fattest passenger car tires at the time in the world.

 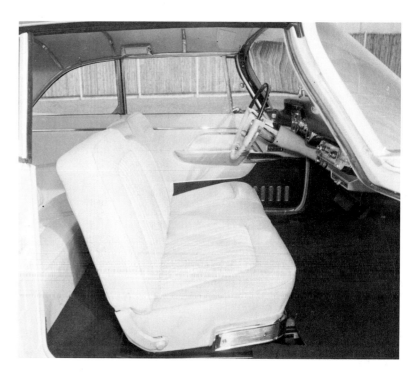

1958 300D styling was mildly changed from 300C; its grille was somewhat simpler.   300D interior.

The racing ban again prevented the 1958 300D from proving itself, but this fourth-generation muscle car from Jefferson Avenue must have been the quickest yet. For $400 extra, one could order the 300D with Bendix Electrojector fuel injection. This was a strange option for those raceless days, born of a desire to answer the injection options of Chevrolet and Pontiac. Though it was a simple, bolt-on affair, the Electrojector caused more problems than praise: Cars were hard to tune, and the system was unreliable even when running well. Of the sixteen 300D's so equipped, nearly all were reconverted to the dual quad carburetor set-up. It is doubtful whether this was done on a recall basis. Possibly one 300D escaped the treatment; if so, it has not come to light.

Chrysler 300 rear axle options for 1958 included 2.93, 3.18, 3.54, 3.73, but 3.31:1 was standard. Power brakes were also standard. The engine was modified with a new valve timing lift and heavier pistons plus a new cam to improve low speed performance. The camming gave the car only 435 foot-pounds of torque compared to the New Yorker's 450. Small carburetion calibration changes were made to match the higher 10:1 compression ratio.

In one of its few competitive outings, the 300D set a new speed record — 156.387 in Class E at Bonneville, with Norm Thatcher driving. Brewster Shaw took one to the Daytona Speed Weeks, and turned a quarter-mile in sixteen seconds at 84 mph. So there was no doubt about the 300D's potential, and Chrysler viewed it seriously enough to warn owners to "respect [it] for its power and control its power with care." Bill Carroll underlined this in some interesting 300D impressions in the February, 1958, issue of *Motor Trend*.

"A man-size 17-inch steering wheel which with power steering flips the Caddy-sized 300 around like a Corvette" was Carroll's first impression. "The dash layout is filled with instruments and gauges (no tach); Torque-Flite buttons are easy to reach. Both pedals fall naturally underfoot. The

Bendix Electrojector fuel injection system was a $400 option on the 300D.

1958 New Yorker hardtop and convertible.

accelerator has a mushy feel compared to other hot cars; but once you begin opening the second carburetor, [the] intakes sound like you're moving at a hundred miles an hour. Hold the button down for 25 seconds and you will be.

"Once moving, the 300's huge 9.00 x 14 Goodyear Blue Streak racing nylons slap at tar strips with solid authority. The low-speed ride is rough on city streets, solid on highways up to 85 or so, and just right at anything you can run over that. There's no body or chassis vibration from either engine or suspension. Dirt or rough pavement, when traveled fast enough to keep tires out of chuckholes, feels as secure as pavement. Belting over grade crossings at 70 caused as much steering disturbance as a bug smacking the windshield. The car *can* be broken loose on corners but the driver would be way over his head when it happens. The entire package is an impressively engineered, confident automobile that knows it's good — and soon lets you know it too."

Interestingly, the 300D responded nicely to a light foot: Carroll recorded 17.6 mpg on an Illinois turnpike, which was approximately the same as the Pontiac Tri-Power. The Tri-Power could, however, run the quarter mile slightly more rapidly than Carroll's (but not Shaw's) 300D. Carroll considered the 300 the second sports car built in Detroit— Corvette was the other. "Few drivers will ever exhaust its ability and even fewer know for sure what to do with four throats or an Electrojector."

The Dart, a striking Exner show car, made the rounds of dealerships and car shows at the same time as the 1957-58 Chryslers. The Dart ran the 392-cubic inch hemi engine with 375 horsepower. Featuring a retractable hardtop on a 129-inch Imperial wheelbase, the Dart was nearly nineteen feet long and bore close resemblance to its name, with towering fins that tapered to a narrow, wind-cheating front end. Later the Dart was modified: The fins were cut down and the retractable hardtop was converted to a standard soft top. The car was then renamed Diablo, in which form it survives today at Paul Stern's Museum in Manheim, Pennsylvania.

"The Dart represented some of the Ghia influence at the time," says Virgil Exner, Jr. "There was a back and forth [interchange of ideas] because Ghia was so talented sheet metal-wise, as well as having an excellent designer, Giovanni Sevenutzi. He was a really terrific engineer who had been involved in racing cars, and was mostly responsible for the Dart's execution.

"Sevenutzi had also designed the Ghia Gilda, a mock-up that was really just one long fin from front to rear — a dramatic, fastback car. He

did wind tunnel studies on it, as it was considered for possible use as a speed record-breaker. Finally Ghia showed it to Chrysler, where it evolved into the Dart. The low front end of the car, the diametric opposite to the big high hoods, was something my father was very much caught up in."

Wind tunnel tests showed that the Dart allowed less than a third the air drag of a conventional passenger car. But it possessed many other remarkable features: a full body underpan; rubber-mounted full bumper protection around the entire body; finned wheel covers for brake cooling; a radically sloped, compound, curved windshield dictated by wind tunnel tests. The narrow air intake was supplemented by two ducted fans for engine cooling; these were ample for the deep-breathing 392 engine.

This writer drove the Dart/Diablo in Manheim during the preparation of this book, and was impressed with its power and quality of construction, fit and finish. Evidently, everything Virgil Exner said about Ghia's ability was true. The Dart performed and handled like a conventional Chrysler, however; we were unable to get up to speeds where its streamlining advantages became apparent. Some features obviously bespoke the Dart's prototypal purposes: There was much distortion in the compound curved windshield, and the considerable brightwork in the cockpit unfavorably affected visibility. The most disconcerting impression was given by the tapering sides; the edges of the side panels were completely invisible from the driver's seat. Since the car had an Imperial chassis, it was no midget; one had to be extremely careful navigating tight quarters. In appearance, the vehicle is unmatched as a head-spinner; it looks like nothing else on four wheels. And that, of course, was Virgil Exner's intent when he built it.

1958 Imperial Crown, readily identifiable by a crown built into fender script; Crown interior.

1958 New Yorker four-door sedan.

Another idea car of the period, but one disliked intensely by Exner, was the 1958 Imperial d'Elegance — a mock-up borrowing a few ideas from the production Imperial, combined with several new design features. The d'Elegance predicted the rear deck slope of the forthcoming Valiant, and in fender and headlight treatment anticipated future Imperials. Features included flush door and window handles, hidden headlamps, and a squared-off steering wheel. The car was finished in metallic blue with matching leather interior, but it was only a styling exercise and had no mechanical underpinnings. Like the concurrent Plymouth Cabana, an

Exner's radical Dart show car, only fifty-four inches high, held four passengers comfortably. Wind-cheating Dart front-end neutralized air drag. Chrysler called the Dart a "hydroplane on wheels." Styling had been aerodynamically tested by Ghia in Turin, Italy.

Dart's retractable hardtop was later deleted, fins were cut down and car was renamed Diablo. It resides today in the collection of Paul Stern, in Manheim, Pennsylvania.

experimental four-door hardtop station wagon, its purpose was strictly investigative.

Ordinarily, what Chrysler called "The Bold, New Look of Success" would have been a salable package for model year 1958. But the times were wrong. Not only had a severe recession hit, with consequent burgeoning of foreign imports and economy cars like the Rambler; but work stoppages seriously curtailed production during peak demand periods. Corporately, Chrysler recorded a $33.8 million loss against its previous year's profit of nearly $120 million — with literally the same line of cars.

The company could not take comfort in a general industry decline, for its share of the market was also down to 14.9 percent, from nearly twenty percent in 1957. Yet Chrysler forged ahead, breaking into the European industry by acquiring a twenty-five percent share in Simca. Chrysler recovered enough to record an $11 million profit in the last quarter of 1958.

Plans were also afoot to further separate Imperial from Chrysler. Since the very first one in 1926, Imperials had been built at the Jefferson Avenue assembly plant in Detroit. Commencing with the 1959 models, Imperial production would shift to its own assembly plant on Warren Avenue in Dearborn (formerly occupied by Graham-Paige and DeSoto). Warren Avenue offered a million square feet and room for the considerable handwork involved in building Imperials. Twenty-seven cars an hour could be produced, using the first automatic body switching assembly system in

Exner later expressed disdain for another 1958 exercise, the Imperial d'Elegance. Cockpit was more functional than outside lines suggest.

1958 Imperial LeBaron.

1958 Imperial Crown convertible.

the industry. Despite low sales in 1958, Imperials still accounted for more than one-fifth of Chrysler-Imperial Division production; but volume was down by almost two-thirds. Division general manager E. C. Quinn picked

The 'Lion Hearted' 1959 Chrysler featured new wedge-head 383-cid engine. Windsor two-door hardtop shown.

1959 Saratoga four-door sedan.

this as a good cue to step aside; he was replaced by former Sales vice president C.E. Briggs. Chrysler dropped to twelfth place in the sales race, and naturally was glad to put 1958 behind and look forward to 1959.

Lead times being what they are in Detroit, model lineups are not as flexible as market conditions. Thus the 1959 offerings were not greatly altered, despite the 1958 doldrums. Car for car, Chrysler and Imperial models were almost exactly the same as 1958. Except for two new spring

colors, turquoise and bright red, few midyear changes occurred either. A 300-like Windsor called the X3 was planned, but was withdrawn at the last minute. However, a revived Windsor convertible was offered in quantity (two had been produced in the 1958 series). Styling revisions were moderate and normal for a two-year-old body design: a new grille, heavier headlight eyebrows and another ill-fitting taillight design. Side trim shifted to an upward-sloping sweep spear on the Windsor and Saratoga, and to a silver spear on the New Yorker. Two-toning was applied in different ways; e.g., to color panels on the roof rather than to the entire roof. The Imperial received a new toothy grille, revisions to side trim and new upholstery.

Model Body Style (passengers)	Price	W.B.(in)	Weight (lb)
Series MC1-L Windsor			
sedan, 4dr (6)	$3,204	122	3,800
hardtop, 2dr (6)	3,289	122	3,830
hardtop, 4dr (6)	3,353	122	3,735
convertible (6)	3,620	122	3,950
Town and Country wagon (9)	3,878	122	4,070
Town and Country wagon (6)	3,691	122	4,045
Series MC2-M Saratoga			
sedan, 4dr (6)	$3,966	126	4,010
hardtop, 2dr (6)	4,026	126	3,970
hardtop, 4dr (6)	4,104	126	4,035
Series MC3-H New Yorker			
sedan, 4dr (6)	$4,424	126	4,120
hardtop, 2dr (6)	4,476	126	4,080
hardtop, 4dr (6)	4,533	126	4,165
convertible (6)	4,890	126	4,270
Town and Country wagon (9)	5,212	126	4,360
Town and Country wagon (6)	4,997	126	4,295
300E hardtop, 2dr (6)	5,319	126	4,290
300E convertible (6)	5,749	126	4,350
Series MY1-L Custom Imperial			
sedan, 4dr (6)	$5,016	129	4,735
Southampton hardtop, 2dr (6)	4,910	129	4,675
Southampton hardtop, 4dr (6)	5,016	129	4,745
Series MY1-M Crown Imperial			
sedan, 4dr (6)	$5,647	129	4,830
Southampton hardtop, 2dr (6)	5,403	129	4,810
Southampton hardtop, 4dr (6)	5,647	129	4,840
convertible (6)	5,774	129	4,850
Series MY1-H LeBaron Imperial			
sedan, 4dr (6)	$6,103	129	4,865
Southampton hardtop, 4dr (6)	6,103	129	4,875
Crown Imperial			
limousine (8)	$16,000+	149½	5,960

1959 Saratoga two-door hardtop looked clean, though taillights seemed a bit unnatural. Note roof insert panel.

1959 New Yorker four-door sedan appeared best in formal black.

What *was* new in 1959 was the Chrysler engine lineup, with less expensive, wedge-shaped combustion chambers replacing the hemispherical and polyspherical configurations. For the Windsor, Chrysler introduced one of its most popular and most reliable V-8's, the 383-cubic inch, 305-horsepower model with 10:1 compression and 4.03 x 3.75 inches bore and stroke. The same engine yielded 325 horsepower on the Saratoga. The New Yorker and 300E used a 413-cubic inch unit (4.18 x 3.75) producing 350 horsepower on the New Yorker and 380 on the 300E. Chrysler developed a new front suspension with widely variable cam adjustments, new torsion bars and anchor point seals and new ball joints. An Imperial option was an automatically self-leveling rear suspension; a compressor acting on nylon-reinforced, flexible rubber air springs was the controlling mechanism.

The Chrysler 300E retained its distinctive trapezoidal grille and clean flanks bearing the traditional 300 emblem and spear, but wore 1959-style taillights, rear bumper and deck. The '59 items did nothing to improve 300 styling; a rumor floated that the 300E had lost its teeth. Dual four-barrel carburetors remained, but the new wedge engine was 101 pounds lighter than the hemi and lacked the wild camming, hydraulic valve lifters and optional Bendix fuel injection.

Chrysler further damaged the 300's image by promoting it as a luxury car. A full range of New Yorker-like equipment was offered, including a new invention — swivel seats that swung outward as the doors were opened. Other accessories included auto pilot, air conditioning, comprehensive radio and heater controls, power windows, seats and antenna, tinted glass and miscellaneous minor tinsel. An attractive but impractical 300 wheel cover was introduced bearing a black-painted center disc and a gear-shaped device to hold the red, white and blue 300 emblem (which also appeared on the rear seat). Leather still swathed the 300's interior in a new, porous, woven texture, and exterior colors were still limited to black, red, copper, turquoise-gray and tan. But all this fluff, and the concentration on such nonfunctional ephemera as brake-heating wheel covers with phoney hubs naturally made many people wonder if the 300E wasn't a paper tiger.

But it appears they were wrong. One of the most interesting evaluations was made by *Motor Trend's* Bill Callahan in March of 1959: "Performance of the 300E tops its predecessor by a good margin," Callahan wrote. "The 300E this year weighs a little over 4,300 pounds at the curb. The big 380 hp engine (with 10.1:1 compression, improved TorqueFlite transmission and 3.31 to 1 rear end) handles this poundage with no difficulty at all. His claim seems to be validated by both his and Chrysler Engineering's performance figures:

	Chrysler Engineering		Callahan
	300D	300E	300E
0-30 mph	3.7 seconds	3.4 seconds	3.4 seconds
0-60 mph	9.7 seconds	8.3 seconds	8.2 seconds
0-90 mph	20.6 seconds	17.6 seconds	not tested

Yet with only 690 300E's produced, the 1959 version could hardly be called a sales success. If profit wasn't its purpose, Chrysler at least expected the 300E to break even. This was the lowest production of 300-letter series cars until 1963, when only 400 appeared; even tail-enders 300K and 300L of 1964-65 sold in much higher quantities.

1959 Imperial two-door Southampton hardtop.

Happily, the breadwinning 1959 Windsor batted higher. It sold well and rated many 'best in class' kudos from test publications. *Motor Trend,* impressed with performance of the 1959 Plymouth Fury but unhappy with its brakes, was agreeably surprised to find the Windsor the equal of the Fury in acceleration and much better on the binders — though Windsor's 230 square inches of braking area (251 inches optional) compared favorably with the Fury's 184. "The seventh of a series of 60-to-20 mph slowdowns in rapid succession required quite a bit of pedal pressure," technical editor Charles Nerpel reported of the Windsor, "and on the eighth stop the brakes were at full fade; all the pressure we could apply produced only 15 feet per second during each second of deceleration. [But] the extra 21 square inches offered in the larger size drum option will provide an additional margin of stopping safety for heavy loads, high speeds and station wagons, and is closer to the 125 square inches per ton that brake engineers consider to be the minimum. . . . Quick steering, good braking, effortless acceleration, and wide visibility fore and aft" was how the Windsor shaped up to *Motor Trend.* "It is not likely that normal road touring will ever produce the need for as much stability as encountered on the test course, but should this happen the front suspension will keep the wheels in good position for control."

The Saratoga and New Yorker models for 1959 were much like those of the past year, with a new variety of jacquard and nylon interiors and revised exterior trims. Back-up lights were made standard for the first time. One option was a rearview mirror mounted sensor; it controlled the headlight dipping formerly tended to by a foot switch or automatic 'seeing eye' units mounted on dashboards. The new swivel seats, which were standard on the 300E and optional on all other Chryslers and Imperials, were commonly found on New Yorkers. The swivel seat was a clever idea, facilitating entry and egress from Exner's low-roofed automobiles. The pivotal point for the seats was the rear center; the unit turned on nylon bearings mounted at the front. The seat could be manually locked into permanent position with a latch on the side, but in the 'automatic' position the seat would swivel outward as the door next to it was opened.

Overall, 1959 was not as good a year as Chrysler had hoped. Another loss, of $5.4 million, was recorded. Even a sales gain of about 20,000 Chryslers and 7,000 Imperials was not enough to offset several problems including a major steel strike and heavy expenses in the fourth quarter for model conversion, warehousing and imported steel to substitute for the domestic product.

Chrysler might have been consoled; 1959 was not much of a year for many standard sized cars. The Edsel, product of untold millions in market research and promotion, was fast proving Ford's biggest mistake since the war. Sales were also uninspiring in the middle-range, full-size car market. Though most makes increased their production over rock-bottom 1958, few were up very strongly; some stalwarts like Buick were actually down.

At the same time, the public was fast warming to the imports and what few domestic economy cars there were. With its Lark, Studebaker sales in calendar year 1959 shot up to 153,000 against a dismal 56,000 (combined with Packard) the year before. Rambler, which had come from literally nowhere, soared from twelfth to seventh place between 1957 and 1958, when it sold 217,000 cars and in 1959 was fourth, with almost twice that many.

"An anticipated rising level of retail demand" was promised for 1960, which would see Plymouth Division's new compact Valiant enter the lists to do battle with the horde of foreign economy cars and domestic rivals like Chevrolet's Corvair, Studebaker's Lark and Ford's Falcon. In 1960 Rambler would forge past Plymouth in the sales race and build nearly one-half million units, while the standard-sized cars continued to lose ground. A revolution was in the making; the 'foreign invasion' scoffed at by Detroit executives as late as 1955 was now full scale, requiring heroic replies by the domestic producers.

The future also seemed limited for the school of styling epitomized by the tail fin. Virgil Exner once recalled, "By 1959 it was obvious that I'd given birth to a Frankenstein. The fins of the Forward Look were copied by

1959 300E, on paper the most powerful letter series yet, used 413-cid wedge head V-8 and featured swivel seat option.

just about everybody, rarely with good results." The reader may recall that by 1959 the fin dominated the industry — modestly on Fords and Mercurys, garishly on Lincolns and Buicks, grossly on Cadillacs and Chevrolets. Even the independents succumbed. Studebaker created heavy, concave, flaring fins on its Hawks beginning in 1957. Rambler designed even uglier bent affairs in 1958. To its credit the Edsel didn't mimic these developments, but it ushered in other styling techniques equally bizarre, to which the public reacted with closed purse strings.

Alex Sarantos Tremulis, famed designer of the Tucker and styling contributor to Kaiser-Frazer and later Ford, is one of those who could say he told them so. As early as 1954, in a Ford styling meeting, Alex told design vice president George Walker, "I see a bomb on the horizon and its name is Volkswagen." Walker had erased Tremulis' comments from the minutes with the admonition that, were they heard by higher brass, Tremulis would be laughed out — or walked out — of the Ford Design Center. Later Tremulis did a sketch of the plug-ugly 1958 Oldsmobile, adding musical notes to the four chrome bars on its glittering flanks. "I thought that summed the situation up perfectly," he said. "We designers were about to suffer the fruit of the seeds we had helped plant — the sins of the forefathers being visited on . . . the forefathers!" Raymond Loewy, whose staff under Bob Bourke turned out the magnificent 1953-54 Studebaker coupes, had feuded with Detroit for years over the same subject. "I had a motto," he told this writer: " 'Weight Is The Enemy.' But everywhere you looked from 1955-60, it was chrome and more chrome, huge excess gobs of metal, immense overhang not only at the front and rear, but also at the sides."

The public finally bit the bullet, and stopped buying these flagrant assaults on the tastes of humanity and resources of the planet. But Chrysler-Imperial Division still seemed to shrug off the blatant proof that old concepts weren't any good. "There will never be," said C.E. Briggs, "a small Chrysler."

CHAPTER 8

Tailfins to Turbines

A CHRYSLER PERSONALITY desiring to remain anonymous in this narrative, views the 1960-64 period as the crux of Chrysler's postwar history. By 1962, the "Never a Small Chrysler" aphorism had become part of the corporate lexicon. It summarized a basic conservatism that had set in with higher management. "Can you imagine what might have happened if we'd decided to retain the initiative?" he asked me after a long discussion of Chrysler in the sixties. "Suppose for example we'd have surrendered to the inevitable and built a small Chrysler — a 1962 Cordoba. Or we could have called it DeSoto — with the big DeSoto gone the name was available. We were still riding on the crest of our engineering and styling leadership; we could have pulled off the greatest coup of the decade. We'd still be riding high today. But it didn't happen. And a radical approach like that will not happen again in the forseeable future. It wouldn't be inaccurate to say, in fact, that after Colbert and Exner left, a sort of hibernation has set in. The company's been going downhill since."

Such a statement bears pondering. Chrysler's history is not one of steady success but of several successes; this implies it has seen as many failures. The 1946-48 period was one of advances, in sales if not in technology — the postwar seller's market saw to that. The 1949-54 period was one of decline, arrested by success again in 1955 and 1957. But 1958 saw Chrysler plunging into difficulty again, as did 1959. Neither the sixties nor the seventies has been exactly appetizing from the standpoint of Highland Park; the history of alternative highs and lows continued in those decades.

From 1960 to 1964 Chrysler could claim a generally improving position, as it blithely sold cars that were — in retrospect — oversized, overweight, dangerously fast yet generally tardy in reacting to driver control, and at times horrendously styled. These cars flew in the face of ultimate reality — Chrysler could and would build a small model eventually — but it was not evident at the time to corporate management. The company had the Valiant and the Dart, with intermediates to follow, which would handle the temporary fetish for little cars. Chrysler, they calculated, would remain the pretentious big car it had always been.

The most important engineering breakthrough for 1960 was the Chrysler unit body (Imperial retained its separate body and chassis). Chrysler Engineering was by now confident that unit construction would provide significant advantages in mass-produced cars: tighter, rattle-free bodies, for example, without the penalty of added expense.

The unit body first appeared in production with the 1922 Lancia. By 1960 it had long been a feature of American Motors, having sprung from AMC predecessors Nash and Hudson. The idea was mainly sparked by the aircraft industry, where technology had proven that a body might be built at great saving of weight and material if the body was engineered to distribute stress over its entire structure: the 'monocoque' principle. Unit

Car A600 was a prototype unit-body model, extensively modified with 1955 Chrysler-DeSoto sheet metal. Note its low build, '55 Imperial front bumpers and '55 New Yorker wheel covers. Lack of windshield wipers may indicate recent wind tunnel testing.

A600 unit construction and torsion bars.   A600 midship transmission.

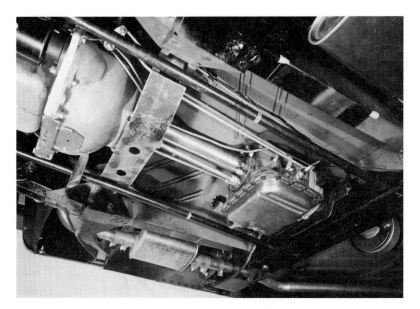

construction also eliminated the traditional method of attaching a body to a frame with flexible mountings, then attempting to later increase frame stiffness by reinforcing the body.

Chrysler envisioned a unit-construction car body made from steel stampings and box- or channel-section steel frames to form a hollow unit. The lower half had to be particularly stiff in order to support the body and drive train, but this rigidity could be attained by the integral, or unitized attachment of the upper half of the body. The weld succeeded the nut and bolt as the main means of sticking the bits together, reducing the chance of bolts working loose as miles piled up. The lack of an underframe aided the stylists by making it easier to lower the floor, and hence the body line.

The unit body had never totally penetrated industry thinking because of several significant drawbacks. Its structural stress distribution, for example, had always been a matter of catch-as-catch-can — one either achieved it when he built his unit box, or he didn't; and if not, he didn't know about it till the job was done. Then he had to resort to reinforcements, which added more weight and cost, often making it more complicated and expensive than a separate body and frame structure. In addition, it was harder to face-lift and retool unit bodies, owing to their all-of-a-piece construction. Finally, unit construction was particularly susceptible to corrosion, which could do little long-term damage to a conventional frame but could disrupt the entire rigidity of the unit body-frame in a startlingly rapid time. Nash especially had suffered from the corrosion problem.

Chrysler's theory on rust was that, in any case, things couldn't be much worse than they were already. Rust was one of the leading problems on the 1957-59 models, possibly the result of the company's relative inexperience in building bodies (which had previously been supplied by Briggs). Some Chrysler executives maintain that sales problems in 1958-59 were the direct result of the rapid-rotting 1957 models, which had sold in droves but had rusted in equally impressive numbers. American Motors had begun dipping its bodies in pools of zinc chromate in 1958; Chrysler also elected to do this. The engineers decided that an eighteen- to twenty-two-inch dip was sufficient, but Chrysler unit shells were also passed through seven baths in the rustproofing process, including cleaners, rinses, phosphate coatings and Bonderite, the last for a better painting surface.

Chrysler engineering prowess was also turned to the problem of calculating unit body stress before the fact, rather than afterwards as had been traditional. Body stress factors were reduced to mathematical equations and then checked by computers, which had just come into their own in 1960. It was a typically Chrysler performance, accomplishing hitherto unreached technical goals with apparent ease. And the cars *were* quieter, more solid and less prone to corrosion than any since the old Briggs units. They were also expensive; the annual face-lifting vogue required costly changes or all-new body jigs every year, the one unit-body problem that even Chrysler couldn't entirely solve.

Some companies had in the past rejected the unit body for a variety of compromises. The 1951 Kaiser, for example, used a series of subassemblies bolted together and attached to body panels of the current style configuration — an arrangement that Kaiser-Frazer engineers felt gave the best of both types of construction. Chrysler's approach involved a front substructure to support the engine and suspension, which was anchored at ten spots; but a boxed longitudinal frame section led rearward, supporting the drive-line and rear suspension. Structural twist tests on four-door sedans indicated a one-hundred percent improvement in rigidity and a forty percent gain in beam strength.

The 1960 Chrysler and Imperial lineup follows:

1960 Windsor two-door hardtop.

Model Body Style (passengers)	Price	W.B.(in)	Weight(lb)
Series PC-1L Windsor			
sedan, 4dr (6)	$3,194	122	3,815
hardtop, 2dr (6)	3,279	122	3,855
hardtop, 4dr (6)	3,343	122	3,850
convertible (6)	3,623	122	3,855
Town and Country wagon (9)	3,814	122	4,390
Town and Country wagon (6)	3,733	122	4,235
Series PC2-M Saratoga			
sedan, 4dr (6)	$3,929	126	4,010
hardtop, 2dr (6)	3,989	126	4,030
hardtop, 4dr (6)	4,067	126	4,035
Series PC3-H New Yorker			
sedan, 4dr (6)	$4,409	126	4,145
hardtop, 2dr (6)	4,461	126	4,175
hardtop, 4dr (6)	4,518	126	4,175
convertible (6)	4,875	126	4,185
Town and Country wagon (9)	5,131	126	4,535
Town and Country wagon (6)	5,022	126	4,515
300F hardtop, 2dr (6)	5,411	126	4,270
300F convertible (6)	5,841	126	4,310
Series PY1-L Custom Imperial			
sedan, 4dr (6)	$5,029	129	4,700
Southampton hardtop, 2dr (6)	4,923	129	4,655
Southampton hardtop, 4dr (6)	5,029	129	4,670
Series PY1-M Crown Imperial			
sedan, 4dr (6)	$5,647	129	4,770
Southampton hardtop, 2dr (6)	5,403	129	4,720
Southampton hardtop, 4dr (6)	5,647	129	4,765
convertible (6)	5,774	129	4,820
Series PY1-H LeBaron Imperial			
sedan, 4dr (6)	$6,318	129	4,860
Southampton, 4dr (6)	6,318	129	4,835
Crown Imperial			
limousine (8)	$16,000+	149½	5,960

Detail improvements for 1960 included the first four-way hazard flashers. Standard on the Imperial and optional on Chryslers was a self-activating version of the 1959 swivel seat, which pivoted outward through an automatic latch release when either front door was opened. An electroluminescent instrument panel was also adopted: Current passed through conductive surfaces, lighting a layer of phosphorescent ceramic material that glowed in the dark. A sprayed-on coating covered an opaque plastic film containing the dial markings. This made them stand out brightly with minimum visual interference.

1960 300F hardtop and convertible.

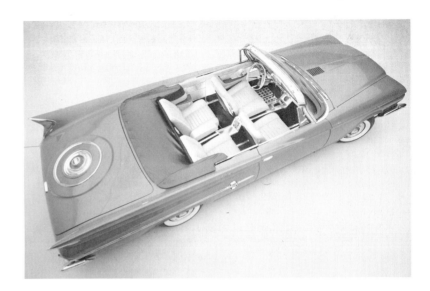

Imperial concentrated on driver comfort for 1960. A high-backed driver seat with added foam rubber padding, adjustable spot air-conditioning beneath the steering column, a six-way power seat with a single rotary knob control, auto-pilot speed selector and automatic headlamp beam changer were all new features. The base Imperial was named Custom, and was upholstered in crown-pattern nylon. A more conservative nylon and vinyl, wool broadcloth or leather upholstery came on the Imperial Crown. The Ghia-built LeBaron again featured wool broadcloth. Virgil Exner's unique two-tone roof finishes now proliferated. The Southampton's were available in solids, two-tones and in combinations with stainless brush-finished steel.

The 300F made a major comeback in 1960, the last before a succession of styling and marketing decisions rendered it near-toothless for 1962. With its restrained styling and handsome blacked-out grille, it wore the flamboyant finned design better than most Chryslers. Thanks to its ram-induction 413-cubic-inch engine and the first four-speed gearbox offered on a postwar Chrysler, it was a hot car indeed. The four-speed was the Pont-à-Mousson box out of the French Facel Vega, for which Chrysler had been supplying a stream of hemi engines since its introduction in 1954. The ram manifolds, optional on Plymouth, Dodge and DeSoto and standard on the 300F, were the first to be used in a passenger automobile.

Ram induction had been applied for some time in racing, and experiments designed to measure its effectiveness in production cars had been going on since 1952. Engineers found it possible to calculate intake manifold lengths by experiments using telescoping tubes and an engine dynamometer, concentrating on the mid-range area of 2000 to 3500 rpm, where they hoped to improve engine performance. Thirty inches proved optimum for each ram tube — one for each port. To avoid a multi-tubular appearance, the left cylinder-bank tubes were routed over the top of the engine aft of the carburetor, while the right bank criss-crossed after leaving the left carburetor. Placing the carbs at the ends of the tubes, rather than somewhere in the middle, gave a steady power increase all along the torque curve, eliminating pulsations. The side-mounted carbs were, incidentally, a lot easier to work on; they ran cooler, decreasing the chance of fuel starvation during hot weather. They were also mounted somewhat lower than conventional mid-manifold carburetors, allowing lower hoodlines without eliminating effective air cleaners.

By adjusting the length of the ram tube inner runners, it was possible to produce a torque peak at any given rpm. The smaller ram engines, for example, peaked at 2800 rpm; but shortening the inner tubes of 300's allowed them to peak at 3600 rpm. This gave the 300 faster legs, at figures of 3600-5000 rpm.

Motor Trend tested a 300F with the 375-hp ram-tuned engine, and found it did the standing quarter-mile in sixteen seconds flat, at 85 mph. It handled as well as ever, "so comfortably [that it] requires an extra concentration which only experienced drivers have proved capable of exerting." The magazine felt that the 300F had "traded a measure of its 'brute, racy' feeling for that of a 'sporty, personal type' car, like the four seater Thunderbird." Yet the 300F was apparently a much more potent road machine than the preceding 300E.

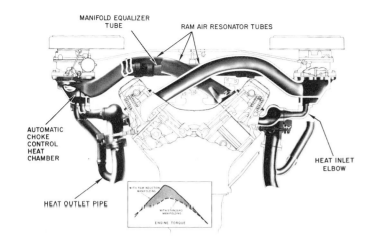

Chrysler diagram of ram induction manifolding, showing long, thirty-inch ram tubes. Short ram 400-hp engines used manual chokes and sweeping exhaust headers without heat riser valves.

1960 Saratoga four-door sedan.

1960 New Yorker four-door hardtop.

1960 New Yorker convertible.

1960 Custom Imperial four-door hardtop.

1960 Custom Imperial two-door hardtop.

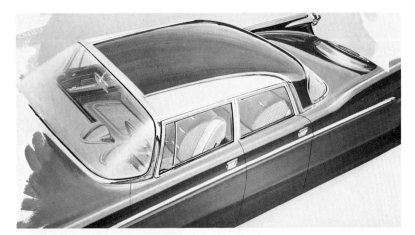

Detail views of 1960 Imperials.

1960 Imperial Crown four-door hardtop.

1960 Imperial LeBaron four-door hardtop.

The optional Pont-à-Mousson four-speed gearbox was fitted to only seven 300F's, all 400-hp models. It was a very tight, notchy gearbox; and its deliberate nature tended to dampen enthusiastic gear-changing, which is probably a blessing to collectors today — parts are virtually unobtainable. Six four-speed cars entered in the flying mile contest at Daytona turned in very consistent performances between 141.5 and 144.9 mph. Hottest was Gregg Ziegler, who scored a best one-way time of 147.783 mph; Ziegler reported that his 300 would do an indicated 60, 90, 120 and 160 mph in the respective gears. Six different axle ratios could be specified between 3.03-3.73:1; Andy Granatelli recorded an average speed of 184.049 mph and a best speed of almost 190 mph with the 3.03. This was hardly in the image of four-seat Thunderbirds.

The 300F's interior was better styled for its purpose than ever before, with the exception of the rev counter. While 300's had never used a tach before, there was a natural spot for one on the 1957-59 models: the hole occupied by the clock, between the speedometer and combination gauge. Except for non-stock modifications, this was never offered. But in 1960, the new Astra-dome instrument panel eliminated so logical a tach position, and Chrysler installed a unit on the center console, well-buried under the dash. Here it was almost useless, certainly no great factor with TorqueFlite equipped models. But it didn't say much for the performance image.

The 300F used four contoured bucket-like seats with the console; both these features were new to the series. Exterior colors were black, red, white and terra cotta. A fake spare tire outline was added to the F's deck, but laughs by the performance press and complaints of enthusiasts would cause it to be deleted again on its successor, the 300G. The latter was a minor update of the F, the four-speed option replaced by a floor-mounted three-speed; Chrysler switched it back to fifteen-inch wheels for the first time since 1956.

The 300G's interior was similar, with a different 'basket weave' seat material and 1961 exterior styling. Again Gregg Ziegler found himself setting the pace at the Daytona trials, 143 mph for the flying mile. Mechanics were unaltered, the G retaining the 375-hp engine and 400-hp option, both with ram induction.

For one final time in 1961, Chrysler styling was of the finned school. The model lineup was again hardly disturbed, making a five-year run of nearly identical offerings — a record for the postwar Chrysler. The changes included listing the 300 as a separate model, elimination of the pillar-type sedans from all Imperial lines and a shuffle of Chrysler model names from Windsor-Saratoga-New Yorker to Newport-Windsor-New Yorker:

Model Body Style (passengers)	Price	W.B.(in)	Weight (lb)
Series RC1-L Newport			
sedan, 4dr (6)	$2,964	122	3,710
hardtop, 2dr (6)	3,027	122	3,690
hardtop, 4dr (6)	3,106	122	3,730
convertible (6)	3,444	122	3,760
Town and Country wagon (9)	3,624	122	4,155
Town and Country wagon (6)	3,543	122	4,070
Series RC2-M Windsor			
sedan, 4dr (6)	$3,220	122	3,730
hardtop, 2dr (6)	3,305	122	3,710
hardtop, 4dr (6)	3,369	122	3,765
Series RC3-H New Yorker			
sedan, 4dr (6)	$4,125	126	4,055
hardtop, 2dr (6)	4,177	126	4,065
hardtop, 4dr (6)	4,263	126	4,100
convertible (6)	4,594	126	4,070
Town and Country wagon (9)	4,873	126	4,455
Town and Country wagon (6)	4,766	126	4,425
Series RC4-P 300G			
hardtop, 2dr (4)	$5,413	126	4,260
convertible, 2dr (4)	5,843	126	4,315
Series RY1-L Custom Imperial			
Southampton hardtop, 2dr (6)	$4,925	129	4,715
Southampton hardtop, 4dr (6)	5,111	129	4,740
Series RY1-M Crown Imperial			
Southampton hardtop, 2dr (6)	$5,405	129	4,790
Southampton hardtop, 4dr (6)	5,649	129	4,855
convertible (6)	5,776	129	4,865
Series RY1-H LeBaron Imperial			
Southampton hardtop, 4dr (6)	$6,428	129	4,875
Crown Imperial			
limousine (8)	$16,000 +	149½	5,960

Prototype evolution of the 1961 Chrysler; from an ornate to a relatively clean approach.

A radically changing Imperial was produced during 1959 through 1961. From left to right: 1959, 1961, 1960 models.

Details of clay models for the 1961 Imperial; the last idea, reviving classic-style headlamps, was seen in production.

The 1961 Imperial line was considerably altered, though it still retained the basic 1960 shell. Its fins were, sadly, more outlandish than ever — Styling seemed to get carried totally away. The classic influence that always hung over Exner drove him to great lengths in 1961: heavily chrome-plated free-standing headlamps and taillamps were adopted, the former pocketed in a curve of the fenders, the latter dangling from towering fins. The 1961

Imperial was an ungainly package, exemplifying everything that was wrong with an era now rightly under fire.

Inside, improvements were more practical: The Imperial gained a better dashboard layout — an upright, fully instrumented, rectangular bank of gauges flanked by the usual set of TorqueFlite buttons and heater controls left and right — and it was well padded. But these improvements were small compensation for the bad taste of the overall design and — despite Mencken's dim view of the taste levels of the American public — the buyers seemed to realize it. While Chrysler in 1961 had its first 100,000-car year since 1957, Imperial dropped, almost twenty-five percent, to less than 13,000 units for the calendar year.

As a Division, Chrysler's business picture was excellent. Aside from its 100,000 cars — against an eleven-percent overall decline in the new car market that year — Chrysler had seemingly justified what general manager Claire Briggs called its "marked disdain for any junior edition of our car." At the end of 1961, Chrysler was the only medium-priced competitor without a scaled-down companion model, while Buick had the Special, Pontiac the Tempest, Oldsmobile the F-85, Mercury the Comet. This was not as singular as it may seem, because every Chrysler dealer was teamed with Plymouth, and the compact Valiant was available to him. (In export markets like Great Britain, the new compact was even called the Chrysler Valiant.) "Instead of risking the Chrysler image in any car-size contest," said Briggs, "we have made capital of our car's tradition. The Newport was introduced as a lower-priced, full-sized Chrysler that offered a tempting alternative to buyers exploring the upper strata of the low-price field." This was markedly important in Chrysler's success, for the Newport sold 57,000

Imperial prototypes envisioned two different window treatments; the less radical won.

In 1961, this was the Imperial Crown Southampton four-door hardtop.

The 1961 four-door hardtop version of the Imperial LeBaron Southampton.

copies in 1961, against only 41,000 Windsors sold in this position the year before.

But Chrysler's upsurge was one of few bright spots for the Corporation as a whole in 1961. With Imperial production removed to the former DeSoto plant in Dearborn, output was sporadic; and the assembly line worked only on alternate weeks. In the hottest sector of the industry, Plymouth and Dodge did not do well. Plymouth, which had run up 484,000 units for fourth place in the production race of 1960, built 310,000 cars for

1961 Newport four-door sedan.

1961 Newport two-door hardtop.

1961 Newport convertible.

seventh place in 1961. Dodge had built 411,000 cars for sixth place in 1960; now it was 221,000 and ninth. Chrysler Corporation's overall share of the domestic new car market dropped from fourteen percent in 1960 to less than eleven percent in 1961; unit sales plummeted some thirty-one percent, from close to a million to only 632,000. Though the company remained in the black, 1961 earnings were only $11 million — about a third of what they were in 1960. Corporately, the best thing Tex Colbert could say about 1961 was that it had seen "the reduction of breakeven levels." This was not enough. Heads would have to roll.

Actually, a management shakeup had been in progress since the late spring of 1960. Colbert had turned the presidency over to his "heir apparent," William C. Newberg, on April 28, 1960. Newberg, a close friend and associate of Colbert, had been the first executive vice president in the history of Chrysler. He had risen alongside Colbert since joining the company as a test driver in 1942. During the war Newberg had been assigned the B-29 engine plant in Chicago (later headquarters of the ill-fated Tucker Corporation). By 1947 he had become president of Airtemp Division, then Dodge vice president in 1951, Corporate v.p. in 1953. The executive prefix had come in 1959. But Newberg had relieved Colbert as president for only sixty-four days when he was forced to retire, following revelations that he had personal financial interests in several of Chrysler's suppliers. Newberg's departure destroyed Colbert's and his rapport. After Colbert reassumed the presidency, Newberg became a bitter opponent of his former colleague — his dislike and that of others proved fatal in the spring of 1961.

Chrysler stockholders met at Highland Park in mid-April. Though he controlled a majority of proxies, Colbert was in trouble: First quarter shipments were down fifty-seven percent from 1960, and almost 7,000 salaried employees had been laid off. Colbert reported, "If we had been able to combine our progress in cost reduction with a comparable improvement in sales, we would have a highly satisfactory report for you." At that point chaos broke loose.

A stockholder stood up, holding a letter from Bill Newberg. "It is my conviction," the letter said, "that we cannot ever again have a strong Chrysler under the czarist rule of Mr. Colbert." Newberg noted that Chrysler's market share had not approached twenty percent in years, that in the past three years the company had lost $7 million on sales of $8 billion, not to mention *$20 million* in the first quarter of 1961 alone. Colbert, Newberg said, "had no policy except that of frequent and unpredictable change that throws off balance not Chrysler's competitors, but Chrysler itself." It was the first time since the founding of the company that anyone had so bluntly challenged Chrysler's chief executive.

Colbert had a searing reply to the Newberg letter: "It is unfortunate that the author of this statement did not see fit to be here." A stockholder answered that Newberg's selection as president "doesn't reflect very well

1961 Windsor four-door sedan. William E. Newberg and Lynn A. Townsend.

1961 New Yorker Town & Country wagon.

on your judgment, sir." "Mr. Newberg concealed his interests," Colbert shot back to a welter of boos.

It was a rough day for the Chrysler president. When a stockholder asked him how much it had cost to investigate company officers in the wake of the Newberg scandal, Tex didn't know. Someone in the audience said, "Don't you know *anything* about your company?" A former executive, Karl Horvath, stood up: "Who are you trying to fool, Mr. Colbert? You've got your head in the sand and your flanks exposed to attack. You do all your planning with one hand on the panic button and the other in the till." Colbert eventually carried the day — the complainers were in the majority only at this meeting — but the word went out quickly afterward that Chrysler was in the market for a new president. Colbert, it was implied, might stay on as board chairman. Chrysler was; Colbert didn't.

In May, UPI reported that a group of directors had asked Tex to resign. Colbert denied it. But on July 27 the expected happened: Colbert retired, not only from the presidency and chairmanship, but also as a director of Chrysler Canada Ltd. and Chrysler Corporation. His replacement as president was former administrative v.p. Lynn A. Townsend; G.H. Love became chairman.

The Colbert years can be viewed as typical of Chrysler's mixed history. When Tex took over from K.T. Keller in 1950, the company was moribund, the products uninteresting and growing unsalable. Colbert pushed the radical styling ideas of Virgil Exner, while continuing to support a forceful engineering program that produced the hemi engine, pushbutton automatic, torsion bars and the unit body. He gamely borrowed $250 million from Prudential to refinance these activities, and he was rewarded with a strong resurgence in 1955 and 1957. Whatever one may think about his controversial last years, and the scandal attached to his temporary successor, one must recognize that Tex Colbert managed to keep surprises coming. It was really the last interesting period for the company in design and engineering. All too soon thereafter, Chrysler products began to follow rather than to lead. Today the Corporation publicly admits that this is the policy. Some officers actually seem to be proud of it.

Another casualty of the management upheaval was Virgil Exner. "It was the change of presidents that caused his departure," Maury Baldwin

1961 300G and engine compartment.

remembers. "Exner's philosophy of design — he really leaned toward the elegant kind of automobile — was not in line anymore. Really I suppose what they [management] wanted was a more conventional type of car. It was a shame, because Exner was one of the more imaginative designers." Virgil Exner, Jr., adds: "Dad was with them until 1964, actually. He maintained an office for a couple of years, but was no longer the vice president of styling." The younger Exner doesn't feel his father's departure had as much to do with product as with politics. "There was all this business about payola going on, and Chrysler was in some pretty big financial troubles. [Exner] was really a total pawn in the whole works, and it was time for a change, their image needed changing. It was the beginning of the 'smart marketing' approach at Chrysler. But it's still his design section that is operating there — he built it up from seventeen to what it basically is today — whatever it is today." Exner undoubtedly left a legacy of styling originality and great imagination at Chrysler. It was never matched before he arrived, and it is safe to say it will never be matched

again. It is also possible to conclude that Exner's was the greatest single influence in making Chrysler the interesting entity it was in the fifties and early sixties.

Virgil Exner left still supporting the tail fin. "It gave our cars a visible difference," he said, while noting that it would not have been useful if the overall designs of the cars hadn't been right. "This same basic concept is being used on our cars today and probably will continue." He referred here to the 1962 cars, whose wedge shape, he said "lends itself to an infinite variation of accent lines. For many years automobile bodies were distributed about fifty to seventy as between hood and rear deck treatment. Many of them still retain that proportion. Starting in 1960 with the Valiant, we lengthened hood lines so that we had about sixty percent of the focus lines directed forward. Our whole line of cars this year features that proportionment with the longer hood line contributing to the appearance of power thrusting forward." Future Chryslers would, he felt, have lower belt-lines but not bubble tops, such as GM had been predicting. "Until glass, or some other clear substance, can be developed to more completely reflect

 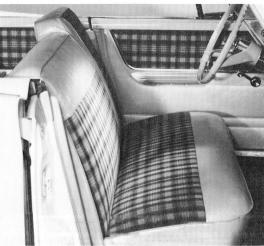

Astra Dome instrument panel of the 1961 Chrysler and Highlander plaid trim in a 1961 Newport.

the sun's heat rays and eliminate glare, stylists might just as well forget bubble domes, see through roofs and the like." Exner received the styling award from the Society of Illustrators for his design of the new 1962 Valiant Signet hardtop. Shortly afterward, his place was taken by Elwood Engel, fresh from Ford and the design of the notably un-Exner-like 1961 Lincoln Continentals. Engel told the press the first thing he was going to do was travel to Cape Canaveral to be inspired for future Chryslers by the NASA rockets. "One presumes," said a commentator, "that he will not look at the rockets with fins."

At the topmost management level, Lynn Townsend moved quickly to usher in a new wave of officers. He created an administrative committee of top decision makers to guide the new firm, among whom was the new administrative vice president, Virgil Boyd. Accountant-trained like Townsend, Boyd had been an American Motors vice president since 1954. Also present in the leadership ranks was 'Flamethrower' John Riccardo, whose nickname was built on his reputation as a tough guy; a hard driver. Riccardo came to Townsend's attention at the company's accountant firm of Touche, Ross, Bailey and Smart, and had joined Highland Park as financial staff executive, International Operations, in 1959. Later Riccardo became Export-Import Division general manager and, in 1961, vice president of Chrysler Canada Ltd. He moved on to head Dodge Sales, manage Chrysler-Plymouth Division and the Corporate marketing staff. Finally becoming vice president in 1967, he succeeded Virgil Boyd as president in 1970. As the dust settled and Townsend's team took control, business improved and stockholders heaved a sigh of relief. The days of turmoil and uncertainty, they thought, were over. But at the product level, the influence of Tex and Ex was present still.

Off the record, Exner was less enthusiastic about the 1962 cars than his press statements implied. "He always referred to them as the picked chickens," Virgil, Jr., says, "because somebody got a wild ass idea up there to make them low in cost. He had a beautiful line designed for '62, but they were cut. He was done out of that series, so he went back and started to develop his next big phase, the short deck-long hood idea mentioned to the press, like the 1962 Dodge. To that he wanted to add a bit of the radiator shape, he saw an opportunity to promote that sort of thing and was dead set on doing it. Of course he never got the chance."

Exner's production 1962 Chryslers lasted only for that model year, being quickly slated for replacement by designs of the Engel team in 1963. Though new-looking, they retained the old body while lopping off the fins. The front end was relatively unaltered from 1961, with the inverted trapezoidal grille and slanted quad-lights; the sides were clean, and the roof lost its contrasting color insert panels.

The model lineup now took advantage of the Chrysler 300's proud reputation. A standard production line of cars bearing the 300 designation was minted, replacing the mid-range Windsor, which in 1961 had replaced the Saratoga. Included in the 300 line were the letter series 300H convertible and hardtop, with a more potent engine — adding some confusion between them and the mass production 300's, which were often nothing

Elwood P. Engel and John J. Riccardo.

Exner's original plans for 1962 envisioned a much more compact, finless Chrysler and Imperial. This is a 300H convertible proposal.

Production '62's shorn of fins; Exner called them "plucked chickens."

more than glorified Windsors with bucket seats. This formula was, however, effective: Chrysler would sell more than 25,000 300's — the highest count for a mid-range model since Saratoga's 37,000 back in 1957.

The power lineup was mainly unchanged from 1961. Newport ran a 361-cubic inch V-8 of 265 hp, the 300 née Windsor a 383-cubic incher producing 305 hp. Standard on the New Yorker, and optional on 300, was a 413-cubic inch unit producing 340 hp, while the 300H came with a 380 hp engine that was also available on the non-letter series 300. The latter lost its ram tubes but actually gained five brake horsepower and, like the 300G before it, retained heavy-duty valve springs, special intake manifold and mechanical tappets, dual four-barrel carburetors and low restriction air cleaners. *Speed Mechanics* listed 0-60 mph in 6.5 seconds for the 300H, holding TorqueFlite in D-2 position. The magazine also reported that the car could achieve 100 mph in less than sixteen seconds. The test car returned 8.5 miles per gallon in city driving and only 13-14 mph on the highway.

The 300H continued to offer four, tan leather bucket seats separated by a center console, a speedometer calibrated to 150 mph, a tachometer and Blue Streak racing tires as standard. Exterior colors were limited to black, festival-red, oyster-white or caramel. Power windows, seats, brakes and steering were fitted to all 300H cars.

To be entirely fair, the non-letter 300 for 1962 wasn't necessarily fangless. One could custom order most of the 300H's performance options, including the largest engine, heavy-duty suspension and — with the 380 power plant — manual transmission. The sporting image was not distorted by offering a 300 station wagon — though no such model had traditionally been part of the mid-range Chryslers — or a pillared sedan, which had

been part of the Windsor range in 1961. Another model deletion, from the New Yorker ranks, was the two-door hardtop. "The New Yorker market was definitely four-door," said a sales executive. Down the line, Newport remained base-priced at less than $3,000, and as in 1961 it offered a Highlander upholstery option in the four-door sedan and hardtop models, with MacDuff tartan interior keyed to five different exterior colors.

In early 1960, these were the 1962 proposals. Left to right: Valiant, Lancer, DeSoto and Imperial. DeSoto, of course, was discontinued early in the 1961 model year.

Dodge, center, emerged relatively the same as it was in this studio photo of February 1960. Imperial, left, was entirely altered.

Model

Body Style (passengers)	Price	W.B.(in)	Weight (lb)
Series SC1-L Newport			
sedan, 4dr (6)	$2,964	122	3,690
hardtop, 2dr (6)	3,027	122	3,650
hardtop, 4dr (6)	3,106	122	3,715
convertible (6)	3,399	122	3,740
Town and Country wagon (9)	3,586	122	4,090
Town and Country wagon (6)	3,478	122	4,060
Series SC2-M 300			
300 hardtop, 2dr (6)	$3,323	122	3,750
300 hardtop, 4dr (6)	3,400	122	3,760
300 convertible (6)	3,883	122	3,815
300H hardtop, 2dr (4)	5,090	122	4,010
300H convertible, (4)	5,461	122	4,080
Series SC3-H New Yorker			
sedan, 4dr (6)	$4,125	126	3,925
hardtop, 4dr (6)	4,263	126	4,005
Town and Country wagon (9)	4,873	126	4,445
Town and Country wagon (6)	4,766	126	4,425
Series SY1-L Custom Imperial			
Southampton hardtop, 2dr (6)	$4,920	129	4,540
Southampton hardtop, 4dr (6)	5,106	129	4,620
Series SY1-M Crown Imperial			
Southampton hardtop, 2dr (6)	$5,400	129	4,650
Southampton hardtop, 4dr (6)	5,644	129	4,680
convertible (6)	5,770	129	4,765
Series SY1-H LeBaron Imperial			
Southampton hardtop, 4dr (6)	$6,422	129	4,725

Like the Chrysler, the Imperial featured only mild die changes but a much-revised appearance. Only a trace remained of the past year's fins; elongated bullet-shaped taillights rode, freestanding atop the rear fenders per the 1955-56 concept. The individually housed headlamps were still present up front, but in general the cars were considerably cleaner looking

1962 300 (non-letter series) four-door hardtop.

1962 Newport Town & Country wagon.

1962 Imperial LeBaron four-door hardtop.

1962 New Yorker four-door hardtop.

and — predictably — they sold better. The Ghia-built limousine was absent for 1962, but would return in 1963. (For details, see the Appendix.)

Nineteen sixty-two was a good year for Chrysler Division — while the marque remained eleventh in the sales standings, close to 120,000 units were built for the calendar year, 12,000 more than in 1961. Earnings by the Corporation, as a whole, increased to $65,400,000 — a reassuring figure after the paltry one of the year before. With the introduction of the 1963 models in October, 1962, sales jumped twenty percent over the fourth quarter of 1961, and the following February the board recommended a two-for-one stock split. Lynn Townsend's administrative committee now included six staff vice presidents — for Engineering, Product Planning, Operations, Administration, Finance and Legal Affairs — and three group vice presidents — for domestic manufacture and sales, international operations and defense/space work. The passing of DeSoto marked the end of combination Dodge-Plymouth franchises: Chrysler-Plymouth became one Division, Dodge another. Each offered its dealers a similar range of Dodges, Plymouths and Valiant-Lancer compacts.

Chrysler model production for 1962 rose 13.8 percent and was the highest since banner year 1955. Again Chrysler remained the only medium-priced competitor without a 'little car,' thanks to the readily available Valiants which shared every Chrysler showroom. But all this was dull business news as far as the public was concerned — the most talked-about Chrysler feat in 1963 was its gas turbine car — certainly the most advanced turbine in the world at the time. An idea the company had been working on for decades now seemed on the verge of production.

Chrysler's interest in gas turbines dated back to before the war, when exploratory investigations concluded that considerable development would be required before such units could be economically produced. After the war, turbine development shifted to aircraft applications, thanks to a grant by the Navy Bureau of Aeronautics. Chrysler built a turboprop engine with fuel economy equal to piston aircraft of the time. Then, in the early fifties, engineers returned to considering a gas turbine for automobiles.

The turbine is not a complex concept, though its feasible production presented — presents — enormous problems. Its main element is a turbine wheel with a ring of blades around its circumference. A mixture of fuel and air flows past the blades, causing the wheel to rotate and produce power. But, while an aircraft turbine usually runs at a steady speed, a car engine

1961 TURBOFLITE, Exner's last show car. Turbine powered, it featured unique canopy roof, flashing light speedometer.

constantly varies speeds: It needs good acceleration for standing starts and passing, plus engine braking to assist in slowing. The automotive device must run quieter, and cooler than the aircraft turbine. And it may not produce exhaust emissions above a certain specified level — though this was not realized then.

All these challenges were tackled by Chrysler's intrepid engineers. A rotating heat exchanger or 'regenerator' was developed that recovered heat from exhaust gases, kept running temperatures low, and fuel mileage acceptable. The problems of flexibility in automotive applications, and production of high-temperature alloys able to withstand the heat of the turbine, were also investigated. Then Chrysler reached the automotive testing stage.

The first turbine car was a stock-looking 1954 Plymouth Belvedere hardtop, its engine rated at one hundred horsepower. It featured the regenerator apparatus to extract heat from the exhaust, transferring heat energy to the incoming air. The car was tested successfully at Chelsea, but only one example was built. A second model, a 1956 Belvedere sedan, was driven cross-country in a test of durability and performance; it was successful in these respects but made only thirteen miles per gallon of fuel. Together these cars made up the 'first generation' turbines; relative to the next generation, their engines were extremely expensive to build.

The 'second generation' began with a 1959 Plymouth hardtop turbine, which first appeared on a 576-mile Detroit-New York run. It produced about 200 horsepower, featured new construction materials and was more efficient; the heat exchanger, for example, was ninety percent efficient against eighty-six percent on the 1956 model. Metallurgical research had now produced fairly inexpensive heat- and oxidation-resistant alloys for engine construction.

The 'third generation' turbines came in three different forms: a stock-appearing 1960 Plymouth, a 2½-ton Dodge truck designed to demonstrate the turbine's versatility and a unique show car designed by Maury Baldwin, which Chrysler called the TurboFlite. "I think this was the last Exner show car," Baldwin says. "We incorporated a lot of interesting things in it. Entrance-wise, the entire cockpit above the beltline lifted to admit passengers. Mounted between the fins was a deceleration flap such as is now used on racing cars, and the headlights were retractable. The car was built by Ghia — we did a three-eighths model and then full-size drawings. It was probably one of the best engineered cars we ever did."

By 1962, Engineering had developed the CR2A gas turbine, first installed in a four-door hardtop Dodge Dart, which again traveled from New York to Los Angeles. This time it scored better fuel economy than a conventional 'control' Dodge traveling alongside. The CR2A differed from earlier turbines by the addition of a variable fuel-nozzle mechanism, which provided engine braking (by shutter action under deceleration) and better performance (by varying the angle of the jet stream to the turbine blades on take-off). The variable nozzles eliminated most of the lag that had accompanied earlier turbines. First-generation models, for example, took seven seconds to go from idle to full output, while the CR2A Dodge did it in 1½ to 2 seconds. Later the CR2A was modified to use twin regenerators,

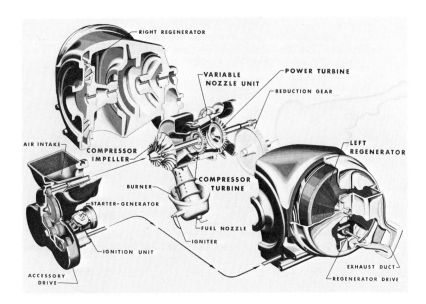

Exploded view of twin regenerator gas turbine engine showing main components.

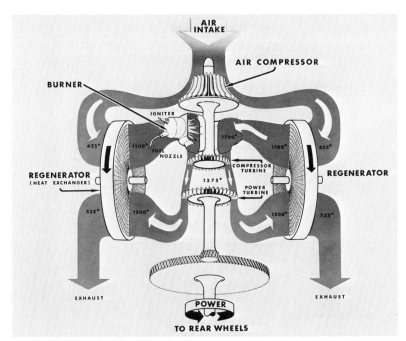

Diagram of twin-regenerator gas turbine engine.

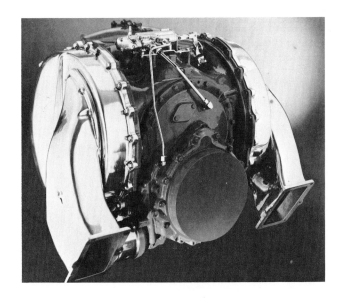

Exterior view of 1962 turbine.

and Chrysler decided to build fifty to seventy-five turbine-powered passenger cars for consumer testing toward the end of 1963.

Aside from its mechanical novelty, the Engel-styled Chrysler turbine unveiled in May, 1963, was a beautifully designed car — though it bore more than a passing resemblance to concurrent Thunderbirds, which Engel had designed for Ford. It was a bucket-seated, four-passenger, two-door hardtop painted turbine-bronze with power steering, brakes and window lifts, automatic transmission and other luxury equipment. Its headlights and back-up lights were in a rotary-blade motif to emphasize its power source; horizontal taillights were set into steeply angled rear fenders. Under the hood was the 'fourth generation' gas turbine.

The new engine's twin regenerators rotated in vertical planes, one on each side, with a centrally controlled burner. It was quieter, lighter and less bulky than the CR2A. Acceleration lag was reduced to 1 to 1½ seconds. Maximum output engine speed after gear reduction shrank from 5360 rpm in the CR2A to only 4680 rpm, and the engine had twenty percent fewer moving parts than a conventional piston powerplant. While its horsepower was down slightly compared to its predecessor, torque was up to 425 foot-pounds, from 375.

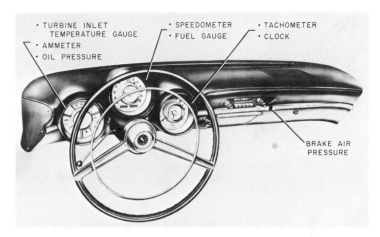

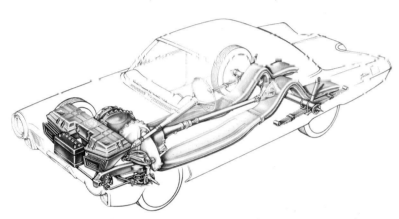

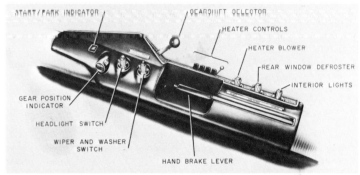

Chrysler had Ghia build fifty turbine cars. They were presented to 'consumer representatives' gleaned from 30,000 inquiries — received after the announcement that the cars would be loaned to the public. Each driver had a car for about three months. All continental forty-eight states were included among locations; owners ranged from twenty-one to seventy years of age. In all, 203 persons drove turbine Chryslers between 1963 and early 1966.

The report issued in 1967 on the testing program noted that the turbine required little or no maintenance compared with the gas engine. But Chrysler never divulged the fuel mileage, which apparently was embarrassing — one out of four drivers complained about it, despite the fact that the cars would run on kerosene, jet fuel, unleaded gasoline or diesel fuel. One out of three drivers disliked the acceleration lag, while the main compliments were directed at the vibrationless acceleration of the turbine cars.

Clean-limbed Chrysler Turbine was an Engel design, built by Ghia.

Turbine's instrument panel, console controls.

Turbine car chassis components.

Chrysler never released a turbine for testing by a motor journalist, though John Lawlor managed to land one surreptitiously toward the end of the research campaign. He was impressed with the car's smoothness, but was disconcerted with the lack of engine braking and the presence of acceleration lag, which he found was about 1-1½ seconds as Chrysler had predicted. Fuel mileage was also disappointing — 11.5 mpg — though the fuel was usually cheap kerosene. Lawlor found sparkling acceleration, reaching 0-60 mph in less than ten seconds. This put to rest the rumor that turbine cars weren't fast.

The 1963 Chrysler emerges. Clay models at various stages represent alternatives considered. They'll try to forget it if you will....

Lawlor wrote in 1973, in *Plymouth-Dodge-Chrysler,* "Getting 11.5 mpg out of a 4,100 pound car that can go from zero to 60 in 11 seconds has begun to look like an attractive proposition, particularly when you consider that the fuel used could be a much cheaper one than today's gasoline." But at the time, Chrysler lost interest in the turbine. The technology to build the cars at mass-production levels still didn't exist, at least not in readily affordable form. The turbine research program went underground again, but it would surface a few years later — as we shall see in the next chapter.

The Chrysler turbine cars suffered a sad fate: All but ten were cut up before the watchful eyes of United States Customs. Since the cars had been manufactured abroad, Chrysler would have been charged duty had it chosen to keep them all on the road — an enormous expense, given the cars' high construction costs. The Corporation did cough up enough to pay the duty on ten, which were dispersed to museums such as Harrah's Automobile Collection and the Chicago Museum of Science and Industry. Two of the ten were retained at the Chelsea proving grounds — and are there yet.

Meanwhile the "crisp, clean, custom look" made its debut with the 1963 Chryslers. "Basically these were done by the Engel regime," Virgil, Jr., comments. There was, however, still a touch of Exner in the sharply creased sides of the front fenders, the bold inverted trapezoidal grilles and the clean flanks. Again the word was passed, "We do not build a junior Chrysler," though the New Yorker wheelbase dropped to 122 inches in a tiny gesture toward the increasing interest in smaller cars. The new grille was narrowed, allowing the dual headlights to be aligned horizontally; wider rear-window pillars cut down on the good visibility of the 1962 models. The rear deck was recontoured, gradually sloping to the fenders,

where there was no sign of a tail fin. Chrysler's revolutionary five year/50,000 mile warranty was featured for the first time — a piece of marketing genius that took the industry by surprise and sent competitors scrambling to announce similar plans. The warranty covered all engine and power-train parts against defects in material or workmanship for five years or 50,000 miles, whichever came first, and was even transferable to a new owner when the car was sold.

No body styles were changed within the individual models. The Newport again carried 265 hp, the 300 model 305 hp, and the New Yorker 340 hp. In the letter series, which was still blended in with the plain vanilla 300's, letter *I* was skipped and the model was designated 300J, available only as a hardtop. The 300J was equipped with the New Yorker 413-cubic inch engine, but it produced 390 horsepower and the same amount of foot-pounds at 4800 rpm, with 9.6:1 compression. Alas, the 300J looked more than ever like a standard Chrysler. This impression was heightened by advertising that dwelled on its comfort, rather than its performance. Even the distinguished red, white and blue 300 emblem was replaced — by a black dot on which the model name and letter *J* were set in thin white lines. As might have been expected, these changes didn't set well with the small but enthusiastic clientele that made up the traditional letter series market — only 400 300J's were sold, a record low.

In the Imperial range, 1963 styling revisions were modest. A new grille was supplied, with a pattern of elongated horizontal rectangles. The roofline was restyled by Engel, who had always resisted roundness at the expense of angles. Above the belt-line, the Imperial was now squared off in the image of Elwood's Lincoln Continentals. The freestanding taillights of 1962 were retained, the rear bumper and back-up lights mildly revised. The

1963 Newport four-door sedan.   1963 300 paced the Indianapolis 500 that year.

1963 300J came only as a hardtop.

model lineup was unchanged except for the re-emergence of the Ghia Crown Imperial. On normal wheelbase cars, Imperials continued to use the 340 hp, 413-cubic-inch engine.

Model

Body Style (passengers)	Price	W.B.(in)	Weight (lb)
Series TC1-L Newport			
sedan, 4dr (6)	$2,964	122	3,770
hardtop, 2dr (6)	3,027	122	3,760
hardtop, 4dr (6)	3,106	122	3,800
convertible (6)	3,399	122	3,825
Town and Country wagon (9)	3,586	122	4,215
Town and Country wagon (6)	3,478	122	4,200
Series TC2-M 300			
300 hardtop, 2dr (6)	$3,430	122	3,790
300 hardtop, 4dr (6)	3,400	122	3,815
300 convertible (6)	3,790	122	3,845
300J hardtop, 2dr (5)	5,184	122	4,000
Series TC3-H New Yorker			
sedan, 4dr (6)	$3,981	122	3,910
hardtop, 4dr (6)	4,118	122	3,950
Town and Country wagon (9)	4,815	122	4,370
Town and Country wagon (6)	4,708	122	4,350
Series TY1-L Custom Imperial			
Southampton hardtop, 2dr (6)	$5,058	129	4,640
Southampton hardtop, 4dr (6)	5,243	129	4,690
Series TY1-M Crown Imperial			
Southampton hardtop, 2dr (6)	$5,412	129	4,720
Southampton hardtop, 4dr (6)	5,656	129	4,740
convertible (6)	5,782	129	4,795
Series TY1-H LeBaron Imperial			
Southampton hardtop, 4dr (6)	$6,434	129	4,830
Crown Imperial			
sedan, 4dr l.w.b. (8)	$18,500	149½	6,000
limousine (8)	18,500	149½	6,100

New Yorker Salon; midyear trim option in 1963.

1963 New Yorker Town & Country.

In 1963 Chrysler retained its hold on eleventh place in sales, though calendar production slipped to 111,000. At the same time, Corporate net earnings broke an all-time record at $161.6 million, and worldwide sales of $3.5 billion were second only to the 1957 total. Lynn Townsend said the improvement stemmed from the five year/50,000 mile warranty, the strengthening of the dealer organization, and a broader spread of product coverage. Chrysler stock split again, this time four-fold. Passenger-car output for the entire company at 1,047,722 units, was the first million-plus figure since 1960, and the largest since 1957. Four hundred sixty-two new dealerships were added, along with a worldwide construction program

Again for 1963, the Imperial ended up far different than it began in the minds of stylists. These two clay models show a very close relationship with Chrysler . . .

. . . but it didn't turn out that way. For 1963 Imperial retained much of its 1962 appearance. Here, various sketches for front end face-lift; the lower one was accepted.

1963 Custom Imperial four-door hardtop.

1964 clay models close to final form. Engel attempted to work-in Chrysler's taillights better.

A complete rework of the rear deck that was not used by Styling.

1964 Silver 300.

1964 Newport Town & Country.

1964 300K.

totalling $160 million. Chrysler had peaked again, perhaps the highest peak in its history. In exuberance later to be regretted, Chrysler purchased controlling interest in Simca of France and began negotiations for a similar deal with the Rootes Group of Great Britain. Chrysler-Cummins Ltd, British manufacturer of diesel engines, also originated in 1963. Finally, Chrysler invested $17 million in Barreiros Diesel, a Spanish builder of trucks, diesel engines and farm equipment.

Two interesting midyear 1963 models were the 300 Pace Setter (two-door hardtop and convertible) and the New Yorker Salon (four-door hardtop). The Pace Setter appeared after a 300 had paced the Indianapolis 500; it was identified with crossed checkered flags below the 300 emblems on its flanks. Prices were $4,129 for the convertible, $3,769 for the hardtop. The New Yorker Salon sold for $5,860. It came equipped with extensive luxury accessories including air conditioning, AM/FM radio, auto-pilot, power brakes-steering-seats-windows, TorqueFlite transmission, color-keyed

1964 New Yorker four-door hardtop.

1964½ New Yorker Salon four-door hardtop.

Imperial for 1964 was to undergo considerable change with the first application of integral headlights, departing from the classic theme of previous models.

wheel covers, a special vinyl covered canopy roof. The word *Salon* was spelled out on its flanks under the New Yorker emblem. Since no more than 1,000 (estimated) Pace Setters and Salons were sold, the cars are potential collectors' items.

For 1964, the Chrysler face-lift was hardly more than a tinsel shift: Model lineup, wheelbases and engine combinations remained the same. Grilles, medallions, wheel covers and side moldings were given different treatments, and the rear windows were enlarged. Taillamps were hexagonal and rear panels slightly modified. The 300 continued to use a black mesh grille with bold cross bars, and now featured a loud, paint-filled side stripe with textured aluminum insert. Midyear special in 1964 was the Silver 300, an option-loaded two-door hardtop with special metallic silver paint, vinyl canopy roof, and a custom bucket seat interior with reclining front passenger seat. Like the 300, the Silver variation could be ordered with a four-speed manual shift as well as TorqueFlite automatic transmission.

Elwood Engel had drastically revised the Imperial for 1964. The old silhouette was now eliminated below, as well as above, the belt-line. The car was squared off, completely Continental in concept, its fender line traced in brightwork like the Engel Lincolns. A divided grille was fitted, the freestanding headlamps deleted. The rear deck was revised, with no suggestion of a spare tire remaining. The Custom series was eliminated; the Crown became the base model Imperial. LeBaron remained the most expensive normal-wheelbase Imperial, while the Ghia Crown limousine was available with either six or four side-windows.

Model Body Style (passengers)	Price	W.B.(in)	Weight (lb)
Series VC1-L Newport			
sedan, 4dr (6)	$2,901	122	3,805
hardtop, 2dr (6)	2,962	122	3,760
hardtop, 4dr (6)	3,042	122	3,795
convertible (6)	3,334	122	3,810
Town and Country wagon (9)	3,521	122	4,200
Town and Country wagon (6)	3,414	122	4,175

Massive, full-width grilles, square protuberances and integral styles were considered; the last was adopted.

Strongly Lincolnesque lines (above) were avoided, and the 1964 Imperial appeared with a trace of the old spare tire on its deck. Crown model shown below.

Series VC2-M 300

300 hardtop, 2dr (6)	$3,443	122	3,850
300 hardtop, 4dr (6)	3,521	122	3,865
300 convertible (6)	3,803	122	4,120
300K hardtop, 2dr (5)	4,056	122	3,965
300K convertible (5)	4,522	122	3,995

Series VC3-H New Yorker

sedan, 4dr (6)	$3,994	122	4,015
hardtop, 4dr (6)	4,131	122	4,035
Town and Country wagon (9)	4,828	122	4,395
Town and Country wagon (6)	4,721	122	4,385

Series VY1-M Crown Imperial

hardtop, 2dr (6)	$5,739	129	4,950
hardtop, 4dr (6)	5,581	129	4,970
convertible (6)	6,003	129	5,185

Series VY1-H LeBaron Imperial

hardtop, 4dr (8)	$6,455	129	5,005

Crown Imperial

limousine (8)	$18,500	149½	6,100

1964 LeBaron four-door hardtop.

Without any question Chrysler Division had a smash year in 1964. Model year production effectively tells the tale:

Model	1963	1964
Newport	75,972	85,183
300	25,065	28,965
New Yorker	27,960	31,044
Imperial	14,108	23,285

Chrysler production was up 10.3 percent, the best performance since the all-time high of 1955. Imperial's year was a colossal sixty-five percent better than 1963, and gave the marque a fifty percent better slice of the market. As a whole, Chrysler Corporation recorded the best year in its history. Plymouth was back in the groove, running fourth in sales at more than 570,000 units for the year, Dodge was sixth at 505,000. Chrysler Division hadn't produced as many cars in a decade. "We actually feel," said new general manager P.N. Buckminster in *Ward's Yearbook*, "that we can set a production record next year, surpassing Cadillac." He was indeed right — 1965 would see 224,000 Chryslers built to Cadillac's 196,000.

In this fabulous year even the declining letter series set a record—3,647 units were sold, including 625 of the reinstated convertible model. But 300K's were equipped with a mild, 360 hp version of the 413-cubic-inch engine, same as the 'regular' 300 line. The 390 hp was available — at extra cost. The final civilizing of the old fire breather was taking place, to be concluded with the last of the letter series, the 300L, in 1965.

In the first half of the sixties, Chrysler dispensed with design and engineering heroics in favor of careful market planning, unified "committee control" at the top and vast — sometimes, as time proved, rash — expansion financed by the wealth that accrued through increasingly successful operations. To his credit, Lynn Townsend had smoothed the roiling waters of the Colbert-Newberg era, and got down to the business of making money — lots of it. If a trend away from the stark independence of the middle and late fifties could be seen in this, no one was complaining much. After all, Chrysler was giving the public what it wanted. The public had declared its wants by attaching itself with fervor to a bucket-seated legion of sports cars that weren't sports cars, stick shifts that weren't stick shifts, 300's that weren't 300's.

In November, 1965, the California Motor Vehicle Pollution Control Board approved a Chrysler air cleaner package — the first emission control system developed by an American manufacturer to receive the approval of an agency of any government. This system was slated for use on Chrysler's high volume models sold in California at the beginning of the 1966 model year, with other models to be phased in as production permitted. Chrysler, market-oriented and more conventional-looking than in many a year, faced the decade of environmental protection.

CHAPTER 9
Into the Seventies, Gingerly

K.T. KELLER SAW the new age coming.

Chain-smoking filter cigarettes in his twelfth floor offices in the Fisher Building, Chrysler's former president and board chairman was relaxing with reporters in late 1958 when he made a prediction. "The present trend in cars has about another year or two to go. Then we'll get back to design for function and there'll be more stress on utility. . . . It takes more than styling to make a successful car. The car must be a good dependable product. Right now we have quite a bit of gingerbread design in automobiles — lots of jigsaw work. We'll go back to simplicity of design, you wait and see."

Old K.T. was still in there pitching for his kind of car, a car Chrysler hadn't been building since 1954, or maybe since 1950. Though nobody listened much to him anymore, the old man was still beloved by Highland Park. Every year he'd celebrate his birthday, with especially big parties at the five-year increments, and every year it came as rather a shock, and a poignant reminder, to realize that this last throwback to the glory days of Walter Percy Chrysler was still around.

K.T. died of a coronary in January, 1966, falling short of the eighty-fifth birthday to which he'd invited everyone he knew. He departed with the respect of many, not only for his achievements at Chrysler but also for his civic activities, including twenty-one years on the Detroit Arts Commission. "We have lost one of industry's great men of our times," said president Lynn Townsend as the motor city mourned. There was no sign, however, that K.T.'s type of automobile was reviving under the Chrysler badge as he had predicted; nor was there much evidence of the old Keller dash and spirit. Detroit's *Free Press* obituary quoted Keller's parting words in what might have been a rebuke to his company: "There is one thing that bothers me as I look back. I wonder if we are counting too much on security as against individual enterprise . . . I have an uneasy feeling that we as individuals are not as spunky as we used to be. We seem not to take the personal chances without which our common American goal is in danger of being mediocrity."

Certainly Chrysler was not as spunky as it had been, a far cry from the days when Keller ruled. But the Corporation and the marque had witnessed enough extremes of success and failure, since the war, to last a century. If management now deemed it wise to settle back into conservative products, perhaps it was high time. (At least it seemed like a good idea then.)

For 1965 the Chrysler line was fully redesigned by Elwood Engel, and an excellent job he did. Edged with brightwork — an Engel trademark — the fenders of the new cars swept cleanly from front to back in an unbroken line, with slightly arching body sculpture between the belt and lower body. The bumpers were molded in at each end; a new, wider grille enclosed the headlights; the side window glass was curved. Inside, TorqueFlite controls reverted to a column lever. Imperial had seen a major redesign the year before, so the only serious change was a new grille with

The Imperial LeBaron D'Or was a flashy show car displayed at the 1965 New York Automobile Show — in the days when Chrysler not only attended the shows, but built specials for that express purpose. The D'Or used gold striping and embellishments and was painted royal-essence-laurel-gold— of course.

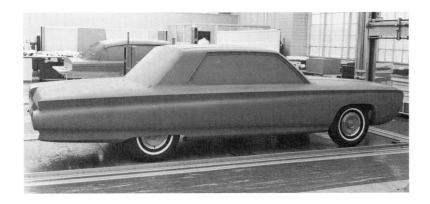

Styling clay shows 1965 Chrysler's basic theme.

Different approaches were considered to the '65 front end . . .

. . . before the production prototype was viewed at Highland Park.

glass-enclosed dual headlamps. The only midyear change of note was the replacement of the New Yorker's white-finish taillight lenses with conventional red units. The white ones were apparently dreamed up to blend better with the rear brightwork; they lit up red on application, but the scrappage rate in their manufacture caused them to be replaced with more conventional lenses.

Nineteen sixty-five saw the last of the letter series 300's, by now the almost stock-looking hardtop and convertible 300L offered only the 360-hp engine. Despite the fact that the 300L was second only to the 300K in letter series sales (2,845 were built, 2,405 of them hardtops), Chrysler's success with the 'regular' 300 line precluded continuance. So the letter series departed unmourned; there was nothing to mourn since the performance models had stopped coming after 1961 or 1962.

Above all, '65 was remembered by the accountants. When the totals were in, 224,061 Chryslers had been built for the calendar year — a monumental fifty-four percent increase over 1964 and a new all-time high — surpassing 1955's 176,000 by a fourth. Since the 1965 models had received two-inch-longer wheelbases and three more inches of length (though wagon wheelbase remained 121 inches), it seemed that the logical thing to do was make 'em longer yet in '66. The 1966's kept the 124-inch wheelbases, but were extended to 221.9 inches on the 300 hardtop. Styling remained much the same except for a shuffle of grille and taillight treatment, though the 300 series did have a crisper, more angular roof-line — the influence of Elwood Engel.

Engel also reworked the 1966 Imperial, coming up with one of the most beautiful, understated designs in many a year. The split grille of past models was replaced by an oblong unit that framed multiple rectangles. The rear deck, which had boasted an ungainly looking pigeon and 'spare tire cover' outline the year before, was smoothed off and cleaned up. Wheelbase and length were unchanged. Another new Imperial design appeared for 1967 and 1968, with the Imperial's adoption of unit body construction on a shorter, 127-inch wheelbase; the 1969 Imperial would be cleaner yet, with a minimum of sculpting announced by a much tidier grille and hidden headlamps.

The lack of Ghia limousines didn't prevent a number of interesting non-mass-production cars from appearing in 1966, for both show purposes and as long-wheelbase models. The show car of note was the Chrysler 300X, a custom convertible with lever steering replacing the traditional wheel — and smiles replacing amazement at this latest demonstration of

Compared to the non-letter 300 (upper), the 300L (lower), last of the letter series, used cleaner side molding but was otherwise almost identical.

1965 New Yorker hardtop.

1965 Newport six-window sedan.

Experimental 300X used a key punch card to turn on ignition, start engine and set driver seat; also provided TV for rear passengers.

Chrysler engineering prowess. The 300X was a sleek affair with a very sharply angled windshield, which could have used any angle at all since there were neither door windows nor a soft top. Exactly what Chrysler hoped to prove with the 300X wasn't too clear: it was impractical for production, not advanced enough to predict any design trends. And a long way from the exciting ideas of Exner.

The supply of limousines was provided by the Stageway Company of Fort Smith, Arkansas, which produced a seven-passenger executive limousine on an extended wheelbase to go with their airport limousines— those with the multitudinous doors. (For further Stageway details, see Appendix.) Chicago's auto show witnessed the Mobile Executive: an Imperial Crown two-door hardtop with special custom interior, including the usual high-priced businessman's toys — radio, telephone, dictaphone, writing table, typewriter, television, reading lamp and stereo. With the latter model Chrysler had a sales pitch in mind, for the Mobile Executive became an option on 1967 Imperials.

Chrysler maintained the tenth-place position it had wrested from Cadillac in 1965-66; and in 1967 it actually rose to ninth, despite diminished volume at 240,000 units. This position was a result of the fall of Rambler, a surprisingly successful independent that had ranked as high as third in production in the early sixties. Chrysler slipped back to tenth in 1968, but a record 263,266 units were built for the calendar year. This surge was temporary, however; for the Division suffered from strikes and the general economic decline in 1969-70, and in 1970 built only 158,614 units.

Model developments in the late sixties reflected what Chrysler saw as the temper of the times. The New Yorker wagons were quietly dropped for 1966, after selling hardly more than 3,000 units the year before; Newport wagons did the selling in the utility sector, though by 1968 all wagons were consigned to a separate Town and Country series with its own (shorter) wheelbase. There hadn't been a New Yorker convertible since 1961. The four-door pillar sedan returned in '65 with six-window models in the Newport, 300 and New Yorker series; then in 1966, in the Newport and

The 1965 Imperial front end is developed...

...and finally emerges in full-scale clay.   1966 Newport four-door hardtop.

1965 Imperial Crown convertible.

Stageway's unique Imperial LeBaron limousine; this 1969 model featured luxurious appointments.

1966 Imperial Crown.

1966 300 — this was the first year the 300 lacked a letter series.

1966 New Yorker four-door hardtop.

Mobile Executive option on 1967 Imperial.

1967 Imperial Crown hardtop.

1967 Imperial LeBaron four-door hardtop.

1967 300 convertible.

1967 Newport Custom.

1967 New Yorker four-door hardtop.

The old Town & Country look, available midyear on specially wood-grained Newport convertibles and hardtops, appeared in February 1968.

New Yorker only. This interesting body style disappeared again in 1967. In 1967 a Newport Custom appeared, sandwiched between Newport and 300 — and Chrysler styling began to get cluttered again. The Newport Custom had unpleasantly bright moldings on the body sides and a new hardtop roof design that succeeded brilliantly in creating a blind spot — for the sake of what the Division called a 'semi-fastback.' This design persisted through 1968 before being erased by the new design of 1969. One must concede that annual model changes at least break even, destroying just as many nasty body styles as good ones. Finding the good ones is a matter of timing and selectivity.

Midyear specials began to get interesting again in 1968. A line of blue Newport hardtops with vinyl trimmed roofs appeared in '67, but in 1968 a flashier Newport could be had with Sportsgrain simulated wood paneling as on the Town and Country wagons — $126 option for hardtops and convertibles only. It was the first wood-grained non-wagon since the old Town and Country Newport had given up the ghost back in 1950. Also in 1968, Newport Special two- and four-door hardtops with turquoise color schemes were offered, and were later extended to the 300 series.

A major styling accomplishment was the 'fuselage-styled' 1969 Chrysler, which the Division proudly announced as 'Your Next Car.' Years ago, Virgil Exner had pioneered the idea of a combination bumper/grille on the XNR sports car — the bumper surrounded the radiator opening and lights. Here it was, on production '69 models. But unlike the XNR, the body lines were free of creases, wrinkles and fins; the cars smooth and fleet-looking. Nineteen sixty-nine was a very good year.

Chrysler and Imperial had downplayed mechanical performance in the last years of the sixties. The 383-cubic-inch V-8 of 270 hp was the base engine in 1965 with the 360-hp 413 the top line product. By 1969 the 383 offered only 20 hp more, and the 413 had been replaced by a 440-cubic-inch engine of 350-375 hp. The Chrysler wheelbase remained at 124 inches, though the cars had now grown to almost 225 inches long and nearly eighty inches wide, about as huge as an American passenger car could get.

At the Corporate level, Lynn Townsend's regime was laboring away to permanently improve the profit picture. Virgil Boyd became president on January 1, 1967, and was relieved by John Riccardo on January 9, 1970. Chrysler Realty Corporation had been established in 1967 by Townsend. Essentially, Realty grew out of the old Dealer Enterprises operation, and was designed to help dealers buy and build stores. Under Riccardo, retail outlets were upgraded. Now company-owned dealerships were commonplace as well. On the production line, quality control had become an end in itself for the first time in Chrysler history. K.T. Keller's tightly centralized Corporate structure was decentralized under Colbert; Townsend recentralized it, but left operations to the two new Chrysler-Plymouth and Dodge Divisions, which were in reality a lot more centralized than the former Dodge, Plymouth, DeSoto and Chrysler Divisions had been.

Midyear 1970 saw the first Cordoba, but Ricardo Montalban could keep his Ferrari awhile longer — the 1970 Cordoba was anything but a 'small Chrysler,' being a two- or four-door Newport hardtop painted gold with special vinyl roof and body side molding, gold wheels and grille, and Aztec Eagle interior design. Newports of all varieties could be ordered with

Virgil Boyd.

1968 Newport Custom hardtop.

1968 Imperial Crown four-door hardtop.

1968 New Yorker four-door hardtop.

1968 300 convertible.

1969 Newport Custom.

1969 300 hardtop.

1969 Imperial LeBaron two-door hardtop.

1969 New Yorker hardtop.

Hurst's custom 1970 300-H, bore no letter series relationship except basic hairy chestedness.

the 440-cubic-inch engine; a special Newport 440 hardtop was offered complete with TorqueFlite, vinyl roof, special interior trim and accessories.

Another flashy product of 1970 was the 300-H — not a new letter series 300, but formally the 300-Hurst. A floor-mounted Hurst shifter controlled an automatic gearbox. Performance options were fitted including special road wheels H-70x15 white-letter tires, 440-cubic-inch engine and heavy-duty suspension. The 300-Hurst was set off by a special gold and white paint job, a customized hood and deck with spoiler, special grille paint, custom interior and pinstriping. It was often displayed in ads with a color-coordinated female, not a mandatory option; the implication was that the 300-H was useful for acquiring such equipage.

One should not overlook among Lynn Townsend's accomplishments his greatest gift to enthusiasts — the Chrysler Historical Collection. First set

Concept 70X, an exciting experimental exercise, is pictured with Chrysler-Plymouth general manager Glenn E. White, Elwood Engel and product planning and development vice president L.B. Bornhauser.

up in 1969 under the direction of Cliff Lockwood, whose tenure dated with Walter Chrysler's, it contained everything from a complete set of shop manuals to the actual office furniture of the founder. Lockwood was relieved in 1971 by John Bunnell, who, on his retirement, passed the collection to C.R. Cheney. Each of the directors has been enthusiastic in recording Chrysler history, and the particular thanks of the writer go to Mr. Cheney for many of the illustrations in this book.

It is unfortunate that higher management's attitude toward the collection has been varied. During particularly bad times in the corporate economy, availability of the collection to researchers has occasionally diminished. This on-again, off-again attitude of top management toward its availability has caused some to suggest that the collection would be better housed in a central repository like the Detroit Public Library. Wherever it is located, it remains unquestionably one of the most complete and best-organized corporate archives in the country.

Not particularly significant to the Chryslers of the seventies, but an interesting idea, was a 1969 show car called the Concept 70X, featuring a unique batch of novel ideas. Typical of most styling mockups, 70X had two doors on the left side and one door on the right; the doors slid open alongside the fuselage on parallelogram hinges. According to L.B. Bornhauser, product planning and development vice president, the 70X was designed "to develop major concepts high in customer appeal," but apparently those doors weren't too appealing or feasible for production. The seventy-inch long door on the single-door side was about twenty-one inches longer than a standard Chrysler door — no small object itself — and rear seat passengers could enter and exit with a shred of dignity. Concept 70X's long door can be likened to a similar design on the passenger side of 1975-76's AMC Pacer. The difference is that the 70X doors swung on their special hinges, too expensive to put into production, while the Pacer's swing on conventional hinges.

High points of the Concept 70X that should not go unremarked were its fingertip controls, placed on each side of the steering wheel column. On the right side were warning lights for the dashboard instruments. The dash consisted of a single-screen read-out system that broadcasted preselected information on a screen under the steering wheel — fuel level, oil pressure, engine temperature and alternator condition could be checked. Speed was constantly projected on the screen. The right-hand console also contained the ignition key slot, radio control knobs and a rotary transmission gear selector. The left side housed controls for the auto pilot, headlights, wipers

70X featured mesh headrest hung from a rollbar and steering column control console.

Other 70X features were: rearview mirror lights indicating position of following traffic, combination armrest and rearfacing child's seat in front compartment, and one of the best workouts of the sliding door idea.

1970 Newport four-door sedan, and convertible.

1970 Town & Country wagon.

Midyear offering in 1970 was Chrysler's Cordoba.

and washers, parking and emergency lights and 'twilight sentinel,' Chrysler's automatic lighting device. Directional signals were controlled from buttons on the steering wheel spokes, and warning lights on each side reported on emergencies. It was a technically interesting and practical dashboard layout that showed considerable ingenuity.

Less exotic technically than the Concept 70X, but still arresting, was the Cordoba de Oro, an Engel design exercise on the normal 124-inch Chrysler wheelbase. It featured the strongest wedge profile since Exner, though it was rather heavy near the back end. Another feature harking back to Exner was a cantilevered roof lacking any sort of A pillars — like the old Norseman had that sunk with the S.S. *Andrea Doria*.

Simultaneously with these bold predictions about the future, the Chrysler turbine program sufaced again. The cause was certainly the government's new concern with clean-burning engines, and the possible replacement of the internal combustion engine with a unit more ecologically acceptable. Chrysler research director George J. Huebner approached the Department of Transportation in 1970 with an analysis of alternate power sources — electric, steam and the now sixth-generation Chrysler turbine. Unsurprisingly, Huebner proved the turbine a better alternative than either rival. Its road behavior had much improved: Throttle lag and fuel consumption had both been reduced from 1966 levels — and

while the high cost of manufacture and exhaust emissions were still problems, Huebner felt they could be licked with an ample dose of federal cash. In late 1972 the newly-created Environmental Protection Agency (EPA) awarded Chrysler a $6.4 million contract to investigate the cost and emission problems of the turbine. Chrysler, said the EPA, would provide "gas turbine automobile engines for use as 'test beds' to establish baseline gas turbine performance and emission levels."

Thus the federal government gave Chrysler powerful impetus toward continuing turbine development. Had it not been for the growing federal concern with emissions, the program might have become moribund. It is noteworthy that, while Chrysler's research on turbines continues under government sponsorship, the tooling for the stillborn General Motors Wankel engine languishes at the Hydra-Matic plant in Willow Run, Michigan — roped off and covered with "keep out" signs. The Wankel, which is heavy on fuel and burns dirty, has been virtually abandoned by GM, and with it a $50 million investment. Perhaps the turbine will prove to be the engine of the future, and Chrysler Engineering will regain its old pre-eminence.

The last Imperial convertible vanished with the 1968 models; the last Chrysler soft top (in the form of a Newport, production 1124) was discontinued after 1970. The 1969 Imperial line was five inches longer, but

Advertised as "the shape of things to come," Engel's radical Cordoba de Oro used a pillarless monocoque design similar to the ill-fated Norseman's. Wide doors allowed easy access to all four seats; headlights were experimental, air-intake thermostatically controlled.

1970 Imperial LeBaron four-door hardtop.

1970 300 four-door hardtop.

1970 New Yorker four-door hardtop.

the models were down to only five: Crown four-door sedan, at midyear two- and four-door hardtop; and LeBaron two- and four-door hardtop. Nineteen seventy was the Crown's last year, and in 1971 the Imperial began to be merchandised as part of the Chrysler line again.

Chrysler had never been able to sell the idea of Imperial as a marque in its own right, since adopting the practice in 1955. As a model of Chrysler, Imperial had been with the company almost since the beginning; people continued to refer to it as the Chrysler Imperial even when it was being portrayed as a separate up-market make. The most strenuous efforts to enhance the separation occurred when Imperial moved to the ex-DeSoto plant in Dearborn. But by 1967 the Imperial was again becoming more and more like a Chrysler; that year it adopted the Chrysler unit body, and was again being built alongside the Chryslers at Jefferson Avenue.

The 1971 model lineup was rejuggled slightly, and the old Royal name was back as a midyear Newport Royal sedan and hardtop, the former selling for $4,078 base price. This marked the first time that no Chrysler could be had for less than $4,000. Government-mandated emission and safety equipment, and customer-desired accessories, were being applied as standard on all models; inflation, too, was taking its toll. The Newport four-door had sold for only $3,414 in 1969; it is interesting to look at the sharp price surge that took place throughout the line between 1965 and 1971:

Price of four-door base line sedan

Year	Newport	New Yorker hdtp	Imperial hdtp
1965	$2,968	$4,173	$5,691
1966	3,052	4,233	5,887
1967	3,159	4,339	5,836
1968	3,309	4,500	6,115
1969	3,414	4,615	5,770
1970	3,514	4,761	5,956
1971	4,078	5,041	6,864

The last year for 'fuselage styling' was 1971 although 1972-73 models were still based on the 1969 shell. To Chrysler's credit, the cars remained relatively clean-limbed, though such changeable items as grilles, taillights and side trim did become a shade more tacky. Chryslers remained on the 124-inch wheelbase for 1972, Imperials on the 127; but a new 400-cubic-inch engine, better adaptable to emission requirements than the old 383, was introduced, while 1971's smaller 360-cubic-inch block for the Newport Royal was dropped. Electronic ignition was now *de rigueur*. New Yorkers and Imperials retained the 440-cid V-8, with added emission controls. Nineteen seventy-two was the first year the manufacturers began listing net instead of gross horsepower, so the contrast in specifications was all the more apparent:

cubic inches	bore & stroke	bhp/rpm	torque/rpm	compression (carburetion)
1971				
360	4.000 x 3.358	255/4000	360/2400	8.7 (2bbl)
383	4.250 x 3.380	275/4400	375/2400	8.5 (2bbl)
383	4.250 x 3.380	300/4800	410/3400	8.5 (4bbl)
440	4.320 x 3.750	335/4400	460/3200	8.8 (4bbl)
440	4.320 x 3.750	370/4600	480/3200	9.5 (4bbl)
440	4.320 x 3.750	385/4700	490/3200	10.3 (3 2bbl)
1972				
400	4.340 x 3.380	190/4400	310/2400	8.2 (2bbl)
400	4.340 x 3.380	255/4400	340/2400	8.2 (4bbl)
440	4.320 x 3.750	225/4400	345/3200	8.2 (4bbl)
440	4.320 x 3.750	280/4800	375/3200	8.2 (4bbl)

Note: California emission package deleted 9 bhp and 5 foot-pounds of torque from 1972 440- and 400-cubic-inch engines. Bhp in 1971 is gross, in 1972 net. Dual exhaust on 1972 New Yorker models adds 20 bhp.

The LeBaron two- and four-door hardtops were the only cars in the Imperial line now; to fill the gap left by the departing Crown series they were

1971 New Yorker with sunroof.

1971 Imperial LeBaron four-door hardtop.

priced down a bit — to $6,550 and $6,778 respectively. The first LeBaron four-door hardtop had cost $1,000 less, back in 1957. A Bendix anti-skid system, which had been a $250 option on Imperials in 1971, was offered on the entire line for 1972.

The one-millionth Chrysler passed through the Jefferson Avenue lines on June 26, 1973. It was a Newport sedan, the base-line car — the Royal version was dropped this year — and 54,146 like it were sold in 1973.

1972 Newport Royal hardtop.

1973 New Yorker Brougham.

1972 Imperial LeBaron hardtop.

1973 Imperial LeBaron four-door hardtop.

Nineteen seventy-two models used entirely new sheet metal. The bumper-framed grille was out in deference to federal impact regulations. Chrysler adopted a more conventional frontal design with bulkier bumpers; it most closely resembled the Chevrolet Impala. Here was an example of the creativity of the 535 senators and representatives in Washington, who suddenly fancied themselves automotive engineers. Prodded by the big insurance companies, Congress mandated a bumper resistant to damage at collisions of up to 5 mph — and the bumper did save on insurance claims in low-speed accidents. It also levied a massive tax on all consumers, who uniformly had to pay for these bulky, heavy, fuel-draining devices for the sake of the minority who would suffer accidents. A car magazine totaled the saving achieved by the 5-mph bumper versus the cost of putting it on every automobile built in 1973. To the surprise of no one, the latter figure outweighed the former by about two to one, not even taking into account the effect on the body shop trade or the increased quantity of imported oil required by heavier cars.

In addition to the benighted entrance of Congress into the automotive design field, Chrysler itself did the cause of energy and raw material conservation little good by extending its 1973 cars to 230 inches — 231 for the New Yorker, 229.5 for the Town and Country. There was a reason beyond Chrysler's control, however: the federal government ordered 'safety' bumpers, that accounted for the increase. The Imperial held the same dimensions (which were certainly big enough), and included all power accessories, TorqueFlite and air conditioning as standard; New Yorkers adopted air conditioning as standard while retaining options like the four-wheel braking system and vinyl roof, along with the sliding sun-roof introduced in 1971 — a sop to the convertible market.

Nineteen seventy-four saw the tide change. Still holding the 124-inch wheelbase, the cars were reduced about five inches and given crisp new styling. Chryslers and Imperials both adopted the pseudo-classic square grille that they had studiously avoided during this fad's proliferation in the early seventies. Engine options were down to the 400 and 440-cubic-inch engines, producing from 185 to 230 net horsepower. The lineup now

On July 26, 1973, a Newport sedan became the one millionth Chrysler. Holding the sign is Chrysler-Plymouth sales manager Francis Hazelroth and plant manager Richard Cummins.

consisted of the Newport ($4,442-4,955), New Yorker ($5,418-5,927), Town and Country ($5,532-5,661) and Imperial ($7,537-7,668). Imperial prices were really galloping — they had jumped $1,000 since 1972, and would increase another $1,000 to a towering $8,698 for the LeBaron two-door hardtop in 1975.

The price spiral was unexpected. In 1974, with U.S. sales lagging by twenty-six percent compared with 1973, a price increase hardly seemed propitious; and Townsend's announcement flew in the face of solemn testimony by Ford and GM that they would hold prices down — if only Washington would go easy on safety and environmental mandates. Townsend's thesis turned out to be the honest one: After Chrysler raised the ante, Ford, General Motors and even American Motors meekly followed. Townsend said his action was "perfectly realistic" in view of spiraling costs of raw materials, but the Cost of Living Council called the move "an act of consummate gall." Townsend replied by raising prices another one percent.

What neither Townsend nor anyone else counted on, however, was the severe recession that hit Detroit following the energy crisis in early 1974, and continued during the massive sticker increases on the 1975 models announced six months later. Sales of the 1975 cars dropped to 1970 levels, and a two-month inventory of unsold models developed. Townsend refused to slash prices; instead he slashed production. By early November of 1974, Chrysler sales were down thirty-four percent. On paper this didn't seem as bad as General Motors' forty-three percent decline, but Chrysler felt the drop more because its fixed costs spread over a much smaller total output than GM's did.

What happened next was inevitable. In mid-November Chrysler laid off 18,000 employees — and more layoffs were contemplated — in an effort to eliminate about $120 million in fixed costs. Again fingers were pointed; Washington said that Chrysler's price increases had caused the problem; Townsend replied that administration had failed to stimulate new car sales, that President Ford had even urged Americans to buy less. Townsend felt that the seven percent excise tax, which Congress had lifted in 1971 to stimulate sales, should be lifted again — but at the same time he admitted that prices would be raised once again by early 1975. They were. And by then Chrysler had an inventory of 300,000 unsold cars.

1974 New Yorker four-door hardtop: Chrysler yields to the Mercedes-Benz look, a style that had long been obsolete.

1974 Imperial LeBaron four-door hardtop. Imperial continued to stubbornly use this body style, that was being quickly abandoned by the rest of the industry.

Symbol of the times, a cartoon from the British weekly *The Spectator* limning Chrysler's troubles, especially those fostered by U.K. losses.

Something had to break this logjam, and something did: Chrysler instituted a cash rebate plan for buyers, the first time in automotive history that a company in effect paid people to buy its cars. The rest of the industry had little choice but to join in, despite the fact that every company lost money on every sale. It was better to do that, Townsend told his board, than to continue to finance the inventory of non-sellers, which was costing the company about $300,000 every week.

Townsend made the news again in February, 1974, when he stated that Chrysler's entire structure was going to be thinned once more — to survive in a long-term market of only six million American-built cars. This was less than two-thirds the record production of 1973. "Such drastic retrenchment," said *Fortune*, "implies a slash of about one-third of the company's facilities and overhead, and it could be quite a gamble. If the market does rebound, say to sales of over ten million a year, Chrysler could get caught short of capacity and lose market share. Nevertheless Townsend seems prepared to err on the side of caution: 'We are not going to permit ourselves to go on rosy forecasts of the future.' "

What did all this mean for the Chrysler car, which from the beginning had survived as a big, luxury machine — never, ever to be issued in a smaller package? It meant a new look at the whole scheme of things, not only at the long-resisted junior edition Chrysler, but at the elimination of some of the senior editions. For Chrysler it was just as revolutionary an idea as Cadillac's bringing out the very un-Cadillac-like Seville. But observers and insiders alike agreed that it was the only action that could guarantee the ultimate survival of the marque. Pessimists held that not only the marque, but the Corporation, was at stake.

It is worth recalling at this juncture that Chrysler's new look in the mid-seventies directly confirmed what K.T. Keller had predicted back in 1958, when most of those who heard him were wont to smile. Chrysler had

1975 Chrysler Cordoba, a new small Chrysler at last; just in the nick of time.

Tribute to a vanished age, the last Imperial, a LeBaron four-door hardtop, leaves the Jefferson Avenue line June 12, 1975. The car holds serial number YM43-T5C-182947, sold for $10,403.35.

at last begun to "get back to design for function, with more stress on utility. It takes more than styling to make a successful car," Keller had said. "We'll get back to simplicity of design, you wait and see."

In Keller's day, simplicity of design meant three-box styling and a marketing disaster. Chrysler had taken a bit more than the two years Keller predicted to get back to thinking in that direction. And, tempered by experience, it wasn't about to offer boxy designs but a beautifully styled smaller Chrysler that would be responsible for a major reversal in the fortunes of the marque.

K.T. would have liked that.

CHAPTER 10

The Present, the Future

LIMNING THE HISTORY of the Chrysler car it becomes increasingly harder to separate the marque from the Division, and indeed from the Corporation. The demise of DeSoto, the creation of the Chrysler-Plymouth and Dodge Divisions and the 1975 merging of Chrysler-Plymouth and Dodge into one Sales Division brought to a close the era of strict separation in price and specification between Chrysler makes; there is a Dodge equivalent to nearly every Chrysler-Plymouth product, and vice versa. While Corporate operations continue to be relatively decentralized, managerial control is still very much unified under one command. There is one Parts Division, one Service Division.

On October 1, 1975, the command changed. Fixty-six year old Lynn Townsend, elected president in 1961 and board chairman in 1967, stepped down nine years in advance of mandatory retirement. His successor was former president John J. Riccardo; Riccardo's successor — Chrysler's new president — was former executive vice president Eugene A. Cafiero. Thus, for the first time since K.T. Keller in 1935, a production man — Cafiero — had risen to the top at Chrysler.

Lynn Townsend was quick to point out that his early retirement was not the result of stockholder or board demand. "There was absolutely no pressure at all," he said. "It was my decision, and my decision alone. There was no pressure from anyone.

"It certainly is a fair statement that any chairman would like to retire during a profitable year, or profitable years, rather than at a time of losses. However, I reviewed this with myself very closely and decided, basically, there were three factors involved in this decision which I believe outweighed the current operating situation at Chrysler.

"The automobile industry is entering a new era in which it is going to have to change, in which it is going to have to change substantially. There will be new products, energy conserving products, brought on by the energy crisis. There are going to have to be new methods. The industry today, worldwide, is in a great deal of difficulty. The decisions being made now respecting the programs for Chrysler are going to be felt for a substantial period of time. Even if I were to stay on to age sixty-five, I would not be here to see the culmination of many decisions being made at the present time. My early retirement is for the benefit of our management team and our company."

John Riccardo just as rapidly emphasized that there would be no dramatic changes in marketing strategy or dealer relations. But the appointment of Cafiero as chief operating manager was seen as an injection of considerable new blood. The Administrative Committee, for example, formed by Townsend in 1961 as the main decision-making body, has now become the Operations Committee. It is composed of Riccardo, Cafiero and four new executive vice presidents, a manifestly young group: Riccardo is fifty-one, Cafiero forty-nine, the average age of the vice presidents barely past fifty. Gene Cafiero is proud of his ability to experiment and innovate — and a little innovation wouldn't hurt as Chrysler

Why mess with a good thing: the mildly face-lifted 1976 Cordoba.

enters its sixth decade. "You need to develop a very flexible organization because no one knows what's going to happen next year," Cafiero says. "We didn't know there was going to be an energy crisis of the magnitude that existed. I'm sure there will be something next year. The organization that is going to survive is the one that has developed the flexibility to move very quickly, yet has a strategy that has some continuity to it, that can take it through a period of time without creating additional static inside the organization." If this occurs at Chrysler, it will certainly be something new.

The problem with the company, many analysts say, is that it has no corporate identity. Worse, Townsend managers did not seem to know where they were going, what they were trying to do. In the mid-sixties, Dodge ads asked people to "Join the Dodge Rebellion," a disastrous ploy with the traditional Dodge buyer, who was older and more conservative than the Plymouth buyer, and anything but rebellious. Dodge was relatively successful with the Dart Swinger — yet the typical Swinger buyer was forty-five years old. Again, more recently, Chrysler asked the public, "What do you think of when you think of Chrysler?" And the public — one assumes the more tempting answers were edited out — obligingly replied, "engineering." Which was fine, except that 'engineering' is not an identity, as is AMC's reputation as a small car innovator, for example; or Ford's tradition as the builder of inexpensive, economical cars for the common man; or GM's role as the provider of a car for every taste and pocketbook — the old Al Sloan concept, which only GM is big enough to pursue.

Engineering has always exercised dominance at Chrysler, and often with good results. TorqueFlite is generally considered the best automatic transmission in the business, and through 1974 Chrysler had better success at emission control without the use of catalytic converters. It was, in fact, Chrysler that first warned of the converters' potential hazards in the form of sulfuric acid mist — a danger which the EPA finally acknowledged. Chrysler gave us the hemi-head engine, torsion bar front suspension and push-button transmission. But it was never able to convert these innovations and skills into a truly marketable corporate image. Says one Detroit marketing executive, "Chrysler is seen as years behind the other companies in styling, and even in engineering. If you ask, 'What's the last company to do anything?' people will say 'Chrysler.'"

Chrysler's confusion about what it is and where it's going began to show in the marketplace after the banner years of the middle sixties. Its corporate market share had climbed back to fifteen percent in 1965-66, where it hadn't been since 1957. It stayed above fifteen percent through 1970, but it hasn't been at that level since. Although Chrysler has a forty-percent slice of the compact car market, it has arrived at this enviable position almost by chance. While Ford and GM replaced and redesigned the compacts they'd built in the sixties, Chrysler simply shouldered on with the Valiant and Dart — their relative consistency of style and improvement in quality made the public buy them: They were good, reliable, tried and proven cars. Meanwhile the big promotional efforts went into the performance market (which collapsed five years before Chrysler stopped building performance cars) and into the image of the Chrysler automobile as an exclusively big car five years after there should have been a small one. In 1974, with the standard-sized car market plunging, Chrysler's main innovation was a redesigned line of standard-sized cars, conceived at enormous expense. "We came with a new car into a declining market to preserve and improve our position in it," Townsend said at the time, "and it's still a substantial market." But Chrysler's share of that market is still less than ten percent.

In 1975, however, Chrysler broke important new ground with the intermediate-sized Cordoba. Never mind that in reality it was a Satellite with a new suit of clothes, that its styling was obviously a cross between an eight-year-old Jaguar and a three-year-old Chevy Monte Carlo — the Cordoba was a beautifully styled car, and a very necessary model in the range. A talk-show commentator in Washington was recently asked to name an extinct dinosaur common to the D.C. area; he replied, "Chrysler." Fortunately, the Cordoba has largely prevented such a disappearance into the tar pits.

Dramatic indicator of a new direction for the marque, Cordoba's 115-inch wheelbase was the smallest on any Chrsyler since the war, and only 2½ inches longer than the very first Chrsyler announced back in 1925. The 1975 Cordoba came as a two-door coupe only, a road car with steel-belted radial tires, front and rear anti-sway bars. Power seats, windows and door locks were optional. Its interiors were beautifully upholstered in crushed velour buckets, or combination brocade cloth and vinyl bench seats with center armrests. Leather upholstery was optional.

The rest of the Chrysler line was unchanged from 1974, except that prices were up. There were the three Newports (four-door sedan and hardtop, two-door hardtop at $4,854-5,008), and the same body styles in Newport Customs ($5,254-5,423); the Town and Country six- and nine-passenger wagons ($6,099-6,244); the New Yorker Brougham four-door sedan and hardtop and two-door hardtop models ($6,277-6,424); and the Imperial-by-Chrysler ($8,698-8,844). The last Imperial, a LeBaron four-door hardtop, rolled off the line on June 12, 1975, with a sticker price of $10,403.35. In case you're looking for it, its serial number is YM43-T5C-182947.

"If you liked Chrysler Corporation's cars in 1974," said *Road & Track*, "you'll like them again in 1975. The accent is certainly off performance

The 1976 New Yorker Brougham. An Imperial by any other name....

and on luxury and economy . . . guns and butter." The New Yorker Broughams were luxurious, with standard leather, velour or brocade upholstery; shag carpets; simulated burled walnut and filligree moldings. Economy was emphasized with low final-drive ratios and the Fuel Pacer system, in which a manifold sensor was connected to a warning light that glowed during heavy-footedness. Chrysler's opposition to catalytic converters caved in, though its engineers publicly worried about the devices lasting past 50,000 miles, or being ruined by two or three tanks of leaded gasoline. Other engineering changes were modest: a 50,000 mile battery, standard on 440-cubic inch engines and optional on others; a sparkplug of similar life span; automatic height control, standard on the Imperial and optional on other large cars.

Despite its engineering heritage, Chrysler's main innovations seem to be new styling trends — a family identity from the top of the line to the bottom, and high style for the first time since the Exner days — cars that stand out from their competitors. This will be a good thing, if the new styling is as good as the Cordoba's — on the other hand, too much of a styling emphasis may well alienate that large group of customers buying Plymouth and Dodge compacts, which Chrysler hopes to augment with its new higher-priced compacts, Aspen and Volare.

As for the Chrysler marque, Cordoba is only a beginning. It must have been evident for some time at Highland Park that the old formula of eighteen- and nineteen-foot-long land whales with ten-foot wheelbases was not the key to success; that if anyone is left in this league by 1980 it will be Cadillac and possibly Lincoln — backed by a small but fiercely demanding market and by corporations with the resources to stick their necks out. But even Cadillac has come up with Seville — a neat trick, using a long-wheelbase Nova and selling it for $13,000 — and very soon now the new Mark V Continental will appear, with much smaller dimensions in many areas. Chrysler *has* recognized the declining market for biggies by dropping the Imperial for 1976, though an almost identical car remains as the New Yorker Brougham. Will its next generation of 'standard' cars be intermediates, or will the Cordoba line proliferate?

Meanwhile Chrysler entered the 1976 model year with no new models and a slightly diminished range of standard-sized cars — both models of Imperial and the New Yorker four-door pillared sedan are gone. Cordoba's sales tripled expectations in 1975, and half of those were 'conquest' sales to owners of rival products; so this newest Chrysler will be expected to perform yeoman duty maintaining the marque's share of sales. As this is written, Cordoba is outselling seven of the eight entries in the personal luxury car market, the exception being the Chevrolet Monte Carlo that it so distinctly resembles.

Cordoba for 1976 again offers a lush interior. Among the new options are a 60/40 adjustable seat — shades of Virgil Exner again — and a tilt steering column. Seatbacks recline, and seats are fitted with a new velour cloth available in six colors. The standard seat with center armrest is available in a cloth approximating cashmere, bearing a Castilian pattern. Corinthian leather and vinyl bucket seats in seven different colors are also optional.

The Cordoba instrument panel has been slightly reworked with new metric readings on all gauges, and is fully instrumented. The only warning lights are supplemental — to indicate low fuel level, for example. Gauges are set into a panel of simulated Brazilian rosewood, which happily looks more like the real thing than certain other imitations. Another option is a 'high rise' soft-cover center console that doubles as an armrest, contains a lockable storage compartment and a tray for incidentals. Cordobas feature jet airliner type trim panels around the opera windows, doors with integral armrests and simulated wood grain, a space-saving spare tire which adds about two cubic feet to trunk space. The Cordoba's engine options are the widest of any Chrysler: Four-barrel carburetor and dual exhausts push a creditable 240 horsepower out of the 400-cubic-inch engine — this engine with 175 horsepower is standard. Also available are a 150-hp, 318-cubic-inch engine, and 360's of 170 and 175 horsepower.

Group vice president Robert B. McCurry says "We won't be participating in the luxury segment, but we will upgrade the appearance and appointment levels of the New Yorker Brougham and Newport entries to the point that they will be a much better value in the marketplace," whatever that means. It appears to amount to an Imperial grille for New Yorker and a New Yorker grille for Newport, plus revised rear-end styling for these two models. The New Yorker offers no less than seven tones of cloth, vinyl and leather upholstery; and the Chrysler line offers all-white trims throughout. Steel-belted radial tires are standard in 1976; brake performance has been improved through larger rear drums and master cylinder reservoirs, and more efficient front discs.

While the New Yorker series is down to only a two- and four-door hardtop, the six versions of Newport (three standard, three Custom) are retained, as are the six- and nine-passenger Town and Country station wagons. A familiar name is the St. Regis, as in the fifties an optional decor package — available since mid-1974. In 1976 it stands for opera windows and padded canopy vinyl roof on the New Yorker Brougham and Newport Custom hardtops. All standard-sized Chryslers are still on the 124-inch wheelbase. Newports use the 360- and 400-cubic-inch engines of 170-200 horsepower and 280-310 foot-pounds of torque.

Obviously 1976 is a transition year, and possibly 1977 too. The real results of the Cafiero administration — the styling, engineering and marketing decisions now being made — will not be fully evident until 1978 or 1979. Given the three-year lead time, changes are already in the works, but the author cannot resist some conjecture and one or two wishes. He does not delude himself that his predictions and wishes will have much weight at Highland Park; but as a long-time enthusiast of the marque he will make them anyway, just for the record. The foregoing pages have perhaps entitled him to do this. In a few years he will be able to say he told you so, or that he hadn't the foggiest idea of what was really happening at Chrysler — in which case he will not be alone.

The departure of the Imperial, he hopes, will be but a temporary aberration. Granted, it may be useful in the short run to get people thinking in terms of smaller, more efficient and affordable Chryslers. But in the long run, Imperial is too good a name, intrinsically and historically. It has been part of Chrysler since 1927; it should be part of Chrysler in the future as well. Some say the New Yorker in Imperial clothing is selling better; of course, it's priced much lower. If Chrysler ever markets an ultra-luxury compact like Cadillac's Seville, its name should rightfully be Imperial.

Newport has proven to be a marketable title. But there is no need for a Newport Custom. The answer seems obvious: Shift the New Yorker name to what is now Newport Custom, and bring back Imperial for what is now the New Yorker. This will be an ideal change in nomenclature for the next generation of 'standard' Chryslers. It is hard to imagine these as other than Ford Granada-sized cars — the times so dictate — but it is almost as hard to imagine the Chrysler line without an Imperial.

If the Cordoba is any indication, the new, practical-sized Chryslers, making the best use of space on a compact wheelbase, will be well-styled cars. Hopefully they will be less boxy than those of Dearborn and Stuttgart. Cafiero and Riccardo say all their cars will soon have a family resemblance; if so it will have to be a pretty good piece of design. So we may soon see a range of 'precision-sized' Chryslers that are leagues better than their Ford or GM rivals, and we shall be the better for them.

The Cordoba will doubtless continue pretty much unchanged — it would incur the wrath of every Chrysler-Plymouth dealer to alter it very much. Still, it could have made better use of tradition: For a time the name considered for it was 300, and Styling came up with a 300-type square grille to carry out the theme. Management rejected the name, allegedly shying away from a performance image. But at Dodge, the same car is called the Charger! One can only conclude that the Dodge boys are the car enthusiasts.

This writer doubts that the Cordoba will proliferate into more utilitarian body styles, for it is a special car designed for a special market. It may become more of a fastback in the future. Whatever happens, one can hope that it will eventually drop its faddish imitation of a classic radiator, a habit Chrysler noticeably shunned until 1975. (Virgil Exner's grilles were sometimes inspired by the classic era, but they were always original in application.) Mercedes-Benz has been stuck with its noble nose for decades — Stuttgart tried to drop it once and was treated to a worldwide uproar by distributors for whom it had attained a certain salable panache. Chrysler has no such albatross to hang about its neck, so a cleaner, less pretentious Cordoba seems the ticket for the late seventies if the firm is serious about developing a dignified style. Who needs those tacky opera windows anyway? Cost Accounting perhaps — they eliminate two window winders and therefore amount to a super cost-cutter.

Finally, a personal wish, albeit a radical one. Back in 1960, when Virgil Exner released the fabulous XNR sports car and rumors circulated that Chrysler was going to market it with a performance version of the Valiant Slant Six, this writer vowed to be first in line for one. The XNR was unquestionably one of the most exciting Chrysler dream cars in history — brilliantly conceived. Fast yet economical, like the typical mid-displacement European performance car. It could have been the stiletto to Corvette's war club. Wouldn't it be nice — for enthusiasts, for the corporate image, and above all for sales (when the financial picture warrants) — to see Chrysler finally produce the sports car it has so long denied us? Of course you can't find a soul at Highland Park, even among the believers, who will dare to hope for such a thing. But anything's possible when a company is making money. *If* Chrysler is ever making money in the future.

For the postwar Chrysler, Camelot was the middle fifties. In those years the marque reigned supreme. No one could challenge its high style, its blazing performance on road and track, its construction quality, its hold

Still pitching for the big car buyer, the 1970 Newport Custom two-door hardtop.

on its market, its enduring worth as pure automobile. In the industry today, despite the depredations of 'government by hysteria,' there are indications that environmental looniness has bottomed out, that maybe — just maybe — cars are getting interesting again. Call it nostalgia for the glory years, or naive idealism, but it seems to this writer that Chrysler could do worse than produce a car in the image of the old rip-snorting, good-looking cars of yesteryear. But a different car, say, on a one hundred-inch wheelbase, weighing perhaps 2,500 pounds, and powered by an engine like the Slant Six — at least until those turbines arrive, if they ever do. A car of exciting, unconventional lines, preferably a two-plus-two, preferably open, or partly open — since convertibles are not now going to be banned as hazardous to our health. If that formula isn't salable, perhaps it could be a fastback. Above all it would be beautiful, nimble and fun to drive — a car that would prove again, as twenty years before, that Chryslers were built by car lovers for people who love cars.

That would be the best of all possible worlds, one suspects: the good looks and performance of Chrysler tradition combined with the size and powerplant that are necessary in this ever more congested and fuel-short world. Undoubtedly it would take great managerial courage to build such a car. Undoubetdly it would be one hell of a Chrysler.

What would they call it? Why, 300, of course!

Appendix I
by Jeffrey I. Godshall

The Ghia Crown Imperials

DURING THE LATE fifties and early sixties, Chrysler Corporation offered one of the most exclusive automobiles ever built. The Ghia Crown Imperial limousine was a classic vehicle, a splendid combination of Chrysler engineering and styling with the sublime body craftsmanship of Carrozeria-Ghia of Italy. From 1957 through 1965, Chrysler and Ghia participated in this unique undertaking that resulted in 132 fine limousines.

Chrysler had always aggressively pursued the limousine and eight-passenger sedan business. Long-wheelbase versions of all the Corporation's cars — including Plymouth — were offered in the late thirties, and Chrysler continued to build such cars long after the competition had abandoned the field. But as demand for the stretched models gradually fell off, the company's offerings were reduced. By 1954 only Chrysler and DeSoto were still building the big cars.

Flagship of the Chrysler limousine fleet was, of course, the Crown Imperial, which was introduced in 1940 (although the company had built Imperial limousines since 1926). From 1940 through 1954 the Crowns rode on a 145.5-inch wheelbase, pioneering such engineering advances as self-energizing disc brakes in 1949, hemi V-8 and power steering in 1951, and PowerFlite automatic transmission and twelve-volt electrical system in 1953.

For 1955 the entire Corporate line sported Virgil Exner's all-new 'Forward Look' bodies. Because of declining demand, Chrysler decided to drop all of its lesser limousines and concentrate solely on the Crown Imperial. The 1955 Crowns (and the mildly face-lifted 1956 versions) were handsome cars indeed, built over a 149.5-inch chassis. During these last two years of domestic assembly, 398 Crowns were produced, mostly limousines except for ninety-six eight-passenger sedans.

For 1957 the Imperial line was to receive a spectacularly styled, all-new body, which presented Chrysler management with a nasty problem. By judicious face-lifting, Chrysler had managed to use the same Crown Imperial body from 1940 through 1948, and a second body from 1949 through 1954. But it wasn't possible to modify the all-new 1955-56 limousine tooling to accept the 1957 styling. If the company was to continue to offer a limousine, it had to be all-new — all over again.

Of course, Chrysler could have simply dropped out of the limousine business, leaving the field to Cadillac (as Packard and Lincoln had done). But the Corporation felt the limousine was necessary to add prestige to the entire Imperial line. So there had to be a 1957 version.

In May, 1956, Chrysler studied the costs involved in producing a Crown Imperial for the 1957-59 model years and found that more than $3.3 million worth of special dies and tooling would be required. Based on projected sales, the company found that it could not price the limousine high enough to amortize the tooling, and so would have to take a loss of several thousand dollars on the sale of each car. Thus, Chrysler decided not to spend the money for the required tooling and instead considered

1952 Ghia limousine built for the Vatican.

making the limousine outside the company on a contract basis, either in the United States or Europe. After some investigation, Chrysler found there was no suitable coachbuilder in the U.S., so the company turned to the Ghia works in Torino, Italy.

Ghia and Chrysler were old friends, the Italian coachbuilder having made many of Chrysler's experimental and show cars and the Dual-Ghia sports car, which had an Italian body mated to Dodge running gear. Ghia had also built a couple of special Crown limousine styling exercises for Chrysler in the early fifties, one of which eventually went to the Vatican. After some study, Chrysler found that Ghia could handbuild the limousines at a reasonable cost, with a total tooling bill of only $15,000.

After the decision to go ahead, Chrysler had to rush the program along in order to get any Crowns at all for the 1957 model year. Dimensions were quickly set — a 149.5-inch wheelbase (same as the 1955-56 limousines, and carried through 1965), overall length of 244.7 inches, height at 58.5 inches and overall width of eighty inches.

Styling was done by Cliff Voss and Bill Brownlie under the direction of Virgil Exner. The clean, high-finned styling of the 1957 Imperial, when adapted to a limousine, resulted in a visually striking automobile. Highlights included a special six-window roof with a black leather rear canopy and 'Hi-Bridge' doors that opened into the roof for easier entry. There

This 1952 Ghia limousine was used for a slightly less exalted purpose.

'Kit car' for limousine construction, 1957.

wasn't time to build a full-size clay, so the styling work was done piecemeal. Sheet metal surfaces were stretched on paper over full-size body drafts drawn by Charlie Walker, a master at surface detailing. The front end, of course, used regular Imperial fenders and hood, while the rear quarters of the car were adapted from the more flowing two-door hardtop quarter panels.

Those involved with the Ghia limousine included Jack Charipar as chief engineer and Dave Cohoe as Ghia coordinator. The company was especially fortunate in having Paul Farago as resident engineer at Ghia, a close friend of Exner and of Ghia president Luigi Segré. Farago had served as Ghia's representative in America beginning with the Chrysler K310 show car and continuing through the Dual-Ghia. Though American by birth, Farago was of Italian background and had a good working relationship with Ghia craftsmen.

Under the terms of its Chrysler contract, Ghia was responsible for building the complete car, ready for delivery. As with any work of art, the building of a Ghia Crown limousine was slow and painstakingly difficult.

The car began life as a 1957 Imperial two-door hardtop mated to a standard 129-inch-wheelbase convertible frame to secure the rigidity of the convertible's additional X-member. Each car was specially prepared for its new life as a limousine. The body was painted in prime with all sheet metal, moldings, bumpers, etc. in place to prevent loss during the trip to Torino. Shipped with each car were a large assortment of special parts, including sedan sill panels (for modification); sedan center pillars; sedan front and rear doors (for modification); all glass parts; completely wired and mounted instrument panel; front and rear seat frames and springs ready for trimming, and structural parts for the jump seats; electric window lifts in doors; heating and special dual air conditioning units; complete body wiring harness; all weather-stripping materials; all door-operating hardware and mechanisms; some ornamentation (the remainder to be made by Ghia); all interior wiring, switches, and lamps; all paint and trim materials including leather, cloth, carpet and paint (lacquer); and unique mechanical components including a longer drive shaft and lengthened fuel, brake and exhaust lines; larger diameter torsion bars; and Chrysler Suburban rear springs.

When this 'kit car' arrived at Ghia, workmen began cutting apart the entire hardtop body and chassis and lengthening it 20.5 inches. This required extending the frame, floor panel and body sills, reinforcing the side rails and X-member, and installing the longer propeller shaft and the fuel, brake and exhaust lines. Next step was to rework the forward end of the hardtop rear quarter panels to mate with the roof and rear door. Rear lock pillars and inside quarter panels were then fabricated and installed. The roof rails, roof panel and rear canopy were formed and installed along with the sedan center pillars. The 'Hi-Bridge' roof doors required new front

Ghia construction sequence.

and rear door uppers and the rear doors also demanded a new outer skin. While all this was being done, other workmen were making the smaller parts: air conditioning ducts; windshield, belt and roof moldings; and interior trim items including door panels, partition structure, seats, armrests, shelf panel and myriad related parts.

While Ghia had to modify or build from scratch many exterior and interior sheet metal components, there were, amazingly, virtually no dies used. All large panels — including the roof — were formed with air hammers over wooden egg crate try-out manikins. Ghia built all the necessary tools and manikins. This kind of panel beating was a lost art in America. The only hard tooling used was for the installation jig fixtures and certain flanging dies.

When the body was finally assembled, the real fun began. The body was carefully metal-finished, using about 150 pounds of lead, and hand-sanded. All body seams were concealed, even inside the doors. As many as seventeen hours per car were spent hanging and fitting doors, fenders and other sheet metal parts to a maximum permissible gap of four millimeters.

Then the entire body was cleaned with an acid solution to eliminate rust and any excess solder.

The limousines were then ready for paint. First to be applied was a pale green, metal glazing zinc chromate paint (called 'stucco' in Italy), followed by a black fog paint that permitted workmen to find and fill any low spots in the surface. Multiple coats of lacquer in either black, maroon, deep green or deep blue were then carefully applied, sanded between each coat, and checked for evenness. All paint was produced in vats at one time to insure uniform color, and enough paint for ten cars was always stocked at Ghia. After the paint had set properly, the whole car was finished with 400-grit sandpaper. As a final step, the body was rubbed down with a solution of water and a soap-like material called 'sepia,' made from the innards of the octopus-like cuttlefish. The result was a mirror finish unmarred by scratches. Finally a hand-painted cream stripe was applied along the side of the body in place of the usual chrome molding.

After painting was completed, the black leather canopy roof was fitted over the rear compartment, and glass and exterior trim parts were installed.

A 1959 Crown Imperial that was built for Queen Elizabeth's Canadian tour.

This was the 1960 LeBaron four-door sedan 'kit car' for limousines.

Proposal for 1960 Crown Imperial by Don Butler.

Since the Crowns were to have a late-1957 introduction, certain pull-ahead 1958 trim items were installed, including front-fender side moldings, wheel opening and sill moldings, rear bumper inserts, the deck ornament, headlamp moldings and the radiator grille. Shaping and attaching of all parts was done by a craft system, where each part had to fit perfectly, regardless of the time involved.

With the exterior covered by protective cloths, the next step was installation of the interior. Five different rear compartment interior designs were offered, ranging from a traditional biscuit pattern to more modern motifs. Each interior scheme had its own unique seats and arm rests, and door, quarter and partition trim panels. The finest quality silk and wool broadcloth in either grey or beige was used for the upholstery, combined with glove-grade milled leather, rare cabinet woods, hand-crafted metal trim parts, and sheared mouton carpeting.

Even the headlining was special. Farago recalls shopping for headlining material in the best men's stores in Torino, eventually selecting a material used for suits. At Ghia, workmen had trouble with its installation since the material didn't stretch well. Farago solved the problem by steaming the headlining to a drum-tight fit with his wife's steam iron!

The chauffeur had to make do with narrow, piped-leather seats with matching door trim panels and black nylon carpeting, which was also used to line the luggage compartment.

It took about a month to complete each limousine, with about half the time spent on paint and finish. And no wonder, since each car was available in any one of thirty-two possible exterior color and interior style combinations. Usually there were a dozen to fifteen cars in process at any one time, and most cars were built in lots according to specific orders. Total time between initial customer order and final delivery was about six months.

After each car was completed, it was road-tested with forty pounds of air in each tire over local cobblestone streets to reveal any rattles. After any necessary corrections had been made, the limousines were individually boxed, loaded aboard trucks and driven to Genoa for overseas shipment. Trucking the lengthy automobiles over the winding, narrow road to Genoa was somewhat tricky until a new road was built by Fiat to handle its own export shipments. While the new road was open to the public on weekends, anyone using the highway during the week — including Ghia — had to pay a toll to Fiat.

When the Ghia Crowns finally began arriving in the United States, a few problems began cropping up. First it was discovered that the cars were too heavy for the tires, so a larger tire was substituted, along with changes in the rear wheel bearings and drive shaft. A heavy-duty electric motor normally used in wagon tailgates had to be installed to properly lift the glass partition between the front and rear compartments. Sometimes the non-adjustable driver's seat had to be reworked to provide enough room for unusually tall chauffeurs.

And then there was the wiring. It seems that the complexity of the limousines' electrical equipment (including dual air conditioning, *three* heaters, power windows, dual radios, speaker phone, etc.) was too much for the Italians, and each car had to be carefully examined upon arrival in Detroit to make sure everything worked properly.

After final testing and adjustment, the limousines were usually shipped to Chrysler Manhattan in New York, who delivered the cars to such wealthy and socially prominent people as David Sarnoff of RCA, author Pearl Buck and heiress Anna Dodge, at a price of more than $12,000 each. The politically powerful also required a car to impress the masses, and Ghia limousines were bought by the king of Saudi Arabia (bulletproof and specially-fitted with low-compression pistons), the rulers of Kuwait and Qatar, Dominican dictator Trujillo, New York Governor Rockefeller, and the White House. During the royal tour of Canada in 1959, a special bubbletop version of the Ghia was used by Queen Elizabeth and Prince Philip.

There were many difficulties, both large and small, involved in the creation of the two-continent Ghia limousines, beginning with the kit car itself. It wasn't easy to fasten the shorter sedan front door to the longer two-door hardtop opening. The interior and trunk of each car had to be carefully packed with all those sheet metal and trim parts, and it was vital to make the kits as complete as possible. Any parts shortage at Ghia meant the necessary parts had to be located, packed and shipped from Detroit, usually by air. And during shipment each car (filled with flammable trims and paint) had to be carried above deck to comply with fire regulations.

1960 Crown Imperial.

When the finished limousines arrived back in the States, a content added tax had to be paid on all labor and parts fabricated at Ghia, so Customs officials had to be satisfied as to exactly what work was done in Italy. This meant the cars had to be inspected both leaving and arriving in this country. When Ghia needed money, letters of credit and bank drafts had to be made up and sent abroad. Then there was the inevitable confusion resulting from Chrysler and Ghia staffs speaking two different languages with different automotive terminologies. Eventually a former Ghia engineer joined Chrysler's Detroit staff to act as interpreter.

But the main problem with the Ghia Crowns was that the custom-built cars were always exceptions to the Chrysler engineering system and a headache to all involved, requiring an inordinate amount of attention and follow-through. After each model run Chrysler management would consider dropping the Ghia program, yet each time another batch of cars would be authorized to satisfy the small demand.

Ghia completed thirty-six cars in 1957, thirty-one in 1958 and seven in 1959. That year Chrysler again considered using a domestic body builder, but after viewing sample cars of two companies, decided the quality wasn't up to Ghia's standards; so the contract with Ghia was renewed.

1960 Crown Imperial with blind rear quarters.

1963 eight-passenger sedan interior.   1963 Crown Imperial.

When the Imperial line was restyled in 1960, the limousines were updated, too. The base kit-car was changed to the LeBaron four-door sedan, again over a convertible frame, making conversion at Ghia somewhat easier. Sedan doors and center pillar were thus already part of the car, although both the doors and rear quarter panel required additional reworking. Black became the standard exterior color (although other colors were available on special order), and only two different interior trim schemes were offered — either gray or beige. The addition of standard items — such as Auto Pilot; automatic headlight dimmer; and electronic, glare-reducing rear-view mirror — combined with higher in-plant costs at Ghia, boosted the price of a limousine to $16,500 f.o.b. Detroit.

During 1960, sixteen cars were assembled at Ghia and an additional nine in 1961, all with 1960 styling. Most of these carried the usual six-window roof, but at least one was built to special order, with a four-window roof and a blind rear quarter.

There were no 1962 models, but in 1963 the program was reinstated and the limousines appeared with updated styling. Thirteen cars were built, twelve limousines and one eight-passenger sedan. Base car was the four-door hardtop, and price rose again — to $18,500.

In 1964 the styling of the Imperial was again changed under the direction of Elwood Engel. The new, more formal lines were especially appropriate for a limousine. This time twenty cars were built, ten of them updated to 1965 models by changing the grille. Two roof styles were

1964 Crown Imperial limousine

available — the regular six-window 'Town' limousine and a special 'Landau' version with blind rear quarter panels and a discreetly small oval rear window.

The 1965 model was the last of the Ghia Crowns. The cost of the limousine had risen fifty-four percent from 1957 to 1965, and Chrysler felt it could perhaps get the limousines produced locally for less. Segré had died in 1963, leaving Ghia in different hands and ending a long association with Chrysler. Too, the new 1967 Imperial was to use unit-body construction, and Ghia was inexperienced in stretching frameless cars. Tooling for the Ghia limousines was shipped to Barreiros in Spain, where ten more cars were built with 1966 grilles and rear decks.

Ghia was out of the picture, but Chrysler was still interested in the limousine business. A joint venture with a local supplier called for 500 limousines in 1967 — but the program was aborted. Finally Chrysler got together with Stageway Coaches of Fort Smith, Arkansas, a major builder of airport limousines. Twelve 1967-68 LeBaron limousines (the Crown Imperial name was dropped) were built by Stageway on an enormous 163-inch wheelbase. This model was justifiably advertised as the largest luxury automobile in the world. Unlike the Ghia limousines, the Stageway cars had an extra window and panel between the front and rear doors. The stretched LeBarons were priced between $12,000 and $15,000, depending on the equipment ordered. Between 1969 and 1971, another fifteen or so

YEARLY PRODUCTION FIGURES
1957.................36
1958.................31
1959..................7
1960.................16
1961..................9
1962..................0
1963.................13
1964.................10
1965.................10

TOTAL.............132

SALES LITERATURE
1957 Folder, 12½x8, black & white
1958 Catalog, 12½x8, black & white, 8p.
1960 Folder, 7½x12½, black, white and gray
1963 Folder, 16x8, black, white and gold
1964 Catalog, 14x12, color, 8pgs. + covers.
1965 Crown Imperial limousine pictured inside deluxe Imperial catalog

1969 LeBaron limousine by Stageway.

Stageway limousine interior, 1967.

1967 LeBaron limousine by Stageway.

1972 Imperial limousine built for U.S. government by Hess & Eisenhardt, used 1973 grille.

Stageway limousines were built, employing the fuselage styling of the current Imperials. The last two Imperial limousines, 1972 models with 1973 grilles, were built for the Secret Service by yet another coachbuilder, Hess and Eisenhardt, noted for its funeral cars.

Of course, there can be no more Imperial limousines because the Imperial itself is no longer made. The last one, a black LeBaron four-door hardtop, came off the line at Jefferson Assembly early in the afternoon of June 12, 1975. Ghia is now a Ford subsidiary and the Ghia crest is splashed indiscriminately on many of Ford's standard production models. But back in the days when the Ghia crest meant Italian craftsmanship at its finest, the Ghia Crown Imperials were the ultimate in luxury transportation. Perhaps they still are.

Appendix II
Compiled by Jeffrey I. Godshall

Chrysler & Imperial Production Figures, 1946-1975

Figures include:
Cars built in U.S. plants for domestic sale
Cars built in U.S. plants for Canada
Cars built in U.S. plants for export
Cars built in U.S. plants dismantled for export
Cars built in Canadian plants
Note: Figures are totaled for Chrysler 1946-54 (with Imperial); thereafter separate totals for Chrysler and Imperial are issued.

PRODUCTION 1946-48
ROYAL C38S
1,117	2-door sedan
1,221	3-pass. coupe
4,318	club coupe
24,279	4-door sedan
626	7-pass. sedan
169	limousine
1	chassis
31,731	TOTAL

WINDSOR C38W
1,980	3-pass. coupe
26,482	club coupe
11,200	convertible
4,034	2-door sedan
161,139	4-door sedan
4,182	traveler sedan
4,390	7-pass. sedan
1,496	limousine
210,721	TOTAL

TOWN & COUNTRY (six) C38W
4,049	4-door sedan
1	chassis (also built one experimental 2-door brougham)
4,050	TOTAL

TOWN & COUNTRY (eight) C39N
7	hardtop coupe
8,368	convertible
100	4-door sedan
8,475	TOTAL

SARATOGA C39K
74	3-pass. coupe
765	club coupe
155	2-door sedan
4,611	4-door sedan
5,605	TOTAL

NEW YORKER C39N
699	3-pass. coupe
10,735	club coupe
3,000	convertible
545	2-door sedan
52,036	4-door sedan
2	chassis
67,019	TOTAL

CROWN IMPERIAL C40
650	8-pass. sedan
750	limousine
1,400	TOTAL
329,001	TOTAL CHRYSLER

PRODUCTION 1949
ROYAL C45-1
4,849	club coupe (includes one body changed to 3-pass. coupe)
13,192	4-door sedan
850	wood wagon
185	8-pass. sedan
19,076	TOTAL

WINDSOR C45-2
17,732	club coupe
3,234	convertible
55,879	4-door sedan (including one Carryall sedan)
373	8-pass. sedan
73	limousine
77,291	TOTAL

SARATOGA C46-1
465	club coupe
1,810	4-door sedan
2,275	TOTAL

NEW YORKER C46-2
4,524	club coupe
1,137	convertible
18,779	4-door sedan
50	Imperial sedan
1	chassis
24,491	TOTAL

TOWN & COUNTRY C46-2
1,000	convertible (also one experimental T&C 2-door hardtop)
1,000	TOTAL

CROWN IMPERIAL C47
40	8-pass. sedan
45	limousine
85	TOTAL
124,218	TOTAL CHRYSLER

PRODUCTION 1950
ROYAL C48-1
5,900	club coupe
17,713	4-door sedan
375	8-pass. sedan
100	steel wagon
599	wood wagon
24,687	TOTAL

WINDSOR C48-2
20,050	club coupe
2,201	convertible
9,925	hardtop
78,199	4-door sedan
900	traveler sedan
763	8-pass. sedan
174	limousine
112,213	TOTAL

SARATOGA C49-1
300	club coupe
1,000	4-door sedan
1,300	TOTAL

NEW YORKER C49-2
3,000	club coupe
899	convertible
2,800	hardtop
22,633	4-door sedan
9,600	Imperial sedan
1,150	Imperial deluxe sedan
1	wood wagon
2	chassis
39,985	TOTAL

TOWN & COUNTRY C49-2
700	hardtop
700	TOTAL

CROWN IMPERIAL C50
209	8-pass. sedan
205	limousine
1	chassis
415	TOTAL
179,300	TOTAL CHRYSLER

PRODUCTION 1951-52
WINDSOR C-51-1
6,735	club coupe
16,112	4-door sedan
633	8-pass. sedan
1,967	wagon
153	ambulance
25,600	TOTAL

WINDSOR DELUXE C-51-2
8,365	club coupe
4,200	convertible
10,200	hardtop
75,513	4-door sedan
850	Traveler
720	8-pass. sedan
152	limousine
100,000	TOTAL

SARATOGA C-55
8,501	club coupe (includes one hardtop with New Yorker body)
35,516	4-door sedan
183	8-pass. sedan
1,299	wagon
1	ambulance
45,500	TOTAL

NEW YORKER C-52
3,533	club coupe
2,200	convertible
5,800	hardtop
40,415	4-door sedan
251	wagon (including four with C-51 bodies)
1	chassis
52,200	TOTAL

IMPERIAL C-54
1,189	club coupe
650	convertible
3,450	hardtop
21,711	4-door sedan
27,000	TOTAL

CROWN IMPERIAL C-53
360	8-pass. sedan
338	limousine
2	chassis
700	TOTAL
251,000	TOTAL CHRYSLER

PRODUCTION 1953
WINDSOR C-60-1
11,646	club coupe
18,879	4-door sedan
425	8-pass. sedan
1,242	wagon
32,192	TOTAL

WINDSOR DELUXE C-60-2
1,250	club coupe
5,642	hardtop
45,385	4-door sedan
52,277	TOTAL

NEW YORKER C-56-1
7,749	club coupe
2,525	hardtop
37,540	4-door sedan
100	8-pass. sedan
1,399	wagon
49,313	TOTAL

NEW YORKER DELUXE C-56-2
- 1,934 club coupe
- 950 convertible
- 3,715 hardtop
- 20,585 4-door sedan
- 21 chassis
- 27,205 TOTAL

CUSTOM IMPERIAL C-58
- 823 hardtop
- 7,793 4-door sedan
- 243 Town limousine
- 8,859 TOTAL

CROWN IMPERIAL C-59
- 48 8-pass. sedan
- 111 limousine
- 1 chassis
- 160 TOTAL
- 170,006 TOTAL CHRYSLER

PRODUCTION 1954
WINDSOR DELUXE C-62
- 5,659 club coupe
- 500 convertible
- 3,655 hardtop
- 33,563 4-door sedan
- 500 8-pass. sedan
- 650 wagon
- 44,527 TOTAL

NEW YORKER C-63-1
- 2,079 club coupe
- 1,312 hardtop
- 15,788 4-door sedan
- 140 8-pass. sedan
- 1,100 wagon
- 20,419 TOTAL

NEW YORKER DELUXE C-63-2
- 1,861 club coupe
- 724 convertible
- 4,814 hardtop
- 26,907 4-door sedan
- 17 chassis
- 34,278 TOTAL

CUSTOM IMPERIAL C-64
- 1,250 hardtop (including one convertible)
- 4,324 4-door sedan
- 85 Town limousine (including two special Town limousines)
- 2 chassis
- 5,661 TOTAL

CROWN IMPERIAL C-66
- 23 8-pass. sedan
- 77 limousine
- 100 TOTAL
- 104,985 TOTAL CHRYSLER

PRODUCTION 1955
WINDSOR DELUXE C-67
- 18,474 Nassau hardtop
- 13,126 Newport hardtop
- 1,395 convertible
- 63,896 4-door sedan
- 1,983 wagon
- 98,874 TOTAL

NEW YORKER DELUXE C-68
- 5,777 Newport hardtop
- 11,076 St. Regis hardtop
- 1,725 300 hardtop
- 946 convertible
- 33,342 4-door sedan
- 1,036 wagon
- 1 chassis
- 53,906 TOTAL
- 152,780 TOTAL CHRYSLER

IMPERIAL C-69
- 3,418 hardtop
- 1 convertible (special body)
- 7,840 4-door sedan
- 1 chassis
- 11,260 TOTAL

CROWN IMPERIAL C-70
- 45 8-pass. sedan
- 127 limousine
- 172 TOTAL
- 11,432 TOTAL IMPERIAL

PRODUCTION 1956
WINDSOR C-71
- 11,400 Nassau 2-door hardtop
- 10,800 Newport 2-door hardtop
- 1,011 convertible
- 53,119 4-door sedan
- 7,050 4-door hardtop
- 2,700 wagon
- 86,080 TOTAL

NEW YORKER C-72
- 4,115 Newport 2-door hardtop
- 6,686 St. Regis 2-door hardtop
- 1,102 300B 2-door hardtop
- 921 convertible
- 24,749 4-door sedan
- 3,599 4-door hardtop
- 1,070 wagon
- 42,242 TOTAL
- 128,322 TOTAL CHRYSLER

IMPERIAL C-73
- 2,094 2-door hardtop
- 6,821 4-door sedan
- 1,543 4-door hardtop
- 10,458 TOTAL

CROWN IMPERIAL C-70
- 51 8-pass. sedan
- 175 limousine
- 226 TOTAL
- 10,684 TOTAL IMPERIAL

PRODUCTION 1957
WINDSOR C-75-1
- 14,027 2-door hardtop
- 17,639 4-door sedan
- 14,354 4-door hardtop
- 2,035 wagon
- 48,055 TOTAL

SARATOGA C-75-2
- 10,633 2-door hardtop
- 14,977 4-door sedan
- 11,586 4-door hardtop
- 37,196 TOTAL

NEW YORKER C-76
- 8,863 2-door hardtop
- 1,918 300C 2-door hardtop
- 12,369 4-door sedan
- 10,948 4-door hardtop
- 1,049 convertible
- 484 300C convertible
- 1,391 wagon
- 37,022 TOTAL
- 122,273 TOTAL CHRYSLER

IMPERIAL IM1-1
- 4,885 2-door hardtop
- 5,654 4-door sedan
- 7,527 4-door hardtop
- 18,066 TOTAL

IMPERIAL CROWN IM1-2
- 4,199 2-door hardtop
- 3,642 4-door sedan
- 7,843 4-door hardtop
- 1,167 convertible
- 16,851 TOTAL

IMPERIAL LEBARON IM1-4
- 1,729 2-door hardtop
- 911 4-door hardtop
- 2,640 TOTAL
- 37,557 TOTAL IMPERIAL

PRODUCTION 1958
WINDSOR LC1-L
- 6,205 2-door hardtop
- 12,861 4-door sedan
- 6,254 4-door hardtop
- 2 convertible
- 791 wagon 2-seat
- 862 wagon 3-seat
- 26,975 TOTAL

SARATOGA LC2-M
- 4,456 2-door hardtop
- 8,698 4-door sedan
- 5,322 4-door hardtop
- 18,476 TOTAL

NEW YORKER LC3-H
- 3,205 2-door hardtop
- 7,110 4-door sedan
- 5,227 4-door hardtop
- 666 convertible
- 428 wagon 2-seat
- 775 wagon 3-seat
- 618 300D 2-door hardtop
- 191 300D convertible
- 18,220 TOTAL
- 63,671 TOTAL CHRYSLER

IMPERIAL LY1-L
- 1,801 2-door hardtop
- 1,926 4-door sedan
- 3,336 4-door hardtop
- 7,063 TOTAL

IMPERIAL CROWN LY1-M
- 1,939 2-door hardtop
- 1,240 4-door sedan
- 4,146 4-door hardtop
- 675 convertible
- 8,000 TOTAL

IMPERIAL LEBARON LY1-H
- 501 4-door sedan
- 538 4-door hardtop
- 1,039 TOTAL
- 16,102 TOTAL IMPERIAL

PRODUCTION 1959
WINDSOR MC1-L
- 6,775 2-door hardtop
- 19,910 4-door sedan
- 6,084 4-door hardtop
- 961 convertible
- 992 wagon 2-seat
- 751 wagon 3-seat
- 35,473 TOTAL

SARATOGA MC2-M
- 3,753 2-door hardtop
- 8,783 4-door sedan
- 4,943 4-door hardtop
- 17,479 TOTAL

NEW YORKER MC3-M
- 3 chassis
- 2,435 2-door hardtop
- 7,792 4-door sedan
- 4,805 4-door hardtop
- 286 convertible
- 444 wagon 2-seat
- 564 wagon 3-seat
- 550 300E 2-door hardtop
- 140 300E convertible
- 17,019 TOTAL
- 69,971 TOTAL CHRYSLER

IMPERIAL CUSTOM MY1-L
- 1,743 2-door hardtop
- 2,071 4-door sedan
- 3,984 4-door hardtop
- 7,798 TOTAL

IMPERIAL CROWN MY1-M
- 1,728 2-door hardtop
- 1,335 4-door sedan
- 4,714 4-door hardtop
- 555 convertible
- 8,332 TOTAL

IMPERIAL LEBARON MY1-H
- 510 4-door sedan
- 622 4-door hardtop
- 1,132 TOTAL
- 17,262 TOTAL IMPERIAL

PRODUCTION 1960
WINDSOR PC1-L
- 6,496 2-door hardtop
- 25,152 4-door sedan
- 5,897 4-door hardtop
- 1,467 convertible
- 1,120 wagon 2-seat
- 1,026 wagon 3-seat
- 41,158 TOTAL

SARATOGA PC2-M
- 2,963 2-door hardtop
- 8,463 4-door sedan
- 4,099 4-door hardtop
- 15,525 TOTAL

NEW YORKER PC3-H
- 2,835 2-door hardtop
- 9,079 4-door sedan
- 5,625 4-door hardtop
- 556 convertible
- 624 wagon 2-seat
- 671 wagon 3-seat
- 964 300F 2-door hardtop
- 248 300F convertible
- 20,602 TOTAL
- 77,602 TOTAL CHRYSLER

IMPERIAL CUSTOM PY1-L
- 1,498 2-door hardtop
- 2,335 4-door sedan
- 3,953 4-door hardtop
- 7,786 TOTAL

IMPERIAL CROWN PY1-M
- 1,504 2-door hardtop
- 1,594 4-door sedan
- 4,510 4-door hardtop
- 618 convertible
- 8,226 TOTAL

IMPERIAL LEBARON PY1-H
- 692 4-door sedan
- 999 4-door hardtop
- 1,691 TOTAL
- 17,703 TOTAL IMPERIAL

PRODUCTION 1961
NEWPORT RC1-L
- 9,405 2-door hardtop
- 34,370 4-door sedan
- 7,789 4-door hardtop
- 2,135 convertible
- 1,832 wagon 2-seat
- 1,571 wagon 3-seat
- 57,102 TOTAL

WINDSOR RC2-M
- 2,941 2-door hardtop
- 10,239 4-door sedan
- 4,156 4-door hardtop
- 17,336 TOTAL

NEW YORKER RC3-H
- 2,541 2-door hardtop
- 9,984 4-door sedan
- 5,862 4-door hardtop
- 576 convertible

676	wagon 2-seat	
760	wagon 3-seat	
20,399	TOTAL	

C-300 RC4-P
1,280	300G 2-door hardtop
337	300G convertible
1,617	TOTAL
96,454	TOTAL CHRYSLER

IMPERIAL CUSTOM RY1-L
889	2-door hardtop
4,129	4-door hardtop
5,018	TOTAL

IMPERIAL CROWN RY1-M
1,007	2-door hardtop
4,769	4-door hardtop
429	convertible
6,205	TOTAL

IMPERIAL LEBARON RY1-H
1,026	4-door hardtop
12,249	TOTAL IMPERIAL

PRODUCTION 1962
NEWPORT SC1-L
11,910	2-door hardtop
54,813	4-door sedan
8,712	4-door hardtop
2,051	convertible
3,271	wagon 2-seat
2,363	wagon 3-seat
83,120	TOTAL

300 SC2-M
11,776	2-door hardtop (includes 435 300H)
1,801	4-door sedan
10,030	4-door hardtop
1,971	convertible (includes 123 300H)
25,578	TOTAL

NEW YORKER SC3-H
12,056	2-door hardtop
6,646	4-door hardtop
728	wagon 2-seat
793	wagon 3-seat
20,223	TOTAL
128,921	TOTAL CHRYSLER

IMPERIAL CUSTOM SY1-L
826	2-door hardtop
3,587	4-door hardtop
4,413	TOTAL

IMPERIAL CROWN SY2-M
1,010	2-door hardtop
6,911	4-door hardtop
554	convertible
8,475	TOTAL

IMPERIAL LEBARON
1,449	4-door hardtop
14,337	TOTAL IMPERIAL

PRODUCTION 1963
NEWPORT TC1-L
9,809	2-door hardtop
49,067	4-door sedan
8,437	4-door hardtop
2,093	convertible
3,618	wagon 2-seat
2,948	wagon 3-seat
75,972	TOTAL

300 TC2-M
10,129	2-door hardtop (includes 400 300J)
1,625	4-door sedan
9,915	4-door hardtop
3,396	convertible
25,065	TOTAL

NEW YORKER TC3-H
14,884	4-door sedan
10,822	4-door hardtop
950	wagon 2-seat
1,244	wagon 3-seat
27,960	TOTAL
128,937	TOTAL CHRYSLER

IMPERIAL CUSTOM TY1-L
749	2-door hardtop
3,264	4-door hardtop
4,013	TOTAL

IMPERIAL CROWN TY1-M
1,067	2-door hardtop
6,960	4-door hardtop
531	convertible
8,558	TOTAL

IMPERIAL LEBARON TY1-H
1,537	4-door hardtop
14,108	TOTAL IMPERIAL

PRODUCTION 1964
NEWPORT VC1-L
10,579	2-door hardtop
55,957	4-door sedan
9,710	4-door hardtop
2,176	convertible
3,720	wagon 2-seat
3,041	wagon 3-seat
85,183	TOTAL

300 VC2-M
13,401	2-door hardtop (includes 3,022 300K)
2,078	4-door sedan
11,460	4-door hardtop
2,026	convertible (includes 625 300K)
28,965	TOTAL

NEW YORKER VC3-H
300	2-door hardtop
15,443	4-door sedan
12,508	4-door hardtop (includes 1,621 Salon)
1,190	wagon 2-seat
1,603	wagon 3-seat
31,044	TOTAL
145,192	TOTAL CHRYSLER

IMPERIAL CROWN VY1-M
5,233	2-door hardtop
14,181	4-door hardtop
922	convertible
20,336	TOTAL

IMPERIAL LEBARON VY1-H
2,949	4-door hardtop
23,285	TOTAL IMPERIAL

PRODUCTION 1965
NEWPORT AC1-L
23,655	2-door hardtop
61,054	4-door sedan
12,411	4-door sedan, 6-window
17,062	4-door hardtop
3,192	convertible
4,683	wagon 2-seat
3,738	wagon 3-seat
125,795	TOTAL

300 AC2-M
11,621	2-door hardtop
2,187	4-door sedan, 6-window
12,452	4-door hardtop
1,418	convertible
27,678	TOTAL

300L AC2-P
2,405	2-door hardtop
440	convertible
2,845	TOTAL

NEW YORKER AC3-H
9,357	2-door hardtop
16,339	4-door sedan, 6-window
21,110	4-door hardtop
1,368	wagon 2-seat
1,697	wagon 3-seat
49,871	TOTAL
206,189	TOTAL CHRYSLER

IMPERIAL CROWN AY1-M
3,974	2-door hardtop
11,628	4-door hardtop
633	convertible
16,235	TOTAL

IMPERIAL LEBARON AY1-H
2,164	4-door hardtop
18,399	TOTAL IMPERIAL

PRODUCTION 1966
NEWPORT BC1-L
37,622	2-door hardtop
74,964	4-door sedan
9,432	4-door sedan, 6-window
24,966	4-door hardtop
3,085	convertible
9,035	wagon 2-seat
8,567	wagon 3-seat
167,711	TOTAL

300 BC2-M
24,103	2-door hardtop
2,353	4-door sedan
20,642	4-door hardtop
2,500	convertible
49,597	TOTAL

NEW YORKER BC3-H
7,955	2-door hardtop
13,025	4-door sedan, 6-window
26,599	4-door hardtop
47,579	TOTAL
264,887	TOTAL CHRYSLER

IMPERIAL CROWN BY1-M
2,373	2-door hardtop
8,977	4-door hardtop
514	convertible
11,864	TOTAL

IMPERIAL LEBARON BY1-H
1,878	4-door hardtop
13,742	TOTAL IMPERIAL

PRODUCTION 1967
NEWPORT CC1-E
20,500	2-door hardtop
2,891	convertible
49,018	4-door sedan
14,247	4-door hardtop
7,183	wagon 2-seat
7,520	wagon 3-seat
107,349	TOTAL

NEWPORT CUSTOM CC1-L
14,193	2-door hardtop
23,101	4-door sedan
12,728	4-door hardtop
50,022	TOTAL

300 CC2-M
11,556	2-door hardtop
1,594	convertible
8,744	4-door hardtop
21,888	TOTAL

NEW YORKER CC3-H
6,885	2-door hardtop
10,907	4-door sedan
21,665	4-door hardtop
39,457	TOTAL
218,716	TOTAL CHRYSLER

IMPERIAL CROWN CY1-M
3,235	2-door hardtop
577	convertible
2,193	4-door sedan
9,415	4-door hardtop
15,420	TOTAL

IMPERIAL LEBARON CY1-H
2,194	TOTAL
17,614	TOTAL IMPERIAL

PRODUCTION 1968
NEWPORT DC1-E
36,768	2-door hardtop (includes 965 with Sportsgrain)
2,847	convertible (includes 175 with Sportsgrain)
61,436	4-door sedan
20,191	4-door hardtop
9,908	wagon 2-seat
12,233	wagon 3-seat
143,383	TOTAL

NEWPORT CUSTOM DC1-L
10,341	2-door hardtop
16,915	4-door sedan
11,460	4-door hardtop
38,716	TOTAL

300 DC2-M
16,953	2-door hardtop
2,161	convertible
15,507	4-door hardtop
34,621	TOTAL

NEW YORKER DC3-H
8,060	2-door hardtop
13,092	4-door sedan
26,991	4-door hardtop
48,143	TOTAL
264,863	TOTAL CHRYSLER

IMPERIAL CROWN DY1-M
2,656	2-door hardtop
1,887	4-door sedan
8,492	4-door hardtop
13,509	TOTAL

IMPERIAL LEBARON DY1-H
1,852	TOTAL
15,361	TOTAL IMPERIAL

PRODUCTION 1969
NEWPORT EC-E
33,639	2-door hardtop
2,169	convertible
55,083	4-door sedan
20,608	4-door hardtop
111,499	TOTAL

NEWPORT CUSTOM EC-L
10,955	2-door hardtop
18,401	4-door sedan
15,981	4-door hardtop
45,337	TOTAL

300 EC-M
16,075	2-door hardtop
1,933	convertible
14,464	4-door hardtop
32,472	TOTAL

NEW YORKER EC-H
7,537	2-door hardtop
12,253	4-door sedan
27,157	4-door hardtop
46,947	TOTAL

TOWN & COUNTRY EC-P
10,108	wagon 2-seat
14,408	wagon 3-seat
24,516	TOTAL
260,771	TOTAL CHRYSLER

IMPERIAL EY-M
- 4,816   LeBaron 2-door hardtop (includes 244 Crowns)
- 1,617   Crown 4-door sedan
- 15,644   LeBaron 4-door hardtop (includes 823 Crowns)
- 22,077   TOTAL IMPERIAL

PRODUCTION 1970
NEWPORT FC-E
- 21,664   2-door hardtop (includes 1,868 Cordobas)
- 1,124   convertible
- 39,285   4-door sedan (includes 1,873 Cordobas)
- 16,940   4-door hardtop
- 79,013   TOTAL

NEWPORT CUSTOM FC-L
- 6,639   2-door hardtop
- 13,767   4-door sedan
- 10,873   4-door hardtop
- 31,279   TOTAL

300 FC-M
- 10,084   2-door hardtop
- 1,077   convertible
- 9,846   4-door hardtop
- 21,007   TOTAL

NEW YORKER FC-H
- 4,917   2-door hardtop
- 9,389   4-door sedan
- 19,903   4-door hardtop
- 34,209   TOTAL

TOWN & COUNTRY FC-P
- 5,686   wagon 2-seat
- 9,583   wagon 3-seat
- 15,269   TOTAL
- 180,777   TOTAL CHRYSLER

IMPERIAL CROWN FY-L
- 254   2-door hardtop
- 1,333   4-door hardtop
- 1,587   TOTAL

IMPERIAL LEBARON FY-M
- 1,803   2-door hardtop
- 8,426   4-door hardtop
- 10,229   TOTAL
- 11,816   TOTAL IMPERIAL

PRODUCTION 1971
NEWPORT GC-E
- 22,049   2-door hardtop (includes 8,500 Newport Royals)
- 44,496   4-door sedan (includes 19,662 Newport Royals)
- 15,988   4-door hardtop (includes 5,188 Newport Royals)
- 82,533   TOTAL (includes 33,350 Newport Royals)

NEWPORT CUSTOM GC-L
- 5,527   2-door hardtop
- 11,254   4-door sedan
- 10,207   4-door hardtop
- 26,988   TOTAL

300 GC-S
- 7,256   2-door hardtop
- 6,683   4-door hardtop
- 13,939   TOTAL

NEW YORKER GC-H
- 4,485   2-door hardtop
- 9,850   4-door sedan
- 20,633   4-door hardtop
- 34,968   TOTAL

TOWN & COUNTRY GC-P
- 5,697   2-seat wagon
- 10,993   3-seat wagon
- 16,690   TOTAL
- 175,118   TOTAL CHRYSLER

IMPERIAL LEBARON GY-M
- 1,442   2-door hardtop
- 10,116   4-door hardtop
- 11,558   TOTAL IMPERIAL

PRODUCTION 1972
NEWPORT ROYAL HC-L
- 22,622   2-door hardtop
- 47,437   4-door sedan
- 15,185   4-door hardtop
- 85,304   TOTAL

NEWPORT CUSTOM HC-M
- 10,326   2-door hardtop
- 19,278   4-door sedan
- 15,457   4-door hardtop
- 45,061   TOTAL

NEW YORKER HC-H
- 5,567   2-door hardtop
- 7,296   4-door sedan
- 10,013   4-door hardtop
- 22,876   TOTAL

TOWN & COUNTRY HC-P
- 6,473   2-seat wagon
- 14,116   3-seat wagon
- 20,589   TOTAL

NEW YORKER BROUGHAM HC-S
- 4,635   2-door hardtop
- 5,971   4-door sedan
- 20,328   4-door hardtop
- 30,934   TOTAL
- 204,764   TOTAL CHRYSLER

IMPERIAL LEBARON HY-M
- 2,322   2-door hardtop
- 13,472   4-door hardtop
- 15,794   TOTAL IMPERIAL

PRODUCTION 1973
NEWPORT 3C-L
- 27,456   2-door hardtop
- 54,147   4-door sedan
- 20,175   4-door hardtop
- 101,778   TOTAL

NEWPORT CUSTOM 3C-M
- 12,293   2-door hardtop
- 20,092   4-door sedan
- 20,050   4-door hardtop
- 52,435   TOTAL

NEW YORKER 3C-H
- 7,991   4-door sedan
- 7,619   4-door hardtop
- 15,610   TOTAL

TOWN & COUNTRY 3C-P
- 5,353   2-seat wagon
- 14,687   3-seat wagon
- 20,040   TOTAL

NEW YORKER BROUGHAM 3C-S
- 9,190   2-door hardtop
- 8,541   4-door sedan
- 26,635   4-door hardtop
- 44,366   TOTAL
- 234,229   TOTAL CHRYSLER

IMPERIAL LEBARON 3Y-M
- 2,563   2-door hardtop
- 14,166   4-door hardtop
- 16,729   TOTAL IMPERIAL

PRODUCTION 1974
NEWPORT 4C-L
- 13,784   2-door hardtop
- 26,944   4-door sedan
- 8,968   4-door hardtop
- 49,696   TOTAL

NEWPORT CUSTOM 4C-M
- 7,206   2-door hardtop
- 10,569   4-door sedan
- 9,892   4-door hardtop
- 27,667   TOTAL

NEW YORKER 4C-H
- 3,072   4-door sedan
- 3,066   4-door hardtop
- 6,138   TOTAL

TOWN & COUNTRY 4C-P
- 2,236   2-seat wagon
- 5,958   3-seat wagon
- 8,194   TOTAL

NEW YORKER BROUGHAM 4C-S
- 7,980   2-door hardtop
- 4,533   4-door sedan
- 13,165   4-door hardtop
- 25,678   TOTAL
- 117,373   TOTAL CHRYSLER

IMPERIAL LEBARON 4Y-M
- 3,850   2-door hardtop
- 10,576   4-door hardtop
- 14,426   TOTAL IMPERIAL

PRODUCTION 1975
NEWPORT 5C-L
- 10,485   2-door hardtop
- 24,339   4-door sedan
- 6,846   4-door hardtop
- 41,670   TOTAL

NEWPORT CUSTOM 5C-M
- 5,831   2-door hardtop
- 9,623   4-door sedan
- 11,626   4-door hardtop
- 27,080   TOTAL

NEW YORKER BROUGHAM 5C-S
- 7,567   2-door hardtop
- 5,698   4-door sedan
- 12,774   4-door hardtop
- 26,039   TOTAL

TOWN & COUNTRY 5C-P
- 1,891   2-seat wagon
- 4,764   3-seat wagon
- 6,655   TOTAL

CORDOBA 5S-S
- 150,105   2-door coupe
- 251,549   TOTAL CHRYSLER

IMPERIAL LEBARON 5Y-M
- 2,728   2-door hardtop
- 6,102   4-door hardtop
- 8,830   TOTAL IMPERIAL

SUPPLEMENTAL PRODUCTION FIGURES:

1970 300 — includes 485 300-Hurst 2-door hardtops.
1970 NEWPORT — includes 1,868 Cordoba 2-door hardtops. 1,873 Cordoba 4-door hardtops.
1969 NEWPORT — includes 195 cars with Sportsgrain wood panelling.
1968 NEWPORT — includes 965 2-door hardtops and 175 convertibles with Sportsgrain wood panelling.
1964 NEW YORKER — includes 1,748 Salon 4-door hardtops.
1963 NEW YORKER — includes 593 Salon 4-door hardtops.
1964 300 — includes 2,152 300 and 255 300K Silver 300 models.
1963 300 — includes 306 2-door hardtops and 1,861 convertibles as Pace Setter Indy 500 replicas.
1962 NEWPORT — includes 5,902 Highlander trim models.
1961 NEWPORT — includes 4,953 Highlander trim models.

The figures above represent cars already *included* in the model year production figures for their respective years. These figures merely represent a further breakdown of existing totals.

    Certain unusual production figures appeared in the mid-1960's, such as the model 300 four-door sedan. In the U.S. no model 300 sedan was made, but in Canada the 300 was called the Saratoga and was offered as a sedan. However, the plants considered these cars as 300's and therefore included Saratogas (including the sedan) in the model 300 figure.

Appendix III
Compiled by Jeffrey I. Godshall
Chrysler & Imperial Literature, 1946-1975

1946:
Folder, 8½x5½, sedan, sepia&w, CS-206 2-46
Folder, 8½x5½, full line, color, CS-207 4-46
Folder, 8x5, Town & Country, b&w&green
Folder, 9x5½, Town & Country, color, CS-209 6-46
Booklet, 9x6, Fluid Drive, color, 20p., c1945
Booklet, 9x6, Superfinish, color, 24p., c1945

1947:
Catalog, 11x8, full line, color, 12p., CS-216 4-47
Card, 6x4, Traveler, b&w

1948:
Folder, 11x8½, Crown Imp. limo., brown&yellow&w, 232 2-48
Folder, 11x8½, Royal/Windsor sedan/limo., brown&yellow&w, 233 2-48
Folder, 11x8½, Crown Imp. sedan, brown&yellow&w, 231 2-48
Catalog, 9x12, "It's a Boy," b&w&blue&orange, 12p., CS-240

1949:
Catalog, 12x9, full line (no Imp.), color, 20p. + covers, CS-250 5-49 w/env.
Folder, 11x7, full line (no Imp.), color, CS-249 4-49
Folder, 10½x7, full line (no Imp.), green&w, CS-248
Folder, 8x10½, Town & Country, b&w, CS-257
Catalog, 12x9, "Pre-Showing," b&w&blue, 24p., CS-247 2-49
Catalog, 8½x6, access., color&sepia&w, 20p., D-12710

1950:
Folder, 10x7, full line (no Imp.), color, CS-258 12-49
Catalog, 12x9, Saratoga/NY/T&C, color, 20p., CS-261 2-50
Catalog, 12x9, Royal/Windsor, color, 16p., CS-260 2-50
Booklet, 7x9, Fluid Drive, color, 16p.
Folder, 8½x11, Traveler, color, CS-270
Catalog, 9x7, 2-tone paint, color, 8p., CS-267
Folder, 6x3, prices, b&w

1951:
Catalog, 11x9½, New Yorker, color, 16p., CS-273
Catalog, 11x9, Windsor, color, 16p., CS-272 1-51
Folder, 10x8, Saratoga, color, CS-284 7-51
Folder, 10x8, full line (no Sara.), color, CS-271 12-50
Booklet, 7x9, Firepower V-8, color, 20p. + covers, CS-275
Catalog, 11x9½, Imperial, color, 20p., CS-274 1-51

1952:
Catalog, 11x8½, full line, color, 12 p., CS-285 11-51
Catalog, 11x8½, Windsor/W Deluxe, color, 12p., CS-286 11-51
Catalog, 11x8½, Saratoga, color, 8p., CS-285 11-51
Catalog, 11x8½, New Yorker, color, 8p. + covers, CS-289 11-51
Catalog, 7x9, Power Steering, b&w&brown, 8p., CS-295

1953:
Catalog, 11x9½, Windsor/W Deluxe, color, 12p., CS-298 10-52
Folder, 9x11, full line, color, CS-297 9-52
Folder, as above, 3-53
Catalog, 14x11, New Yorker/NY Deluxe, color, 24p., CS-299 10-52
Catalog, 11x14, Imperial, color, 12p. + covers, CS-300 w/env.
Folder, 10x6, Imperial Newport, b&w, CS-307
Card, 6x3, Bermuda Beauty, color
Catalog, 7x9, Power Steering, b&w&green, 8p., CS-305 11-52
Mailer-Folder, 7½x4, "An Invitation," color
Mailer-Folder, 8½x4, "Streamlining," color
Mailer-Folder, 8½x4, interiors, color

1954:
Booklet, 5x7, "Winner," 12p., b&w, CS-321
Folder, 7x9 *Popular Science* test, b&w&blue
Catalog, 12x9, Windsor Deluxe, color, 16 p., 10-53 CS-309
Booklet, 8½x11, "Leadership," color, 24p., CS-230 3-54
Folder, 10x10, full line, brown&b&w, CS-308 10-53
Folder, 10x9½, full line, sepia&w, CS-324 4-54
Catalog, 11x14, New Yorker/NY Deluxe, color, 24p., CS-310 10-53
Catalog, 11x14, Imperial, color, 20p. + covers, CS-311 10-53
Folder, 12½x9½, Golden Falcon/Bluebird, color, CS-322
Card, 8x5, Bluebird, color
Card, as above, Golden Falcon, color

1955:
Folder, 11x9, 300, color, CS-339 2-55
Folder, 9½x11½, full line, b&w&green, CS-328 10-54
Card, 8x5, Blue Heron, sedan, color
Card, as above, Green Falcon, hdtp., color
Folder, 12x9, Blue Heron/Green Falcon, color, CS-341 3-55
Catalog, 12x12, Windsor Deluxe, color, 16p., CS-329 10-54
Catalog, 12x12, New Yorker Deluxe, color, 20p., CS-330 10-54
Folder, 8x5½, New Yorker Deluxe, b&w&orange w/color pic.
Folder, 7½x5, Imperial, b&w, CS-345 4-55
Catalog, 14x14, Imperial, 20p. + tissues + covers, CS-331 10-54 w/env.
Portfolio, 14x11½, Crown Imperial, 5 b&w plates w/purple&gold covers
Sheet, 8½x11, 300 race records/specs., b&w
Folder-Mailer, 8x6, full line, color

1956:
Folder, 10x6, full line, color, CS-349 8-55 Chrysler only
Folder, 4x9, access., b&w&orange, CS-365
Catalog, 12x12, New Yorker, color, 16p., CS-351 9-55
Catalog, 12x12, Windsor, color, 16p., CS-350 9-55
Folder, 14x11, 300B, color, CS-369 1-56
Catalog, 6½x8½, Power Steering, b&w&blue, 8p., CS-358 10-55
Folder, 9½x6, air cond., b&w&yellow&blue, CS-370 1-56
Folder, 5x3½, full line Chrysler, color, CS-362 10-55

Folder, 4x7, "250-HP Power Train," b&w&red, CS-372
Folder, 18x12, Crown Imperial, sepia&yellow, CS-362 w/env.
Folder, 5x6, "Act 2" Imperial, b&w, CS-366
Catalog, 9½x6, Imperial, b&w, 8p., CS-360-55
Catalog, 14x14, Imperial, 16p. + tissues + covers, CS-352-55 w/env.
Folder, 13x11½, Highway Hi-Fi, b&w&purple
Booklet, 5x7, Questions/Answers, b&w w/green covers, 28p., CS-359

1957:
Folder, 5x3½, full line Chrysler, color, CS-385 11-56
Folder, 13½x9, 300C, color, CS-386 12-56
Catalog, 13x9, full line Chrysler, 24p., CS-374 9-56
Folder, 10x6, full line Chrysler, CS-373 9-56
Catalog, 4x7, access., b&w&blue, 16p.
Folder, 11x10, "New Fine Car Leader" Imperial, color, CS-399
Folder, 7½x5, full line Imperial, b&w, CS-388 1-57
Folder, 9½x11, full line Imperial, color, CS-376 9-56
Folder, as above w/notation on LeBaron 4-dr. hdtp.
Catalog, 11x14½, Imperial, color, 20p. + tissues + covers, CS-375 9-56
Folder, 12½x7½, Crown Imperial limo., b&w w/env.
Folder, 9x4, "Chrysler Firsts," b&w&blue, Nov. 15, 1956
Folder, 3½x8½, colors, color, b&w&red
Catalog, 4x7, Imperial access., b&w&red, 12p., CS-391 Feb. '57

1958:
Folder, 12½x9½, Windsor Dartline, color, CS-418
Catalog, 14x11, 300D, b&w, 8p., CS-415 11-57
Folder, 4x3½, full line Chrysler, color, CS-413 12-57
Folder, 12x7, full line, color, CS-406 10-57
Catalog, 14x10½, full line, color, 24p., CS-405 10-57
Folder, 11½x7½, full line Imperial, CS-408 10-57
Folder, 10x7, Imperial, b&w, CS-414 11-57
Folder, 7x8½, Auto-Pilot, b&w&yellow, CS-416
Catalog, 14x11, Imperial, color, 28p., CS-407 10-57 w/env.
Catalog, 12½x8, Crown Imperial, b&w, 8p.
Catalog, 11x7, Imperial, color, 8p. + covers

1959:
Folder, 10½x14, full line Chrysler, color
Folder, 9½x9, full line Chrysler, color, CS-421
Catalog, 12x12½, 300E, b&w, 8p., CS-427
Catalog, 12x13, full line Chrysler, color, 16p. + foldouts, CS-422
Folder, 9x8½, Chry/Imp opt. equip., b&w
Folder, 8½x11, spring colors, color
Catalog, 12x9, Imperial, color, 12p., CS-424
Catalog, 11½x8½, "Your Next Fine Car" Imperial, color, 16p.
Catalog, 15x11, Imperial, color, 16p. + mini-pgs. + covers, CS-423 w/env.
Folder, 10x13, Imperial Warren Ave. plant, color
Folder, 10x7, full line Imperial, b&w, CS-426

1960:
Catalog, 12x12½, full line Chrysler, color, 20p. + mini-pgs. + foldout, CS-433 9-59 81-005-0002
Catalog, 8x11, full line Chrysler, color, 16p., CS-434 9-59 81-005-0003
Booklet, 9x7, "Anchors, Bezels, etc.," b&w&red, 12p.
Folder, 8x11, 300F, b&w
Catalog, 13x10½, 300F, b&w, 12p., CS-349 2-60
Catalog, 10x9, Imperial, color, 20p., CS-436 9-59 81-005-0005
Folder, 7½x12½, Crown Imperial limo., b&w w/env.
Catalog, 14x12, Imperial, color, 20p. + covers, CS-435 9-59 81-005-0004
Mailer-Catalog, 8½x11½, Imperial, color, 12p.

1961:
Catalog, 10x8½, Chrysler, color, 16p., CS-441 9-60 81-005-1008
Folder, 7x10, Newport, b&w
Catalog, 13½x10, 300G, b&w, 12p., CS-446
Catalog, 12½x10½, full line Chrysler, color, 16p. + mini-pgs., 81-005-1009 CS-440
Folder, 8½x11, "Enforcer" police cars, b&w, 4-27-61
Catalog, 11x8, Imperial, color, 16p., 9-60 81-005-1007 CS-443
Catalog, 14x10, Imperial, 16p. + foldout, 81-005-1006 CS-442 9-60

1962:
Folder, 8½x11, Chrysler, color, 81-005-2013 CS-448 9-61
Folder, as above, 1-62
Folder, 9x4, air cond., color, 81-610-0288 Sept. '61
Folder, 11x8½, "Enforcer" police cars, b&w
Catalog, 14x10½, Chrysler, color, 20p., 81-005-2011 CS-447 9-61
Booklet, 4x8½, comparisons, b&w, 24p.
Folder, 8½x11½, 300H, b&w
Card, 8½x6, 300, color
Card, 8½x6, Newport sedan, color
Folder, 5½x3, Newport sedan, color
Catalog, 11x8, Imperial, color, 16p., 81-005-2014 CS-450 9-61
Catalog, 14x10, Imperial, color, 12p + mini-pgs., 81-005-2012 CS-449 9-61
Folder, 14x11½, "Test Drive" Imperial, color
Booklet, 8½x4, comparisons (Imperial), b&w, 20p.
Folder, 9x4, LeBaron 4-dr. hdtp., color

1963:
Card, 10x4, warranty, b&w
Catalog, 11x5, Chrysler, color, 12p., 9-62 81-005-3016 CS-631
Catalog, as above, CS-631 R
Catalog, 11x11, 300J, b&w, 8p., CS-363 11-62 w/env.
Folder, 11x14, "300J Wows Press," b&w
Catalog, 9½x12½, Chrysler Styling Comments, w&color, 12p. w/env. w/4-pocket-sized selling cards
Catalog, 8x11, New Yorker Salon, color, 8p.
Folder, 6x9, *Mechanix Illustrated* Chrysler test, b&w
Catalog, 14x10½, Chrysler, color, 20p., 81-005-3015 CS-360 9-62
Catalog, 11x8, Imperial, color, 20p., 81-005-3018 CS-633 9-62 w/warranty card
Catalog, as above, CS-633 R
Catalog, 14x10½, Imperial, color, 20p. + covers, 81-005-3017 CS-632 9-62
Folder, 16x8, Crown Imperial limo., b&w&gold, w/env.
Portfolio, 11x8½, "Legendary LeBarons," color, 5 plates w/env. w/mailing env.

1964:
Folder, 8½x11, "Enforcer" police cars, b&w
Folder, 8½x11, Chrysler order codes, b&gray, rev. 10-63
Card, 8½x6, 300 2-dr. hdtp., color
Folder, 8½x5½, Trailer Towing, b&w&brown
Catalog, 8½x11, Chrysler, color, 20p., 9-63 C-640 81-005-4019
Card, 8½x6, "Silver 300," color
Folder, 8½x11, Chrysler, color, 9-63 C-641 81-005-4020
Catalog, 13x10, Chrysler, color, 12p., C-641 E
Folder, 9x3½, Auto-Pilot, b&w&blue
Mailer-Folder, 12½x9, "Custom-Build" Chrysler, color (w/correct NY side mldg.)
Folder, 8x11, "Silver 300," b&w&blue
Folder, 8½x11, Imperial order code sheet, b&pink, R-10-63
Catalog, 10½x9, Imperial, color, 16p., 81-005-4022 11-63 I-643
Catalog, 14x12, Imperial, color, 16p. + tissues + covers, 81-005-4021 9-63 I-642 w/plastic wrapper
Catalog, 14x12, Crown Imperial limo., color, 8p. + covers, w/env.

Mailer-Folder, 13x101, "First Look" Imperial, color, w/env.
Mailer-Catalog, 13½x7½, "What Do You Consider..." Imperial, color, 6p.
Mailer-Catalog, same as I-643 w/env. & letter
Mailer-Folder, 12x8, "Unusual Offer," Imperial, color

1965:
Mailer-Catalog, 9x12, Chrysler, color, 12p., w/letter, 81-005-5034
Catalog, as above, w/o letter
Folder, 4x6½, prices Chrysler, b&w
Catalog, 16x8, "Considering New Car" Chrysler, color, 20p.
Catalog, 11x14, Chrysler, color, 24p., 81-005-5033
Sheet, 8x10, warranty/specs. Chrysler, b&w&blue
Folder, 5½x11, Trailer Towing, b&w&blue
Catalog, 8½x11, Trailer Towing, b&w, 8p.
Card, 9x7, Newport hardtop, color
Card, 8½x6, Newport sedan, color
Catalog, 10x10, Imperial, 12p. + covers, 81-005-5036
Card, 4x6½, prices/equip. Imperial, b&w
Sheet, 22x24, Blueprint-Crown Coupe Imperial, blue&w
Catalog, 12x12½, Imperial (w/Crown Imp. limo.), 20p. + covers, 81-005-5035

1966:
Catalog, 8½x11, Trailer Towing, b&w, 8p.
Folder, 4x6, prices Chrysler, blue&w, R-10-65
Catalog, 8x11, Chrysler, color, 32p., 81-005-6034
Catalog, 10½x13½, Chrysler, color, 36p., 81-005-6033
Card, 8½x6, 300, color
Card, 4x6½, prices/equip. Imperial, blue&w, R-10-65
Catalog, 8½x11, Imperial, color, 16p., 81-005-6036
Catalog, 11x14, Imperial, color, 16p. + foldouts + covers, 81-005-6035

1967:
Folder, 6x4, equip./prices Chrysler, b&w&blue, R-10-66
Folder, 4x5½, warranty, b&w&blue
Folder, 6x10½, 300-X show car w/full Chrysler line, b&w
Folder, 10x11½, Trailer Towing, b&w
Catalog, 11x8, Chrysler, 40p., 81-005-7034
Catalog, 14x10, Chrysler, color, 40p., 81-005-7033
Catalog, 9x6, Chrysler "Bonus Days," color, 8p.
Folder, 5½x4, prices/equip. Imperial, blue&b&w
Folder, 4x5½, warranty, b&w&blue
Catalog, 8½x11, Imperial, color, 28p., 81-005-7036
Catalog, 11x14, Imperial, color, 28p., 81-005-7035
Folder, 8x4, Chrysler Facts, b&w&blue&orange
Folder, 8x4, Imperial Facts, b&w&blue&gold

1968:
Catalog, 4x8½, Chry/Imp/Ply prices, b&w, 12p.
Catalog, 11x11, Chrysler, color, 44p., 81-005-8033
Folder, 8½x11, Chry/Ply "Success Celebration," color
Mailer-Catalog, "Success Sale," 12p., color
Catalog, 9x9, Chrysler, color, 44p., 81-005-8034
Catalog, as above, revised
Folder, 11x12, Trailer Towing, b&w
Catalog, 9x9, Imperial, color, 24p. + covers, 81-105A, 8036
Catalog, 12x12, Imperial, color, 24p. + covers, 81-105A-8035
Catalog, 11½x9, LeBaron limo., b&w, 8p., 81-105A-8037 w/env.

1969:
Catalog, 9x10½, Chrysler, color, 36p., 81-005-9034 8-68
Folder, 11x10, Trailer Towing, b&w, 81-005-9035

Catalog, 11x13, Chrysler, color, 36p., 81-005-9033 8-68
Catalog, 11x14, Imperial, color, 24p. + foldout, 81-105A-9035
Catalog, 9x11½, Imperial, color, 24p. + foldout, 81-105A-9036

1970:
Folder, 8½x11, Cordoba, color
Card, 10x8, 300-H (Hurst), color (3/4 front, interior)
Card, as above, front/rear
Catalog, 8x5, 300-H (Hurst), b&w&gold&brown, 16p.
Sheet, 15½x11, Newport 440, b&w&blue
Catalog, 11½x11½, Chrysler, color, 12p., 81-010-0001 rev.
Catalog, 11½x12, Chrysler, color, 36p., 81-005-0033
Catalog, 11x12, Imperial, color, 20p., 81-105-0035

1971:
Sheet, 8½x11, Chry/Ply product changes, b&w&blue, 4-1-71
Catalog, 8½x11, Chry/Ply Trailer Towing, b&w, 81-505-1032
Folder, 8x11, Newport Royal, color, 81-005-1036
Catalog, 11x11, Chry/Imp, color, 42p. + foldout, 81-005-1035
Catalog, 8½x11, Chry/Ply full line, color, 28p., 81-505-1027
Catalog, as above, rev.
Folder, 7x8, Chry/Ply full line, color
Catalog, 8½x11, "More Value" Chry/Ply, color, 20p. + foldout

1972:
Catalog, 8½x11, Chry/Ply, full line, color, 28p., 81-505-2027 8-1-71
Catalog, as above, rev. 12-1-71
Folder, 8½x11, Trailer Towing, blue&gold, 81-505-2032 8-1-71
Folder, 8½x11, Chry/Ply wagons, color
Catalog, 9x4, Trailer Towing, b&w w/yellow&w covers, 20p., SP 72-6 Sept.'71
Sheet 8x10 product changes, b&w&blue, 9-20-71
Catalog, 11x11, Chry/Imp, color, 38p., w/foldout, 81-005-2033

1973:
Catalog, 11x11, Chrysler, color, 24p., 81-005-7035 8-1-72
Catalog, as above, rev. 12-1-72
Catalog, 8½x11, Trailer Towing, b&w w/color covers, 12p., 81-005-7064 9-1-72
Folder, 7x3, Chry/Ply full line, color, 9-1-72
Catalog, 11x7½, Chry/Ply full line, color, 36p., 81-005-7036 9-1-72
Catalog, as above, rev. 12-1-72
Catalog, 11x11, Imperial, color, 16p., 81-005-7037 8-1-72
Folder, 11x8½, "Gold Sticker Values" Newport Special Edition, color

1974:
Catalog, 12x12, Imperial, color, 12p. + tissues + covers, 81-005-7067 8-1-73
Catalog, as above, without tissues
Catalog, 6½x4, colors, color, 12p. + covers
Catalog, 10½x8, Chry/Ply full line, color, 40p., 8-1-73 81-005-7069
Catalog, 11x11, Chrysler, color, 24p., 81-005-7068 8-1-73
Catalog, 8½x11, Trailer Towing, color, 12p., 81-005-7076 8-15-73
Portfolio, 9x12, mid-year Chry/Ply models (NY St. Regis), color, 6 inserts

1975:
Folder, 3½x8, "Clincher," b&w&blue
Folder, 8x11½, Newport Custom Highlander/Silver Duster, color
Catalog, 6½x3½, colors, color, 16p. + covers
Catalog, 10½x8½, Chry/Ply full line, color, 32p., 81-005-7080 8-15-74
Catalog, 11x8½, Cordoba, color, 8p., 81-005-7079 8-15-74
Catalog, as above, 12-15-74 (rev)
Catalog, 11x11, Chrysler, color, 16p., 81-005-7078 8-1-74
Catalog, 11x11, Imperial, color, 16p., 81-005-7077 8-1-74
Catalog, 8½x11, Chry/Ply Trailer Towing, color, 12p., 81-005-0007 8-15-74

Index

Airtemp air conditioning, 95-96, 115
Allison, Bill, 121
Anderson, Robert, 81
Ascari, Alberto, 73
Automatic transmission, *See* TorqueFlite, PowerFlite
Auto Manufacturers Association, 126
Auto Specialties Manufacturing Co. (Ausco), 48

Bakelite, Inc., 24
Baldwin, Maury, 82, 85, 103, 117, 119, 153-154, 159
Baird, Richard, 120
Barreiros Diesel, 167, 205
Bettenhausen, Tony, 73, 75
Boano, Mario, 84, 87
Bond, John, 67
Bornhauser, L. B., 183
Bourke, Bob, 141
Boyd, Virgil, 155, 180, 181
Boyertown Body Works, 28, 30
Brakes
   Ausco-Lambert, 48
   Center plane, 113
   Chrysler self-energizing disc, 47-48, 68
   Crosley Hot Shot, 47-48

Breer, Carl, 6, 65
Bridle, Allen, 34, 37, 38
Briggs, C. E., 138, 141, 151
Briggs Manufacturing Co., 15, 23, 92, 99, 102, 144-145
Briggs, Walter O., 92
Brownlie, Bill, 199
Buck, Pearl, 203
Buckminster, P. N., 171
Bunnell, John, 183
Butler, Don, 202

Cadwallader, Robert, 14-15
Cafiero, Eugene A., 192, 194, 196
California Motor Vehicle Pollution Control Board, 171
Carillo, Leo, 29
Carpentier, M. L., 65
Carroll, Bill, 133-134
Cash-rebate plan, 190
Charipar, Jack, 200
Chelsea, Michigan (proving grounds), 99, 117, 159, 162
Cheney, C. R., 183
Chesebrough, H. E., 81
Chika, John, 14

Chrysler Canada Ltd., 153, 155
Chrysler Corporation
  Facilities
    Conner Ave., 93
    Detroit, MI, 77, 92
    Evansville, IN, 10, 92
    Grand Rapids, MI, 47
    Highland Park, MI, 7, 10
    Indianapolis, IN, 10, 77
    Kokomo, IN, 10
    Los Angeles, CA, 51
    Lynch Road, 10
    Marysville, MI, 10
    Newark, DE, 10, 77
    New Castle, IN, 10
    New Orleans, LA, 10
    Nine Mile Press, 10
    Trenton, MI, 10, 78
    Warren Ave., 10, 137, 186
    Winfield, IL, 10
    Youngstown, OH, 92
    See also Jefferson Ave.
  Historical Collection, 182-183
  Marine and Industrial Division, 78
  Realty Corporation, 180

Chrysler Cummins Ltd., 167
Chrysler-Plymouth Division, 158, 192
Chrysler, Walter Percy, 6, 8, 9, 15, 51, 61, 62, 95, 183
Chrysler's Wonderful Woodie, 36
Clark, Oliver H., 15, 42
Clearbac rear window, 53-54, 55, 56, 115
Cohoe, David, 200
Colbert, Lester Lum 'Tex,' 61, 62, 64, 80, 85, 102-103, 110, 113, 127, 129, 142, 152-153, 171
Cole, Roy, 62
Combustion chambers
   Hemispherical, 64-68, 103, 110, 113, 122, 127, 153
   Polyspherical, 103-104
   Wedge-shaped, 139
Crown Imperial limousines, 25, 26, 115, 127, 158, 164, 198-206
Cummins, Richard, 109
Cunningham, Briggs, 90-92, 110

Derham Custom Bodyworks, 25-26, 50, 55, 60, 109
Detroit Public Library, 183
Dietrich, Raymond H., 6, 9, 15, 47
Di-Noc, 34, 46, 54
Dodge, Anna, 203
Dodge, 10, 158, 192
Dodge-Plymouth franchises, 158
Doern, Ray, 110
Drinkard, W. E., 65, 66
Drisdale, Tommy, 89

Earl, Harley, 62
Eisenhower, Dwight D., 95
Elizabeth II (queen of England), 202, 203
El Paso, TX, 75
Emission control, 171, 185, 194
Engel, Elwood, 155, 156, 160-161, 162, 163, 166, 169, 172, 174, 183, 185, 186, 205
Engineering Achievement Award, 73-74
Environmental Protection Agency (EPA), 185, 194
Evans, C. D., 89
Exner, Virgil, 61, 62, 64, 80, 82, 84-85, 87, 96, 97, 99, 101, 103, 110-111, 113, 115, 117, 118-120, 122, 123, 125, 134-136, 137, 140, 142, 146, 150, 153-156, 159, 162, 180, 185, 197, 198, 199
Exner, Virgil, Jr., 80
Eyston, George, 15

Farago, Paul, 82, 200, 202

Farina, Pinin, 80
FirePower V-8, 63, 64-67, 69, 72, 78, 91, 103-104, 110, 129
Fitch, John, 89
Flock, Tim, 116, 117
Fluid Drive, 8, 20-21, 25, *See also* Prestomatic
Fluid-Matic, 68
Fluid-Torque, 68
'Ford Blitz,' 101
Ford, Gerald R., 189
Ford, Henry, II, 101
Frazer, Joe, 14
Frère, Paul, 90
Fuselage-styling, 180

Gable, Clark, 28
Genoa, Italy, 203
Ghia, Carrozzeria, 80, 81, 82, 85, 86, 87, 96, 99, 115, 117, 127, 134-136, 146, 158-159, 161, 164, 198-206
Ghia GS1, 84-85, 86, 87
Godshall, Jeff, 34
Goodyear Tire & Rubber Co., 23, 47, 134,
Granatelli, Andy, 148
Gregg, Lloyd, 56
Grisinger, Arnott B. 'Buzz,' 14, 15, 33-34, 38

Hafer, Paul, 28, 30
Harrah's Automobile Collection, 29, 162
Harris, William B., 10
Hazelroth, Francis, 189
Hess and Eisenhardt Co., 206
Higgins, James, 120
Highland Park, MI, 7, 9, 10
Highway Hi-Fi, 117
Hope, Bob, 28
Huebner, George J., 185
Hutchinson, B.E., 9
Hydraguide, 68

Imperial 'kit car,' 200-203, 205

Jefferson Ave. plant (Detroit, MI), 10, 20, 51, 61, 92, 137, 186-187, 191, 206

Keene, Henry, 120
Kiekhafer, E. C., 89
Kiekhafer Mercury Outboard Racing Team, 116, 117

King, Henry, 44, 64, 80, 81, 82, 120,
Keller, Kaufman Thuma 'K. T.,' 6, 9-11, 14-15, 25-26, 30, 42-43, 61, 62, 64, 79, 80, 94, 98, 100, 102, 103, 153, 172, 190-191, 192
Korean War, 75-77
Korf, Bob, 89

Lambert, H. L., 48
Lamm, Mike, 23, 24
Lawlor, John, 161-162
Lee, R. K., 65
Leslie, Joan, 28
Lockwood, Cliff, 183
Loewy, Raymond, 141
Love, G. H., 153

Manheim, PA, 103, 134, 135
Mansfield, John, 81
Maxwell-Chalmers, 6
McCahill, Tom, 90, 109-112, 114, 116, 126
McCurry, Robert B., 196
McFee, Regie, 89
McGrath, Jack, 99
Mexico City, Mexico, 75
Milland, Ray, 28, 32
Motor Trend's Car of the Year,
   See Engineering Achievement Award
Mundy, Frank, 89
Murray, Ken, 98

Narus, Don, 36
Newberg, William C., 152-153, 171

Oaxaca, Mexico, 75
Olley, Maurice, 120
O'Malley, J. A., 61

Paramount Studios, 25
Plants, *See* Chrysler Corporation Facilities
Plymouth, *See* Dodge-Plymouth, Chrysler-Plymouth
Poirier, Tom, 110
Pont-à-Mousson gearbox, 146, 148
Post, Marjorie Merriweather, 25-26
PowerFlite transmission, 89-90, 91, 104-105, 115-117
Prestomatic, 44, 56, *See also* Fluid Drive
Prudential Insurance Co. of America, 102, 110, 153

Quinn, E. C., 93, 110, 137-138

Races
  Bonneville, 133
  Daytona, 110-111, 112, 116-117, 126, 133, 148, 149
  Francorchamps, Belgium, 90, 92
  Indianapolis 500, 92, 163, 167
  Le Mans, 8, 73, 90-92, 110
  Mexican Road Race, 73, 75, 89, 112
  Mille Miglia, 73, 90
  Mobilgas Economy Run, 56, 114
  NASCAR, 112, 117
  Nurburgring, 73
  Targa Florio, 73
  Tourist Trophy, 73
Red Head Engine, 64
Reno, NV, 29
Reynolds, Fred, 51
Ricardo, Sir Harry, 103
Riccardo, John J., 155, 156, 180, 192, 196
Rodger, Robert MacGregor, 109-110
Rootes Group of Britain, 167
Ruttman, Troy, 73

Safety Rim wheels, 44, 46
Sarnoff, David, 203
Scott, Lizabeth, 28
Segré, Luigi, 82, 200, 205
Sevenutzi, Giovanni, 134
Shank, James W., 23
Shaw, Brewster, 116, 126, 133, 134
Sheard, Edward, 69
Simca Automobiles S. A., 137, 167
Skelton, Owen, 6, 65
Smith, Clay, 89
Society of Illustrators' award, 155
Society France Motors of Paris, 85
Sommerville, R. C., 81
Specials
  A109, 40, 42, 45
  A116, 42, 45
  A600, 143, 144
  Adventurer I, 85
  Adventurer II, 87, 97, 117
  Belmont sports car, 99
  C-2, 91-92, 110
  C-4R, 91-92, 110
  C-5R, 92, 110
  C200, 84-85, 87, 98
  C300, 109, 111-112
  Cabana, 135-136
  Chrysler 300X, 174, 176
  Chrysler Special (the SS), 84, 87
  Concept, 70X, 183-185
  Cordoba de Oro, 185, 186
  CR2A, 159-160
  Dart/Diablo, 134, 136
  Dual Ghia, 99
  d'Elegance (Chrysler), 84-85, 87
  d'Elegance (Imperial), 135, 137
  Explorer, 96, 99
  Falcon, 117
  Firearrow, 97, 99
  Flight Sweep I and II, 117, 119
  LeBaron D'Or, 173
  LeBaron Thunderbolt, 14-15
  Le Monstre, 91
  K310, 80, 82-85, 87, 103, 110
  Newport, 14-15
  Norseman, 117, 185
  Number 613, 120, 123, 125
  Number 618, 124
  Parade Phaetons, 101, 102, 103
  Plainsman, 117, 125, 126
  TurboFlite, 159
  XNR, 180, 197
  XX500, 80, 81, 84
Spitfire Eight, 22, 33, 67
Spitfire Six, 22, 30
Spitfire V-8, 103-104
S. S. *Andrea Doria*, 117, 185
Stageway Company, 176, 178, 205-206
Stanwyck, Barbara, 28
Sterling, Bill, 73, 75
Stern, Paul, 103, 134, 136

Superfinish, 9, 10, 23
Superior Coach Corp., 25

Tail fins, 85, 113, 118-119, 120, 140-141, 150, 154, 155, 157, 163
Thatcher, Norm, 133
Thomas, C. B., 84, 86
Torino, Italy (Turin), 136, 199, 200
TorqueFlite, 122, 126, 127, 194
Torsion-Aire Ride, 122
Torsion bar construction, 120-122, 194
Townsend, Lynn A., 153, 155, 158, 164, 171, 172, 180, 182, 189, 190 192, 194
Tremulis, Alex Sarantos, 14, 15, 141
Trujillo, Molina, 203
Truman, Harry S., 78
Turbine-powered cars, 158-162, 185

Unit body construction, 142-144, 145

V-8 engines, 65, 72-73, 77, 78, 84
Volkswagen Karmann-Ghia, 84-85, 87
Voss, Cliff, 82, 110, 199

Walker, Charles G., 43, 52, 200
Walker George, 141
Wallace, David, 10, 23, 28, 30, 34, 37, 38, 59, 93
War production, 12, 14
Warranty program, 163, 164
Weissinger, Herb, 15
West, Ted, 21, 22
White, Glenn E., 183
Willys, John North, 6
Wilde, Cornell, 28
Wood, Vicki, 117
Woron, Walt, 56-57

Zeder, Fred M., 6, 10, 15, 42, 64-65
Zeder, James C., 64, 66, 67, 85-87, 110
Ziegler, Gregg, 148, 149